MULTICULTURAL EDUCATION SERIES

James A. Banks, Series Editor

(continued)

Streetsmart Schoolsmart

Urban Poverty
and the
Education of Adolescent Boys

Gilberto Q. Conchas
James Diego Vigil

Teachers College
Columbia University
New York and London

Published by Teachers College Press, 1234 Amsterdam Avenue,
New York, NY 10027

Library of Congress Cataloging-in-Publication Data

Conchas, Gilberto Q.
  Streetsmart schoolsmart : urban poverty and the education of adolescent boys /
Gilberto Q. Conchas, James Diego Vigil.
    pages cm. — (Multicultural education series)
  Includes bibliographical references and index.
  ISBN 978-0-8077-5318-7 (pbk. : alk. paper)
  ISBN 978-0-8077-5319-4 (hardcover : alk. paper)
    1. Teenage boys—Education—United States. 2. Urban teenagers—Education—
United States. 3. Minority teenagers—Education—United States. 4. Teenagers
with social disabilities—Education—United States. I. Vigil, James Diego, 1938–
II. Title.
  LC1397.C66 2012
  373.182351—dc23

                                                                      2011053264

ISBN 978-0-8077-5318-7 (paperback)
ISBN 978-0-8077-5319-4 (hardcover)

Printed on acid-free paper

Manufactured in the United States of America

19 18 17 16 15 14 13 12   8 7 6 5 4 3 2 1

To my carnalito,
Jesus (Jessie) Quintero Conchas,
whose determination, courage, and strength
fuel my passion to work in the name
of economic and social justice.

To my compañera, Polly A. Vigil, in love and in work.

Contents

Series Foreword

This informative, timely, and heartfelt book focuses on the problems and possibilities of one of the most marginalized populations in U.S. society and schools—low-income adolescent boys of color. The litany of problems experienced by this group of youth is legendary: They make up disproportionately high percentages of students who are disciplined and expelled from school, who populate special education, who are members of gangs, and who glide on the school-to-prison pipeline. This book is significant not only because it illuminates the daunting challenges these youth experience but also because it presents complex and myriad explanations of the social, cultural, and economic factors that combine to victimize them. Conchas and Vigil also illustrate ways in which the unrealized potential of marginalized males of color can be harnessed and enriched by schools, community agencies, and society writ large.

The authors' central concern in this book is how to create interventions that will facilitate the transition of young men of color who belong to gangs from the culture of the street to the culture of the school. Conchas and Vigil explicate a number of salient issues that need to be understood by education researchers, practitioners, and policymakers to facilitate the academic achievement of boys of color. Echoing the seminal work of William Julius Wilson (1996), the authors make it clear why joblessness among parents and youth in the inner city is an important root cause of the problems youth in low-income schools and communities experience. With a keen sociological eye, Conchas and Vigil explain why joblessness is tightly connected to truancy, dropout rates, low-academic achievement, and student disengagement from school. Consequently, their rich and sophisticated sociological analysis of society and schools is a pointed and compelling challenge to the critics of teachers and schools who blame them, and not other stakeholders, for the low academic achievement of marginalized youth of color.

Conchas and Vigil argue convincingly that while schools have a powerful effect on student academic achievement, schools by themselves cannot circumvent the cogent influences of the social, political, and economic structures of the society in which they are embedded. This is a propitious, constructive, and needed counter argument to the standards advocates and critics who want to hold teachers accountable for student test scores. The authors' discussion of the ways in which schools reflect and mirror society reveal that accountability for student achievement must be shared by teachers as well as by other stakeholders in the community, including business leaders and political decision-makers at the local, state, and national levels.

Conchas and Vigil conclude that schools—working with other agencies—can construct success or failure for marginalized students and that they have a cogent influence on the lives of low-income young men of color. However, they are careful to point out that schools are most effective when they work collaboratively with other stakeholders such as community organizations and are provided the resources they need by local, state, and federal decision makers.

The authors skillfully combine street socialization theory and research with social capital theory and research to formulate intervention strategies that will facilitate the transition of Vietnamese, African American, and Latino male youth from the gang culture of the street to the culture of the schoolhouse and learning. The authors explain why the concept of multiple marginality is required to understand the complex factors that influence the journey of these youths from the street to the schoolhouse. The research reported by Conchas and Vigil indicates that students with stable ethnic and cultural identities are more likely to achieve academically than students with fragile ethnic identities. This finding suggests that it is important for schools to recognize and validate students' ethnic and cultural identities rather than eradicate them.

This sobering but hopeful book can enable researchers, policymakers, and practicing educators to respond thoughtfully and creatively to the challenges and possibilities of young men of color. American classrooms are experiencing the largest influx of immigrant students since the beginning of the 20th century. Almost fourteen million new immigrants—documented and undocumented—settled in the United States in the years from 2000 to 2010. Less than 10% came from nations in Europe. Most came from Mexico and nations in Asia, Latin America, the Caribbean, and Central America (Comarota, 2011). A large but undetermined number of undocumented immigrants enter the United States each year. The U.S. Department of Homeland Security (2010) estimated that in January 2010, 10.8 million undocumented immigrants were living in the United States, which was a decrease from the estimated 11.8 million that resided in the United States in January 2007. In this year, approximately 3.2 children and young adults were among these 11.8 million undocumented immigrants, most of whom grew up in the United States (Pérez, 2011). The influence of an increasingly ethnically diverse population on U.S. schools, colleges, and universities is and will continue to be enormous.

Schools in the United States are more diverse today than they have been since the early 1900s when a multitude of immigrants entered the United States from Southern, Central, and Eastern Europe. In the 20-year period between 1989 and 2009, the percentage of students of color in U.S. public schools increased from 32% to 45% (Aud, Hussar, Kena, Blanco, Frohlich, Kemp, & Tahan, 2011). If current trends continue, students of color will equal or exceed the percentage of White students in U.S. public schools within 1 or 2 decades. In 2009, students of color exceeded the number of Whites students in the District of Columbia and in 12 states: Arizona, California, Florida, Georgia, Hawaii, Louisiana, Maryland, Mississippi, New Mexico, Nevada, New York, and Texas (Aud et al., 2011). In 2009, children of undocumented immigrants made up 6.8% of students in grades kindergarten through 12 (Pérez, 2011).

Language and religious diversity is also increasing in the U.S. student population. The 2010 American Community Survey indicates that approximately 19.8% of the school-age population spoke a language at home other than English (U.S. Census Bureau, 2010). The Progressive Policy Institute (2008) estimated that 50 million Americans (out of 300 million) spoke a language at home other than English in 2008. Harvard professor Diana L. Eck (2001) calls the United States the "most religiously diverse nation on earth" (p. 4). Islam is now the fastest-growing religion in the U.S., as well as in several European nations, such as France, the United Kingdom, and The Netherlands (Banks, 2009; Cesari, 2004). Most teachers now in the classroom and in teacher education programs are likely to have students from diverse ethnic, racial, linguistic, and religious groups in their classrooms during their careers. This is true for both inner-city and suburban teachers in the United States as well as in many other Western nations such as Canada, Australia, and the United Kingdom (Banks, 2009).

The major purpose of the Multicultural Education Series is to provide preservice educators, practicing educators, graduate students, scholars, and policymakers with an interrelated and comprehensive set of books that summarizes and analyzes important research, theory, and practice related to the education of ethnic, racial, cultural, and linguistic groups in the United States and the education of mainstream students about diversity. The dimensions of multicultural education, developed by Banks (2004), provide the conceptual framework for the development of the publications in the Series. They are content integration, the knowledge construction process, prejudice reduction, an equity pedagogy, and an empowering institutional culture and social structure.

The books in the Series provide research, theoretical, and practical knowledge about the behaviors and learning characteristics of students of color, language minority students, and low-income students. They also provide knowledge about ways to improve academic achievement and race relations in educational settings. Multicultural education is consequently as important for middle-class White suburban students as it is for students of color who live in the inner city. Multicultural education fosters the public good and the overarching goals of the commonwealth.

The engaging narratives in this book describe the challenges facing low-income young men of color as well as reasons for hope. Several of the vivid and moving case studies reveal how some marginalized young men of color are resilient and succeed despite daunting odds. Conchas and Vigil also document how career-related school academies and community-based organizations can become beacons of hope for low-income males of color. If the cogent messages of this searing and compelling book are heeded and implemented by educational researchers, policymakers, and practitioners our nation will be greatly enriched by the abundant gifts of young men of color.

James A. Banks

REFERENCES

Aud, S., Hussar, W., Kena, G., Bianco, K., Frohlich, L., Kemp, J., & Tahan, K. (2011). *The condition of education 2011* (NCES 2011-033). U.S. Department of Education, National Center for Education Statistics. Washington, DC: U.S. Government Printing Office. Retrieved from http://nces.ed.gov/programs/coe/pdf/coe_1er.pdf

Banks, J. A. (2004). Multicultural education: Historical development, dimensions, and practice. In J. A. Banks & C. A. M. Banks (Eds.). *Handbook of research on multicultural education* (2nd ed., pp. 3–29). San Francisco: Jossey-Bass.

Banks, J. A. (Ed.). (2009). *The Routledge international companion to multicultural education*. New York and London: Routledge.

Camarota, S. A. (2011, October). A *record-setting decade of immigration: 2000 to 2010* Washingtgon, DC, Center for Immigration Studies. Retrieved from http://cis.org/2000-2010-record-setting-decade-of-immigration

Cesari, J. (2004). *When Islam and democracy meet: Muslims in Europe and the United States*. New York: Pelgrave Macmillan.

Eck, D. L. (2001*). A new religious America: How a "Christian country" has become the world's most religiously diverse nation*. New York: HarperSanFrancisco.

Pérez, W. (2011). Americans by heart: Undocumented Latino students and the promise of higher education. New York: Teachers College Press.

Progressive Policy Institute. (2008). *50 million Americans speak languages other than English at home*. Retrieved from http://www.ppionline.org/ppi_ci.cfm?knl gAreaID=108&subsecID=900003&contentID=254619

U.S. Census Bureau. (2010). *2010 American community survey*. Retrieved from http://factfinder2.census.gov/faces/tableservices/jsf/pages/productview. xhtml?pid=ACS_10_1YR_S1603&prodType=table

U.S. Department of Homeland Security. (2010, February). *Estimates of the unauthorized immigrant population residing in the United States: January 2010*. Retrieved from http://www.dhs.gov/files/statistics/immigration.shtm

Wilson, W. J. (1996). *When work disappears: The world of the urban poor*. New York: Knopf.

Preface

*One thing is clear: what we're doing is not working. Society's efforts
to deal with the "problem" of young men of color have been largely
reactive. In California, for example, one in thirty-six people is behind
bars today—the majority of them being young men of color. Yet when
these young men and boys of color are released, they are unprepared
and unsupported to assume the responsibilities that come with being
a productive member of their communities. At the same time they
bring with them the harmful health challenges that burden their
respective communities and the community at large.*
—Robert Phillips, from the foreword, *Changing Places*,
C. Edley & J. Ruiz de Velasco (Eds.)

On a research trip to San Francisco, Diego and I strolled from a café near
the Civic Center Plaza to a new restaurant in the South of Market for an
early dinner. It was a remarkably warm evening as we walked down the his-
toric Golden Gage Avenue. We were so captivated in conversation about our
research on youth and urban poverty that we hadn't paid much attention to
our surroundings. We suddenly stopped and observed the unfamiliar neighborhood around us. The buildings were older and many were boarded up.
There were adult cinemas and many liquor stores, and, to put it mildly, the
area was not as manicured and aesthetically pleasing as the rest of the city. We
were in the middle of the urban neighborhood called the Tenderloin.

The Tenderloin is known as San Francisco's poorest and most marginalized neighborhood. Many people claim that it is the worst neighborhood
in San Francisco. On our particular rendezvous, we observed drug dealers,
addicts, prostitutes, and mentally unstable street people. Most were Black
and Latino, but we did see some Native Americans and a few White men and
women. We were struck by the many black and brown bodies congregating
on street corners and in the small park in the heart of the Tenderloin. These
folks had it rough. They had no jobs, they had no health care, and most were
homeless. They had the streets. Lady Luck had not crossed their paths.

Compared to our lives as university professors, who enjoy comfort in Irvine, one of the safest cities in the United States, these folks were not the lucky ones; we were. Unlike the other black and brown faces on the streets of San Francisco—or any other large urban city—we had climbed the social and economic ladder. Luck, in terms of educational opportunity, had crossed our paths, and these men, similar to the many men of color throughout the nation, had not experienced such a windfall. For us, education has been kind to us; and through education, we developed, over the years, the networks that led to our social mobility. We have good jobs despite the nation's current economic malaise and devastating unemployment levels.

However, if you can get past the social strains in poor neighborhoods like the Tenderloin, you'll find excitement and diverse locales. We observed cultural attractions, restaurants, shopping, and nightlife. Most significant, we noticed a long line of men trying their luck to find assistance and work at the St. Anthony's Foundation, one of several community-based organizations that serve the poor and the homeless. These men clearly wanted to work and to contribute to society, but jobs simply were scarce to none. They, nonetheless, tried, and the community-based organizations were there to provide assistance and comfort.

We observed that even within urban deterioration, people are hopeful and are active agents in their struggle for social mobility. However, poor people in ghettos and barrios do not have the "acknowledged" cultural and social capital necessary for economic success. In part, institutions like schools, churches, and community-based organizations serve as the channel for many poor people to acquire the "accepted" capital and use it. Many individuals successfully acquire the capital, while the majority does not.

StreetSmart SchoolSmart is a scholarly attempt to shed light on this dynamic and emphasize the importance of schools and community-based organizations in poor communities. Often, these are the only institutional support systems that provide networks of encouragement, information, and support to low-income youth and young adults. While schools do not equally serve the needs of most students, often, because of the lack of resources, they are still the best hope for our nation's poor. Likewise, many community-based organizations, in concert with schools and other neighborhood institutions, are able to deal with the students that schools have pushed out. Taken together, schools and community-based organizations can provide the necessary scaffolds to lure youth back into conventional paths and also keep those doing well off the streets.

Acknowledgments

Our collective work over the years seeks not to be reactive when dealing with "efforts to deal with the 'problem' of young men of color." We look to solutions that eradicate the "roots" of the problems facing the urban poor. Such efforts are not accomplished in isolation. First, we acknowledge that portions of Chapter 1 first appeared as "Multiple Marginality and Urban Education: Community and School Socialization Among Low-Income Mexican-Descent Youth" (*Journal of Education for Students Placed at Ris [JESPAR]*, 2010, *15*[1], 51–65); portions of Chapter 6 first appeared as "Preventing Truancy and Dropout Among Urban Middle School Youth: Understanding Community-Based Action from the Student's Perspective" (*Education and Urban Society*, [2009] 41[2], 216–247); and, we thank doctoral students Alex Lin and Sean Drake for their research assistance with Chapter 8. Second, we acknowledge the people and schools who on a daily basis struggle against the tides of inequality, but manage to do well despite the odds. Third, we acknowledge our combined research efforts and our participatory work in communities and schools to address inequality. Fourth, we thank our broad and diverse communities of scholars, leaders in education, and friends that continue to have a profound impact on our intellectual endeavors. Finally, we thank the many individuals in the "field" who work long hours developing theories of action and strategic plans centered on school and community improvement efforts. The CASN team at U.C. Berkeley—David Stern, Charles Dayton, Patricia Clark, Susan Tidyman, Carrie Collins, and Erin Fender—deserve special recognition for their determination to eradicate inequality and promote college and career opportunities for all.

We give our sincere gratitude to Professor James A. Banks, who has been a great colleague, friend, and champion of our work. At numerous and highly enjoyable lunches and dinners, Professor Banks embraced this book project and encouraged us to produce a candid and honest academic narrative on boys of color. We are very fond of Professor Banks, appreciate his wisdom, and are humbled to be among his circle of friends. Another important voice came from Joan Rakhshani, who was our fearless editor from the beginning to the end. Her probing and expertise resulted in a clear, concise, and creative narrative. In addition, we give special credit to Polly A. Vigil and Leticia Oseguera, who never hesitated to listen and offer important theoretical and practical insights that undoubtedly sharpened the focus of the book. Finally, we thank our families for their encouragement and love.

Introduction

Poverty and the Creation of Hope and Despair

*Many of today's problems in the inner-city ghetto neighborhoods—
crime, family dissolution, welfare, low levels of social organization,
and so on—are fundamentally a consequence of the disappearance
of work.*

—William Julius Wilson, *When Work Disappears*

*The social conditions seen by many contemporary researchers as
signs of social disorganization, like violence, crime, an inordinately
high number of female-headed households, and illicit drug use, were
used by the residents of these neighborhoods to build a functional
social structure.*

—Martín Sánchez-Jankowski, *Cracks in the Pavement*

Poverty creates vast disparities among populations, regardless of race and
ethnicity. Poverty and its by-products—joblessness, homelessness, violence,
urban decay, and inadequate health care—segregate poor people into economically deprived neighborhoods (Blackwell & Pastor, 2010; Rothstein,
2004; Sánchez-Jankowski, 2008; Wilson, 1996). Race and ethnicity matter;
however, poverty and racism remain the devastating linchpins of inequality.
Latinos, Native Americans, Blacks, Whites, and Asians in disenfranchised
neighborhoods struggle to access the hopes and dreams of those born into
privilege (Moran & Carbado, 2010).

Over the years, William Julius Wilson's seminal texts, in particular *When
Work Disappears: The World of the New Urban Poor* (1996), have highlighted the devastating effects of joblessness on inner-city Blacks. Unemployment dismantles the foundation of family life and leads people, especially men
of color, into lives full of violence, drugs, and disorganization. Wilson sensibly
argues that this culture of apathy and hopelessness results from poverty and,
specifically, joblessness. Apathy and hopelessness are not features inherent in
Black or Latino ethnic cultural traditions. Instead, the consequences of poverty and inequality are presented to explain the harmful social and behavioral

1

conditions present in poor neighborhoods. Wilson, ultimately, promotes a universal policy agenda—advocating for large-scale economic reform—targeted at the disadvantaged and not any one specific racial group.

Today, in agreement with Wilson, we are not witnessing the declining significance of race. Instead, we are witnessing the enduring significance of poverty and inequality as the sources of social disorganization in low-income communities. Joblessness, in particular, lies at the root of the problems facing the urban poor, especially among Black and Latino men. Joblessness and economic deprivation continue to inflict damage on communities and their populations. This book provides a path to the consideration of workable solutions.

Structural, cultural, and psychological issues are interrelated, and we need to examine how they coalesce and affect people. Oscar Lewis's research, published in 1959 and in 1965, on the Mexican and Puerto Rican poor suggested that a culture of poverty—-similar to Wilson's social disorganization—reproduces cycles of privation. Lewis's work was dismissed for blaming the poor for their plight. A careful reading of his thesis, however, suggests that he was not blaming the poor but arguing how that material conditions of poverty within a capitalist system sustain a long-term culture of poverty.[1] "Culture of poverty" does not refer to Mexican or Puerto Rican ethnic cultural behaviors and/or norms, but to behaviors and/or norms that are the consequence of persistent and concentrated privation. In this book, we locate poverty at the root of the problems faced by marginalized communities. The victim will not be blamed.[2]

In addition to examining inequality through a structural lens, we identify hope among the hopeless. We seek to unearth the processes within poor urban communities that may lead to success. *StreetSmart SchoolSmart* departs from the Chicago School explanation, which posits that poor urban communities are disorganized (as a result of ethnicity, industrialization, or urban development) and pretty much stay unchanged. In the Chicago tradition, the social disorganization of these communities remains fixed, and individual actions or inactions provide little, if any, opportunity for change.

Sánchez-Jankowski (2008), however, uncovered in his 9-year comparative urban ethnography that structure and social order existed "even on the most hectic of days" (p. 9). He describes a theory of urban ethnography that explains the dynamic between social change and perseverance. In many cases, disadvantaged people manage to emerge upright in the worst of circumstances. Martin Sánchez-Jankowski's important contribution to the study of the urban poor points out that:

> there is no way to understand the longevity of poor neighborhoods through disorganization theory. Poor neighborhoods are generally structured rather than disorganized, and they feature both social mechanisms through which social change is initiated and brought to fruition and social mechanisms that work to preserve the existing social order and structure. (p. 8)

We follow this observation to suggest factors that may enhance human agency in poor inner-city communities facing despair.

THE SIGNIFICANCE OF SOCIAL CAPITAL

One critical question, yet not adequately unanswered, is, Why do some disenfranchised youth fail or underachieve in school and society while others do not? Or, how has society failed them? This is an old question for researchers, but a driving, perplexing one, especially when studies examine youth who have been socialized within the same communities or within the same families. To unravel these sociodevelopmental dynamics, we initiated a series of studies over a number of years. These studies utilize a community and school orientation to street ethnography. Some studies concentrate on gangs, some on community-based organizations, and some on schools that seek to reengage urban youth. One common research finding, when examining the lives of youth, is the importance of the resources gained from social networks.

"It's who and what you know" was a common phrase used by many of the boys in this book. When asked how they managed to leave gang life or how they avoided gang life, the typical response was "making the proper connections to people who can help." These boys are referring to social capital, that is, the resources gained from relationships and social networks. Social capital is described as the less tangible properties—information, power, and knowledge—acquired through social relations that positively impact educational outcomes (Coleman, 1988; Daly, 2010). Social capital is defined by its function and framed around the value of social networks that contribute to beneficial outcomes (Uslaner, 2001).

Social capital is not synonymous with financial wealth; instead, it represents the knowledge acquired through social contacts and networks that may result in social and economic mobility. Additionally, human relational resources support people in many different ways as they navigate the various institutions in society, such as schools, financial institutions, and workplaces. Nuanced and complex, social capital must be conceptualized as multidimensional to have any useful explanatory significance (Bolivar & Chrispeels, 2011).

There are many community-based programs and schools in poor communities that attempt to promote positive relationships among adults and peers. Suárez-Orozco, Pimentel, and Martin (2009) suggest, "Connections with teachers, counselors, coaches, and other supportive adults in the school [and out of school] are particularly important to the academic and social adaptation of adolescents in general" (p. 718). The idea of deliberately bridging institutions, such as community-based organizations and schools is, in part fundamentally rooted in social capital theory (Putnam, 2000). In order to effectively build capacity among people across various institutions and around any issue, such institutions need to make connections, partnerships, and meaningful relationships with one another.

Institutions within enduring pockets of poverty build functional social structures based on networks and relationships, which may lead to various forms of social capital. On the one hand, some networks may be advantageous (i.e., teachers and other supportive adults), but on the other hand, some networks may promote negative consequences (adults socialized in the criminal justice system or others adults who follow a street lifestyle). In this book, the various forms of social capital available to youth in distinct contexts are highlighted.

StreetSmart SchoolSmart points out the resources, gained through relationships in communities and schools, that promote the social mobility of boys who grew up in poverty. These resources have the potential to structure productive pathways for boys of color and aid in the healthy transition to adulthood. Unfortunately, they are scarce and most boys in economically deprived circumstances do not currently benefit from healthy and positive networks. As poverty and neglect continue to push boys of color further into the margins of society, this book exposes the approaches that work.

BOYS OF COLOR IN COMPARATIVE PERSPECTIVE

The fundamental contribution of our book is to synthesize two research approaches that have traditionally remained separate in the literature. The book merges street-socialization research with social capital research in schools and communities. We suggest that there exists a fluidity of youth movement between these contexts, which means that no context should be studied in isolation. The impact and variety of links between school and community demand further investigation. We seek to stress systems and processes that promote positive networks and relationships that may lead to social mobility. In so doing, we advocate for new policy and practice formulations throughout the targeted communities and schools—formulations that embrace a systemic approach to education reform.

We focus on Vietnamese, African American, and Latino boys in our comparative assessment. We contend that it is valuable to provide a comparative framework for understanding unique histories and both specificities and differences in the situations facing racially marginalized groups in the United States. Therefore, a comparative approach allows us (1) to discern variability between and within groups, (2) to challenge stereotypes of each group, for instance, complicating the "model minority" stereotype among Asians or highlighting that many Black and Latino youth can and do succeed, and (3) to identify structural factors and influences that work to move youth toward success and to keep those doing well off the streets.

Three contexts of low-income boys are presented, specifically, the impact of (1) marginalized poor communities in the formation of gang-oriented youth, (2) community-based organizations in the reengagement of low-income boys, and (3) high schools in the construction of success among low-income boys. Although all youth in these communities are exposed to the street, with many of them becoming street-socialized, some nevertheless succeed in graduating from high school and transitioning into careers. Some do not. We contend that even low-income boys who demonstrate levels of success remain subject to the social ecology of poverty and racism. It is imperative that we unearth the institutional processes in poor marginalized communities that keep boys productive throughout society instead of stagnating inside prison walls—even if we only assist a few.

THE "BOY CRISIS"

This book concentrates on boys and men of color for fundamental reasons. Male students of color are typically overrepresented at the bottom rungs of the achievement ladder on most measures of student performance. Boys of color are more likely than any other group to be suspended and expelled from school (Conchas & Noguera, 2004) and more likely to be classified as mentally impaired or suffering from a learning disability (Harry, Kingner, & Moore, 2000). They are more often tracked into remedial and low-ability courses and more likely to be absent from Advanced Placement and honors courses (Oakes, 2005). Even class privilege and the material benefits that accompany it fail to inoculate boys of color from low academic performance. When compared to their White peers, middle-class boys of color lag behind, both in grade point average and on standardized tests (Noguera, 2008).

The polar shift in the gender gap in education accentuates the challenges facing males of color. For many years, male students were privileged over female students. In an 1894 book by Burstall, a principal of a large public high school discusses a typical view of the time:

> When the girls enter the High School, they are more mature, more honest in work, with greater power of concentration, and are more apt in acquiring information. This lasts for a year or two; then the boys develop, and become at 16 thinking beings. At 18 years of age, the girls' work in general becomes worthless, other interests claiming their attention. Boys excel in mathematics, economics, and civics; girls hold their own in languages and history, and many do well in science. Girls always do rote work better than their brothers. (p. 164)

The tide has turned. In the early days of the 20th century, less than 20% of all college degrees were earned by women. Today, women are more highly represented than men in higher education. Data from the 2010 United States Census shows that when counting adults 25 or older, women have for the first time obtained more advanced degrees than men—10.6 million versus 10.5 million. In 1996, women passed men in obtaining bachelor's degrees. Now, 20.1 million women over the age of 25 have bachelor's degrees compared to 18.7 million men. However, it is important to note that in spite of their gains in education, there is still a persistent wage gap between men and women. Women earn about 77 cents on the dollar that men earn, and the gap is more dramatic for women of color. They also don't make it to the upper echelons of leadership at the same rate men do (Hegewisch, Williams, & Henderson, 2011).

While this increase in female college degrees may not come at the expense of males receiving degrees, it is important to note why this rising tide does not raise all ships. Researchers have isolated some of the reasons. When girls enter the classroom, they engage more quickly than males—especially minority males (Rong, 1996). Research shows that these young girls, who show an early, intent interest in school, will likely have a higher rate of subsequent achievement, resilience, and adaptation to school policies. Minority girls have proven to have another advantage—social and cultural capital. This social and cultural capital, which includes higher parental expectations, control, and fluent bilingualism, contributes to female success by maintaining ease of movement between the multiple identities of school, home, and community (Goyette & Conchas, 2002; Portes & Hao, 1998). Female minority students are more likely to synthesize the cultural resources of home and community with the resources provided at school. Neither sphere is sacrificed. This helps prevent, for female minority students, the undermining of cultural resources—also known as "subtractive schooling" (Valenzuela, 1999). Minority females seem to be able to access school resources without sacrificing the pride and benefits of culture.

Young men of color do not easily demonstrate an ease of movement between school, home, and community. Ethnographic studies reveal that when minority males enter school, their relationship with school authorities is often marked by antagonism and hostility (Noguera, 2003; Vigil, 2007). School is more likely to be perceived as a place of conflict and racism, not of support (Cammarota, 2004; Lopez, 2003). With female participation and achievement increasing, there is growing concern about the underachievement of boys in the United States. For minority males, the situation is dire. In order to concentrate available resources and attention on the challenge, the fact must be acknowledged: a "boy crisis" exists.

THE EPISTEMOLOGICAL UNDERPINNINGS OF THIS BOOK

Community members and academics are both important contributors to the research process. Academically trained insiders integrate multiple perspectives into the research paradigm. Community members, who have experienced or are experiencing the social problems under consideration, are invaluable primary sources. Utilizing both types of insider perspectives provides benefits that accrue to the community under study. However, the contributions and perspectives of the outsider should not be unilaterally abandoned in favor of a strictly insider view. Rather, a blended research framework would seem to offer the most promising results for studies conducted in low-income communities. Data collection methods that afford the researcher multiple tools and perspectives to compile and interpret data provide a broader and deeper picture of reality.

In this book, we embrace a community orientation to street and school ethnography, but with a different thrust. With lessons learned from early exploratory years, in combination with the mission of ethnic studies and research, self-reflexivity integrates school and community perspectives and advocates for policy change. Conchas, the first author and the son of Mexican immigrant farm workers, has established a strong record by conducting school and community case studies. These studies utilize a social capital framework that sheds light on what works for the social mobility of all low-income populations. Vigil, the second author, provides research on youth identity and gangs, which proves particularly fruitful for our purposes.

Our combined work elucidates street-socialization and the influences that frame school failure and success among Asian, African American, and Latino boys who grew up in poverty. The aim is to suggest recommendations and/or solutions to help break the insidious conditions of poverty that lead to disengagement and impact the education and social mobility of ethnic minority youth.

THE ORGANIZATION OF THIS BOOK

This book comprises nine chapters and two autobiographical appendices. The first chapter 1 discusses the theoretical foundation of the book and the following chapters 2–8 address original research studies related to boys affiliated with gangs; boys once disaffected but then reengaged via linked efforts between communities and schools; and boys doing well in school despite disparities in economic and social opportunities. The aim of these chapters is to offer a clear sense of how boys from different ethnic backgrounds approach schooling, how contextual factors affect such development, and how the decision-making process varies among them. The final chapter of the book, Chapter Nine, summarizes the crucial messages that emerge from the research. The names of individuals and programs, as well as identifying characteristics, have been changed in each research study presented to ensure confidentiality.

Finally, Appendix A and Appendix B present the authors' narratives—both grew up in neighborhoods prone to street-socialization in Southern California during different times, in different places, and with different people. Conchas and Vigil, in telling their stories, present a personal yet critical discussion about growing up poor and eventually becoming university professors.

Chapter 1

Street-Socialized Boys in Low-Income Neighborhoods

A Cross-Ethnic Framework to Promote Success

Three tracks should be pursued vigorously and simultaneously if we are to make significant progress in narrowing the achievement gap. First is school improvement efforts that raise the quality of instruction in elementary and secondary schools. Second is expanding the definition of schooling to include crucial out-of-school hours in which families and communities now are the sole influences. This means implementing comprehensive early childhood, after-school, and summer programs. And third are social and economic policies that enable children to attend school more equally ready to learn. These policies include health services for lower class children and their families, stable housing for working families with children, and the narrowing of growing income inequalities in American society.
—Richard Rothstein, *Class and Schools*

Many conditions—including familial, biological, and societal—affect the growth and development of low-income youth. Early on, the quality of engagement in family life—language development, security, stability, and nutrition, among other factors—determines health and learning readiness. While early education contributes to the chances of later success, we find that as boys reach adolescence, the weight of the influence of the school environment increases. No longer merely a positive or negative factor in the life of a child, schooling can make or break the future of youths.

By puberty, ethnic identity formation is well underway, especially in the contexts of gender and age clarification. Influences during this time period may resonate into adulthood as identity sources. The vast majority of youths navigate through puberty to evolve into mature and productive young adults. But poverty, racism, and social inequality undermine the maturation process and generate especially stark options and rigid barriers to success (Suárez-Orozco & Suárez-Orozco, 1995). Of these, poverty deals the greatest damage (Rothstein, 2004).

In this chapter we conceptualize how poverty among boys and men of color leads to "street-socialization." Street-socialization, in turn, undermines and transforms the otherwise normal course of human development for marginalized youth in ways that institutionalize a street subculture. Before policymakers, educators, and social service providers can develop effective strategies for gang prevention and intervention, they must first examine the historical and cultural root causes of street-socialization among youth who grow up poor. Establishing how street-socialized youth experience time, place, and people informs the formulation and implementation of a balanced strategy that is aligned with Richard Rothstein's (2004) call to eliminate inequality in U.S. society through in-school and out-of-school policies and practices.

All youth and young adults in economically deprived neighborhoods must confront and come to terms with economic, environmental, racial, and cultural forces. Street socialization affects all youth in distinct ways. Even school smart youth are not immune to the hazards of poverty and street socialization. However, the most disadvantaged and culturally conflicted individuals and groups must command our attention. These youth are most prone to becoming disconnected and eventual gang members—victimized by the various pressures of the streets. We argue that educational initiatives and reform efforts ought to address the street socialization that impacts all low-income ethnic youth and young adults. We employ a framework to guide our understanding of socio-developmental issues. This, in turn, relates and intersects with the educational failure and success of young adults who are street socialized. Gang and non-gang youth in poverty stricken neighborhoods are subjected to street socialization. These youth demand our immediate attention.

THE GANG ISSUE

The gang issue throughout the United States has worsened in the past few years, as more street children are generated during times of economic crisis. Most gang-control efforts since the 1980s have been conducted by law enforcement agencies; regrettably, these efforts come too late—that is, after youths have disengaged. All too often, debate over the correct response to youth gangs has devolved into an either-or response in which gang members are expected to shape up or go to jail. Police threaten youths hanging out on street corners with arrest unless they disperse. Youths who commit crimes are arrested, prosecuted, and jailed without any attempt by authorities to understand the root causes of the crime. Often, many of these young men are victimized, jailed but never arraigned—yet these arrests remain on their records (Rios, 2011). Jails are filled with youths who have been prosecuted based on suppression tactics that are ineffective at stopping gangs (Vigil, 2010).

A better strategy to address the gang problem is through an open and balanced approach that offers positive activities, outlets, and role models— one that addresses the complex problems facing youth who are vulnerable to gang membership. For a large segment of youth in the United States, punishment is far more common than reward. This imbalance stems not only from law enforcement policies and strained police relations but also from stressed families, overburdened schools, apathy, and the lack of positive role models (Vigil, 2010).

We must right this imbalance. We must create a climate in which fear of poor young men of color does not consume us. Fear forces us to rush to ill-advised strategies that satisfy emotions, but that have no clear evidence of success. A keener approach would identify and deal with the causes behind the problems generated by high concentrations of poverty. We must provide strategies of reason and balance that ultimately will lead to real, lasting results.

It is a false belief that conservative pundits like Glenn Beck, Rush Limbaugh, and Newt Gingrich have often pontificated, that there are no consequential inequities and that everyone begins life from the same starting point. If that were true, there would not be disparities in education, health, occupation, and opportunity in general. Instead, tremendous gaps exist between the fortunate and less fortunate members of U.S. society (Darder & Torres, 2004; Rothstein, 2004). The race, simply, is not even.

MULTIPLE MARGINALITY AND STREET SOCIALIZATION

We offer a *multiple marginality framework* that captures the multilevel factors and influences of the Asian, Latino, and African American youth who grew up in poor neighborhoods (Vigil & Yun, 1990). The framework reflects the complexities and persistence of many forces. As a theory-building framework, multiple marginality addresses ecological, economic, sociocultural, and psychological factors that underlie street gangs and youths' participation in them (Vigil, 1988a). Macrohistorical and macrostructural forces and processes—those that occur at the broader levels of society—lead to economic insecurity and lack of opportunity. These forces also compound the adaptation of ethnic minorities, who face fragmented institutions of social control, stable homes and families, and psychological and emotional barriers.

Academic and social disengagement is an outcome of marginalization; it is the relegation of certain persons or groups to the fringes of society, where social and economic conditions result in powerlessness. This process occurs on multiple levels as a product of forces in play over a long period of time. Some of the most street-socialized youth come from such stressed and unstable circumstances that one wonders how they have survived; however, many youth from the same communities and families manage not only to survive, but to thrive and succeed (Conchas, 2006).

The theory of *multiple marginality* reflects social and economic complexities and their persistence over time and allows us to examine (1) the failure and success of low-income young adults in communities and schools and (2) the variations that exist among all youth and young adults. Therein lies the strength and utility of the framework. Multiple marginality works as a tool because it encompasses the disengagement and reengagement that occur on multiple levels, both macro and micro, over long periods of time.

Poverty and marginalization lead to a cohort of youth being raised principally in the streets. This phenomenon, known as "street socialization," helps to explain the emergence of street gangs and gang members. We define "socialization" as the process by which a person learns the behaviors and norms of a given social group and is molded into an effective participant. Street socialization emerges and continues as social controls break down and human development processes are undermined by stressful situations and conditions that seem hopeless. In order to give readers a better idea of how successful community and school strategies can work for all street-socialized youth, specific examples of new ways to address these destructive and detrimental events and episodes are offered throughout the chapters of this book. These approaches center on time, place, and people. They focus on encouraging urban youth to spend their time in more constructive ways, using age-appropriate interventions; changing the pressures and demands of place (the home and street); and introducing a new supporting cast of people to guide and supervise the urban children most prone to the negative effects of street socialization.

Why do some boys and men of color join street gangs? We argue that physical situations (for example, inferior, crowded housing and exposure only to run-down and spatially separate enclaves) and social conditions (such as low or inadequate income, lack of or limited identity with dominant institutions, and social and cultural conflicts between first- and second-generation family members) compel many urban youths to seek the peer bonding and social support that street gangs provide. Often, boys and men of color in impoverished circumstances perceive that they have very few alternatives to gangs.

Street socialization is a principal characteristic of established gangs and occurs, to a considerable degree, away from home, school, and other traditional institutions (Vigil, 1988b). The most disadvantaged youth are often the most unsupervised and reside in crowded housing conditions where private space is limited; and, therefore, they are the most street-socialized (Vigil, 2007). These youngsters are driven into the public space of the streets, where multiple-aged males and peer groups, with whom they must contend, dominate. These peers and older males provide a new social network and models for new normative behaviors, values, and attitudes. Gang membership makes youngsters feel protected from competing gangs that pose a possible threat.

Once in the streets, the young person must determine where he fits within the hierarchy of dominance and aggression required for survival. Being from a family that has gang members—a brother, an uncle, or another relative—helps in gaining entrance into a gang and offers generational continuity for the gang itself. Otherwise, a young male will only get protection by seeking out associates who are streetwise, experienced, and willing to be friends: namely, gang members (Vigil, 2007). This, in turn, prompts the new gang member to return the favor by demonstrating willingness to think and act in ways approved by his friends. The newly established social bonds are reinforced, a sense of protection is gained, and new behavior patterns and values are learned. Let us be clear that all street-raised youths do not join gangs, but those who *do* join gangs come to terms with the often violent and antisocial peer norms that characterize the street gang. We contend that the most street-socialized youth often join gangs; whereas the least socialized youth, as we shall discuss later in this book, do not join gangs. All youth caught in concentrated pockets of poverty are exposed to street socialization. We suggest, therefore, that all youth—gang and non-gang—emand our attention.

In the absence of positive adult supervision, preadolescent youths also look to the streets for adventure and for the freedom to undertake those adventures. A boy can wander where he wants and return when he wishes, answering to no one or, at worst, facing a verbal or physical reprimand from his parents working long hours—if employed—when he returns home. In this atmosphere of freedom, other children become his reference group, and the values and guidelines of this group encourage activities outside the limits of adult approval. Experimentation with alcohol and drugs occurs, weapons are accepted as a power equalizer when needed, deviant actions are taken on a dare, and bonds with similarly street-active peers who are also school classmates are intensified.

This early interaction provides the fertile ground for later adolescent bonding, when more serious gang activities are introduced. Many of the street incidents, such as exhibiting protection, daring, managing fear, and conducting mischievous acts are seared into the memories of preadolescent youth. The remembrance of a shared past is often a basis for instilling loyalty and comrade-in-arms friendships that build strong bonds for later gang affiliations. Street socialization thus becomes the basis for entrance into the gang and for the perpetuation of gang lore and traditions. It is the first phase of the integration into the gang subculture that for some individuals evolves into steady and uninterrupted development.

The multiple marginality framework is nuanced and embraces the facets of time, place, and people as important prisms to aid future researchers. These will help them to understand the dynamics of street socialization and develop meaningful alternatives to the streets. Time reflects the economic, social, and political habits that shape people and events, whereas place—such as the neighborhood or school—represents local, immediate, and often changing realities. People shift in time and place, and new and/or different forces come into play, such as immigration or economic restructuring. These forces can significantly alter an individual's feelings, thoughts, and actions. As Spindler and Spindler (1990) noted, such shifts can tax and strain enduring (past), situated (present), and endangered (stress between the previous two) notions of self.

Families, schooling, and law enforcement situate the adjustments of individuals in the context of the broader and deeper forces of a modern society. By focusing on these socialization experiences, we can gather facts, describe transformations, and offer interpretations of how and where family life and its structures unravel, how schools fail, and why law enforcement remains disconnected and criminalizes youth (Rios, 2011). Policy and practice, therefore, ought to elevate the importance of understanding street socialization in order to offer solutions that work for all youth in poor neighborhoods. Once we understand street socialization, we are better informed on how to approach ethnic minority schooling.

DIFFERENCES BETWEEN STREET-SOCIALIZED MALES

A comparison of the specific environments of the most street-socialized young adults, which includes a survey of both active gang members and non-members living in the same neighborhoods, reveals a wide gulf (Huff, 2002; Vigil, 2007). Gang members are usually reared in disorganized homes, have more single-parent-centered family situations, have more siblings, and face marginal, unstable economic conditions, such as unemployment and welfare (Vigil, 1988a). In a study exploring differences between gang and non-gang families in a public housing development, Vigil reported notable contrasts between them (2007). These differences considered together strongly suggest that families with histories of gang involvement are more at risk to fall prey to existing local problems, like violence, than most of their neighbors. There are also indications of greater economic stress in the gang families, including the fact that a significantly smaller proportion of those households have access to social and cultural capital. Therefore, attenuated parenting and inadequate policing, along with voids in schooling, have cumulatively added up to leave children free to seek and find their own street-controlling influences, especially among boys. Consequently, gang involvement is associated with an increase in destructive behavior compared to most non-gang youth.

Violence against others, in the form of rampant gang fights and slayings, and against the self, through the careless use and abuse of drugs and other chemical substances, represents the destructive, debilitating habits that separate gangs from other adolescent peer networks. Put another way, gangs foster both public and private destructive acts, meaning that the *locura* (i.e., quasi-madness) orientation common in gangs can take both external and internal paths. The violence brought about by these acts is by no means insignificant (Vigil, 2003).

Nevertheless, even these activities can be understood as an altered type of *sturm und drang* response during adolescence—a time when daring, excitement, courage, and adventure are valued by peers. Indeed, participation in these activities earns one respect and recognition as a dependable gang member with street capital. Notwithstanding their attempts to conform to such expectations, however, most youths remain conscious of, and concerned with, the detrimental effects of this behavior. It should be underscored that often the negative results of this type of behavior accelerate the "maturing out" process, hastening one's exit from the gang (Vigil, 1988a). Despite any respect or recognition earned, most youth remain conscious of the detrimental effects of violence.

If we follow a human developmental model, examining the various facets of growth and maturation, it is fairly obvious that the social dimension of the gang, for gang and non-gang youth alike, is perhaps its most important feature. In particular, the desire to be well liked and accepted is common across most adolescent groups, but this human aspiration takes on a different meaning with gang members. For a gang member, his stage, where he will search for respect and popularity, is the street.

Group psychology is a key aspect of low-income life and plays an important overall role for street children bereft of home and school moorings (Suárez-Orozco & Suárez-Orozco, 1995). Gang members often hold a poor view of themselves. Because of their low self-esteem and fragile and fragmented egos, the street group or gang becomes personally valuable and helps make members feel complete. Self-identification and ego development for them have been radically different processeses than those experienced by non-gang youth, consisting of even more ups and downs accompanied by hits and misses. When a critical mass of similarly unevenly developed youth undergoes street socialization, the outcome is a street identity that is strongly group-based.

On the emotional plane, the crisis passage of puberty is accompanied and strongly affected by bodily changes and hormonal adjustments and imbalances. Becoming more self-conscious of these developments in the context of street life, where the pressures and demands are sometimes overwhelming, leads to a tremendous amount of ambiguity and confusion. This is especially the case because of the developmental tension that exists between early household socialization, during which solely females often rear males, and street socialization, which occurs under the aegis of a male, multiple-aged peer group. Obviously, this makes one even more peer-dependent; members must maintain the emotional stability necessary to keep up the gang front, which is part of the role psychology of the gang (Vigil, 1988b). That is, the physiological changes of puberty, mother-centered households, and street socialization are a potent mix.

As a result of these strains, children from such homes attend school with physical and emotional habits and handicaps that negatively affect their learning and behavior. To compound matters, they also carry an inner rage imbued with a heightened anti-authority edge, an attitude that the streets help forge and bolster. Severely strained households generate negative habits, handicaps, and rage, especially against authority.

Seeking friends to like you and relying on them almost exclusively for guidance and direction can also wreak havoc on the cognitive level of a gang member. There are many physical and mental inconsistencies exhibited by low-income young adults that reflect this tendency. Some gang members often maintain gang and non-gang associations; many adopt a *streetsmart* and *schoolsmart* duality. In fact, although more common among Asian American gang members, the shifting nature of being schoolboys by day and street boys by night—as we will present with the portrait of Jared in Chapter 2—is a balancing act that shows the precarious, flexible identities that youngsters assume as gang members. For some, it is not uncommon to hide their schoolbooks in lockers or to make sure they are never seen carrying books home; such behavior would show fellow gang members that they are not serious about belonging to the gang. The *streetsmart* and *schoolsmart* balancing act of youth embraces dual identities.

The bonding that takes place in the classroom thus often augments what is learned in the streets. As a strategy of survival, street identification is nurtured when youth learn that they need protection, friendship, and support from one another (Vigil, 2007). In the classroom, this identification is intensified, with new dimensions added. Protection and friendship, among other gang attributes, can also mean that you stand up for your friends if the teacher is picking on them, regardless of whether the treatment is deserved or not. When these individuals are singled out by authority figures because of some particular deed or trait, group bonding increases exponentially. Such phenomena as inappropriate behavior, poor study habits, dislike for reading, lack of academic preparation, cultural differences, a need for remediation, and so on generally characterize street children when they arrive in school. Sharing certain backgrounds and personal and home problems, these children are placed in a behavioral and learning category in which teachers strive to give them special help. The teacher, in making sometimes heavy-handed attempts to do so, faces the additional problem of being seen as a usurper of parental authority (which, in any case, the child has by now begun to defy). In the minds of gang members, bonding to defy an unsanctioned authority contributes to the group and gang, adding another objective to the already well-honed gang repertoire. Protection and friendship of the gang extends into the arena of school, fostering behavioral and academic difficulties—the school environment augments the bonding of the gang.

Finally, much of what is true of the emotional state of mind during puberty applies to concurrent physical changes. Although the interior of a person is undergoing mostly hidden changes, it is obvious when physical appearance makes a tell-tale statement about ambiguity and uncertainty. Voice deepens, height increases, and other bodily alterations remake the person and, especially, threaten the sense of confidence associated with control and management of these physical developments. All of these physical changes send a message to onlookers that the adolescent is a work in progress. During this time, the adolescent needs to show mastery by achieving or shining in some capacity. For males, sports become a very important avenue and outlet for such status recognition; females gain attention by wearing makeup and dressing in more adult styles. However, in contrast to the dominant society, where teenagers are socialized in conventional areas of accomplishment, such as academics, sports, and so on, the streets dictate a different set of feats for many gang-prone youth. Showing toughness is a particularly important characteristic for street children, and a few are demonstrably combative. Such individuals are usually those who have experienced early childhood traumas.

Certain developmental phases unfold on their own, such as hormonal and physical transformations. Other phases, by contrast, depend on the ecocultural system that a person lives in—such as home, school, or the streets—and the role models found therein. For example, how the ego is shaped and grows determines whether it develops an overreliance on the group, in which case a person becomes peer-dependent and surrenders to the group. To complicate matters, aside from developmental issues, it is fairly obvious that most adolescents and youth have specific needs and indulge in what many consider to be normal activities. These outlets include striving for friendship, the selection of social gatherings, participation in the daily gossip of their cohort, and even drinking alcoholic beverages and taking drugs. Developmental phases and normal adolescent patterns pertain to all youth. However, the streets in high-poverty neighborhoods present different obstacles and dictate various options to skew such phases and normal activities. We must understand these in order to promote the successful socialization of all youth both in and out of schools.

THE SIGNIFICANCE OF IMMIGRATION
IN A CHANGING SOCIETY

Although migrations certainly include people of means looking for better opportunities, the large-scale movements of people in the 19th and 20th centuries typically were represented by poorer populations seeking a better life. Immigration to the United States certainly has followed this pattern.

With the closing of the western frontier, readily available land for settlers became increasingly scarce and newcomers consequently settled in urban environments, lured by the promise of employment during the Industrial Revolution. Most were forced by their limited means to take up residence in run-down sections of these urban areas. The limited employment and overall opportunities, combined with the prejudices of earlier generations of Americans, made their task that much more difficult.

Beginning in the 1840s and continuing into the 20th century, young immigrant men of Irish, Italian, German, Jewish, and Polish origin gathered on the street corners of their respective neighborhoods to form gangs and confront together the rigors of their new life in the industrialized cities of the Eastern and Midwestern United States. Later, other immigrant groups from Latin America and Asia repeated this experience of establishing ethnic enclaves characterized partly by youth gangs. In this context, a holistic, integrative assessment and interpretation of street gangs must recognize the historical strands and sources of gang delinquency. For immigrants, adapting to a new culture and place affects family structure and stability, schooling readiness in the context of language and cultural differences, and level of involvement with police and the criminal justice system.

Remarkably, in examining the past, we find similarities. Then and now, major pressures force the children of immigrants into the streets. For well over 100 years, the presence of immigrants has generally aroused resentment in sectors of American society. Seldom, however, has this hostility reached such a high pitch as at present, and what is different today is the intensity of the anti-immigration backlash, especially against Mexicans (Chavez, 2008). Of course, anti-immigrant sentiments are heightened during economic instability (Suárez-Orozco & Suárez-Orozco, 1995).

The United States recently underwent a census count that demonstrated drastic demographic changes within its borders, with disproportionate increases in the population of non-Whites. These population changes have not gone unnoticed and have elicited a variety of responses from xenophobic and nativist groups alike. Recent examples reflecting negative and damaging sentiments include the anti-immigrant bill (H.R. 4437) proposed by Wisconsin congressman Jim Sensenbrenner in 2005, as well as current attempts by conservative state legislators in Arizona. These legislators have introduced two separate bills that, if passed, would eliminate Ethnic Studies programs in the K-12 public educational system and deny non-citizen students access to public education. Consequently, these developments have led to the wholesale deportation of many immigrant gang youth and, in their wake, the exportation of gang culture to their homes in Mexico, Central and South America, the Dominican Republic, Haiti, and Belize.

Immigration, both documented and undocumented, and the experiences of immigrants adapting and adjusting to city life form the basis for all else that follows, including and especially the maladaptation that so often occurs as a result. As immigrant families encounter problems in their adjustments to life in new settings, youths often seek respite in the streets from problems in their communities and schools.

As previously mentioned, the contexts of time, place, and people are important parts of the equation. For example, some gangs have been around for generations and are found in various large and middle-sized cities in the United States (Vigil, 2010). Studies in larger cities show a tradition of an age-graded gang structure (Moore, 1991). This network of cohorts works to maintain the size of the gang as older members mature out or go in and out of prison; consequently, the younger novitiates are more likely to fill the void. Newer gangs have emerged in urban, rural, and suburban enclaves as a result of continuing large-scale global immigration from Asia and Latin America, where increasingly more street youth are pushed and seduced into the gang lifestyle (Telles & Ortiz, 2009).

THE ROOTS OF ETHNIC MINORITY SCHOOL EXPERIENCES

Researchers for over half a century have grappled with understanding ethnic minority school achievement (Valencia, 2010). The consequent academic pursuits led to important developments and findings (Conchas, 2006; Suarez-Orozco & Suárez-Orozco, 1995). In general, researchers have focused on either structural or cultural foundations as the causes for poor student performance (Feliciano, 2006a). According to the structural theorists, America's long history of economic dislocation and oppression creates a "caste" educational system that works to exclude ethnic minority children. According to some of these theorists, this exclusion has created a countercultural reaction, an "oppositional" culture (Ogbu, 1987; Willis, 1977) of distrust and suspicion of dominant institutions and authorities—a sort of turning off from a social system that has traditionally and historically oppressed these children. Other theorists argue that cultural barriers or acculturation strains, either language difficulties or a conflict in norms/behaviors/values with mainstream society, serve as the primary problem source. The cultural difference viewpoint takes a bottom-up (micro) perspective, whereas the societal viewpoint prefers a top-down (macro) assessment.

The debate for too long has been cast between the structuralist and culturalist camps (Feliciano, 2006b). A blended model—one that integrates both the structuralist and culturalist viewpoints—is needed to explain the complex relationship between ethnicity and academic performance. Previous studies have too often neglected the tremendous variability found among ethnic Americans in the largest settings in the nation, regions undergoing rapid demographic and cultural changes even at this moment. Researchers have conducted investigations in mid-sized cities or rural towns, rendering their findings similar with larger, more diverse populations such as those found in Los Angeles. Limiting the debate to either structural or cultural explanations ignores the significance of an individual's persona, actions, and motivation.

Social scientists noted long ago that minority groups, natives and immigrants alike, often fashion strategies of acculturation or cultural integration that entail retaining the original culture while learning the new one (Chávez, 2008; Warakoo, 2011). Writers also noted that individuals who take this path of biculturalism often find school success (Gándara & Contreras, 2009). Even as the debate between the structuralists and the culturalists sometimes takes center stage, the overwhelming evidence compiled supports the idea that an *expansionary* rather than a *contracting* acculturation pathway results in successful school performance. Gibson and Ogbu (1991) referred to these concepts as *additive* and *subtractive acculturation*. The case for an expansionary mode of acculturation can be found in the academic success of many immigrants, such as Mexicans (Conchas, 2006), Cubans (Portes & Bach, 1985), and Punjabi (Gibson, 1988). However, although there may be general agreement on the value of expansionary acculturation, the clash between structuralists and culturalists continues to drive much of the debate.

It is time to move beyond the either/or framework dividing structuralists and culturalists. The multiple marginality framework, conversely, shows the actions and reactions among various forces. These generate and sustain an extremely tenuous and uneven educational experience for ethnic minorities. Our work integrates both the structuralists' and culturalists' viewpoints, striving to explain the academic performance in poor inner-city centers.

STRENGTHENING COMMUNITY-SCHOOL PARTNERSHIPS

For the nation's hopeful, education continues to be viewed as the great equalizer, particularly among the most marginalized groups. As a society, we expect schools, particularly in urban areas, to level the playing field amid the larger social and economic ills present in such contexts—poverty, residential segregation, and health care disparities (Noguera, 2003). We challenge urban schools to diminish or, at least, resist the pervasive achievement gap while facing inequitable funding formulas, high administrative turnover, and underprepared and inexperienced teachers (Kozol, 2005). In this context, schools are charged to invest their limited human and economic resources in circumventing such inequalities (Conchas, 2001), while teaching children the new basic skills to thrive in today's complex economy (Murnane & Levy, 1996). However, educators and administrators across the country, by themselves, continue to struggle to serve all youth well.

Schools and external agencies, such as community-based organizations, execute distinct out-of-school approaches in an attempt to reduce truancy and dropout rates among young people. The research on in-school programs, after-school programs, and community-based programs is promising (Fashola & Slavin, 1997). Such initiatives are often committed to utilizing rigorous, proactive strategies and processes to engage youth. Some are adamant about making critical linkages between communities/programs and schools, for the purpose of building an expansive network of support for the students (Noguera, 2001). Both dimensions to truancy and dropout intervention, in-school and community-based, provide students with opportunities to empower themselves while boosting student achievement and school engagement.

The idea of deliberately bridging institutions, such as community-based organizations and schools, is rooted, in part, in social capital theory (Putnam, 2000; Rodríguez & Conchas, 2009). The theory is that to effectively build capacity among people across various institutions around any issue, institutions and people need to connect and partner with one another. In the case of marginalized inner-city youth, community-based organizations and schools are two of the many stakeholders that show the most promise in collaboratively and effectively addressing their needs.

CONSTRUCTING SCHOOL SUCCESS

Schools can have a powerful effect on inner-city youths' experience of social conditions. Schools by themselves, however, are hard-pressed to circumvent structural inequality at the larger social and economic level. Specific school programs construct school failure and success among low-income populations. The findings from our years of combined research extend our understanding of the fluidity and nuance of low-income students' within- and between-group variations in inner-city school contexts. Our collective work reveals that institutional mechanisms have an impact on school engagement and achievement among a diverse low-income student population.

Recent studies provide important empirical evidence that low-income Mexican-descent youth are not monolithic, but instead complex and diverse (Conchas, 2001; Vigil, 2007). In Chapter 5, for instance, we will assess the variations in acculturation and schooling achievement across two generations of Chicano students in the greater Los Angeles area that have implications for other immigrant groups. We classify youth along an acculturation spectrum that includes Mexican-oriented, Intermediate, and Anglo-oriented.

Within the acculturation spectrum, we identify four major profiles of Chicano youth in Los Angeles. The first profile includes low-income first-generation Mexicans, with high goals but limited resources. The second profile comprises the children of the small segment of the petty bourgeoisie, those who were neither Mexican- nor Anglo-oriented. The third profile represents most of the at-risk Chicano youth, those who fashioned a street *cholo* style with the local gang. Lastly, a large number of Chicano youth are Anglo- and surfer-identified students known as the "Chic-Anglos." We depict not a generic Chicano youth population, but a diverse and complex one. A stable ethnic and cultural identity signaled positive school outcomes for many of these urban youth. Importantly, however, students who were in the middle culturally—the cultural marginals—were more prone to join and identify with the *cholo* population or another youth subculture.

Despite variability, research indicates that the school context has a tremendous impact on poor school performance among low-income students (Datnow, Hubbard, & Mehan, 2002). Studies usually point the finger of blame at the aesthetically unpleasant and ill-equipped surroundings, the inadequate instructional materials, the unmotivated teachers, and the defiant peer subcultures, such as youth gangs, that low-income urban students face (Vigil, 1998b). Others specifically implicate school factors—such as teacher expectations, lack of cultural awareness, and a curriculum that does not reflect the lived experiences of minority youth—as contributors to low academic performance (Mehan, Villanueva, Hubbard, & Lintz, 1996). Yet in spite of the all-too-familiar problems of unequal schools in poor neighborhoods and overall dismal performance, many low-income youth can and do defy the odds (Conchas, 2006; Gándara, 1995; Mehan et al., 1996). School context, which includes environmental aspects as well as pedagogy, curriculum, and quality of teachers, contributes mightily to student performance in school.

Mehan et al. (1996) employed the concept of *social scaffolding* as institutional support systems that the AVID program (Advancement Via Individual Determination) promotes to increase school success for low-achieving students. The term refers to "the practice of combining heterogeneous grouping with a uniform, academically rigorous curriculum enhanced with strong supports" (p. 78). Concentrating on the organizational arrangement provided through the AVID program, Mehan et al. demonstrated how social scaffolding mediates student agency and positive academic outcomes. AVID provides low-achieving Latino and African American youth with both the cultural capital (Bourdieu, 1986) and the social capital (Stanton-Salazar & Dornbusch, 1995) essential for social mobility. Similarly, Conchas (2006) and later Conchas and Rodríguez (2008) found that social scaffolds within small schools foster student identities, peer cultures, and social capital responsible for academic success among Asian, African American, and Latino youth.

We suggest that particular units within schools may reinforce the patterns of student (dis)engagement laid out by the multiple marginality model, whereas others may disrupt these patterns and account for some of the variation in street youths' social and academic engagement. Programs and conditions in schools can unwittingly construct failure or success for many low-income young adults. Our combined research demonstrates the importance of school cultures that structure learning environments that link academic rigor with strong collaborative relationships among students and teachers. Our work reveals the necessity of establishing strong links between low-income youth and the institutional support systems necessary for academic success and positive expectations. Most important, school processes and structures play a significant force in reengaging youth in the face of limited opportunity.

As a way forward, we need to take street socialization into consideration and structure success for all youth. Our work suggests that we need to devise institutional support systems and pedagogical methods that embrace difference and create a positive disposition toward school success. Although certain school effects begin to foster positive educational experiences, they do not equally transform students' perceptions of the opportunity structure, especially among the most marginalized street kids. Before tangible progress occurs, as we will demonstrate in Chapter 8 in the case study on African American boys, we must wrestle with the weight of larger social and economic inequality and the creation of street socialization. These processes have a devastating impact on the experiences and perceptions of boys of color concerning social mobility. The success of new institutional support systems and pedagogy depends, to a great degree, on successful progress in addressing social and economic inequality.

CONCLUSION

Schools have generally failed in addressing the needs of low-income, ethnic minority children. Nowhere are the effects of this failure more visible and intractable than in the lives of street-socialized children. These street-identified children typically score poorly on tests and exhibit behavioral problems in the classroom, often compounded by street pressures that infiltrate the schoolyard. Conventional efforts at intervention through such mechanisms as parent-teacher conferences often meet with apathy. As these children get older and their behavioral problems become more serious, often under the influence of gang membership, the usual institutional response is to attempt to suppress the problem behavior and/or to remove the child from the school. This response not only often constitutes abandoning all hope for the child's future, but also does little to prevent other youth from following the same unconventional path.

Educators have struggled to develop new strategies in the school environment to address the educational needs of street-socialized children. The various school-based strategies that have been formulated and are constantly being reformulated often do not target the street-socialized segment. In general, conventional school strategies, which have found minimal success, address behavioral problems, focusing on suppression, removal, and generic "at-risk" students, while failing to address poverty and street-socialization.

Multiple marginality is an important conceptual tool to inform educational policy and practice as we devise strategies and interventions for success along the educational pipeline. We must clearly understand how youth spend their time, with whom, and where—that is, we must consider time, people, and place. In addition, educational strategies ought to consider social, emotional, cognitive, and physical facets of human development among all low-income street-socialized youth. Embracing a multiple marginality framework in education takes us in the right direction.

Although it is difficult to change larger structural economic and racial inequalities, communities and schools have the potential to circumvent the damaging effects of forces that lead to disengagement and failure for too many of our youth. As we will observe throughout this book, communities and schools have the potential to reengage youth back on track to productive lives. We suggest that communities and schools ought to push for an ecology of opportunity to minimize the devastating effects of inequality. School success among all youth ought to be the norm, not the exception.

Chapter 2

To Compete in This World

A Vietnamese American Portrait
of Loss and Liberation

> *The model minority stereotype was used . . . to silence claims*
> *of racial inequality. The stereotype set standards for how Asian*
> *American students and all other students of color should behave,*
> *and it hid the problems faced by some Asian American students. And*
> *finally, the stereotype influenced the way Asian American students*
> *viewed themselves, and when that happens, they may, as one student*
> *reminds us, 'just lose your identity . . . lose being yourself.'*
> —Stacey L. Lee, *Unraveling the Model Minority'Stereotype*

Orange County in Southern California is home to one of the world's largest concentration of Vietnamese immigrants. An estimated 130,000 Vietnamese refugees and children of refugees reside within the county (Vigil, 2010). In particular, the Little Saigon district in the city of Westminster, the heart of Orange County's Vietnamese community, has seen a tremendous amount of commercial and residential growth.

Refugees from Vietnam migrated to Little Saigon in two stages. The different historical and socioeconomic circumstances of these two sets of refugees considerably influenced their respective adaptive responses to life in America (Conchas & Pérez, 2003). The first wave of emigration began in 1975, when news of the Communist takeover first spread through Saigon. The story of the second wave of refugees—the "boat people"—is less sanguine (Conchas & Pérez, 2003). Unlike their predecessors, these refugees, unable to escape during the fall of Saigon, were forced to endure Communist rule for some time before they, too, made their exit.

Unlike their earlier-arriving counterparts, these second-wave individuals, emigrating in the late 1970s and 1980s, were generally less prepared for life in America. Data indicate that the boat people, in comparison with first-wave refugees, were generally poorer, younger (over half were children or teenagers), less educated (often illiterate), and less urbanized (many were rural farmers); fewer of them had job skills useful in this economy (Vigil, 2002b). Most notably, many of them came without their families—relatives either had died en route or were too poor to pay for their own escape. Thus, the familial social capital, crucial to the success of the first wave of refugees, was unavailable for many of the boat people (Oseguera, Conchas, & Mosqueda, 2010). Finally, the second wave of immigrants suffered, due to the privations of war, occupation, and perilous sea passages, much more trauma (Zhou & Bankston, 1998).

The boat people arrived during a time of massive cutbacks in government aid to Vietnamese immigrants. The powers-that-be terminated job training for Vietnamese immigrants. English as a Second Language (ESL) and programs for English Language Learners (ELL) ground to a halt. Many social workers maintain that most refugees have little time for such training when they are already working 12 to 14 hours in menial jobs to support their families. This parental absence, necessary for survival, combined with poverty and trauma related to the violence and loss of war, generated some of the conditions sufficient for gang formation in the Vietnamese community. This chapter presents a general overview of that gang formation and a real-life portrait of a young man struggling to adapt within a Southern California community.

VIETNAMESE GANGS IN SOUTHERN CALIFORNIA

Against a backdrop of socioeconomic duality, crime has asserted a prominent and persistent presence in Little Saigon (Vigil & Yun, 1990). The rise of Vietnamese youth gangs coincided with the influx of the second wave of refugees into Orange County. In fact, among youth who are involved in gang activity, all are second-wave refugees. The police estimate that there are anywhere from 500 to 3,000 Vietnamese gang youths in Orange County, but even these broad estimates are highly speculative. Social workers, community activists, and Vietnamese businessmen estimate that no more than 10% of the Vietnamese youth population is engaged in crime; the gang youths themselves estimate that the figure is much higher (Vigil, 2002b).

Vietnamese gangs differ from traditional ghetto and barrio gangs of other ethnic groups in many ways (Vigil, 2002a). Many, but not all, of these new gangs did not adopt gang names. They are rarely territorial—they don't claim "turf." Not associated with any colors or symbols, many of these youth are straight-A students, and a perception exists that if these youth do participate in criminal endeavors, they tend to have a high rate of success (Vigil, 2002b). To the casual American observer, it may seem as if Vietnamese gangs are acculturating to American gangs, but observers of history must recognize that China occupied Vietnam for over a millennium. In China, for thousands of years, criminals have formed highly developed secret societies, impermeable to outsiders, known as "triads" or "tongs." Many modern Asian gangs maintain similar traits, including well-honed strategies to avoid detection.

The idea of gang "membership" is different in Asian gangs. Many youth claim that they are not part of a "gang" at all, but instead claim that they are part of a loose collection of friends. These groups have an amorphous and fluid structure. Membership is determined almost arbitrarily; "jumping-in" and other initiation rituals are absent. This dynamic gang structure continues to prevail, although there are recent indications that Vietnamese youth are starting to copy characteristic behaviors from Black and Chicano gangs. Hand signs, clothes displaying a gang name, and even graffiti are becoming more common among Orange County's Vietnamese gangs (Vigil & Yun, 1990).

Vietnamese youth gangs seem to commit different types of offenses from organized crime groups and other ethnic street gangs. Unlike Black and Chicano gangs, drug dealing is relatively uncommon, although, as we see in the portrait of Jared below, not unheard of among this population. However, Vietnamese gang members are often drug users. Extortion, or the requirement of money for "protection," is also rare; Vietnamese youth gangs have been reluctant to trespass in an area staked out by older, more organized criminal organizations. Most of our informants have engaged in property crimes, especially auto theft. At one time, Vietnamese gang violence was relatively uncommon. Most gang youths were more focused on the "business of obtaining money," and violence or "gang-banging" was simply not a profitable endeavor.

More recently, however, several outbursts of violence caught the media's attention, including a series of incidents at cyber-cafes in the Little Saigon area and a major gang fight that erupted at a popular shopping mall. The rise of gang-related violence in Little Saigon corresponded to the rise in a singularly terrifying crime perpetrated by Vietnamese gangs—the home invasion robbery. This crime sometimes results in the torture and murder of homeowners. Leery of currency instability in their own home country, as well as institutional authority, many Vietnamese have preserved the practice of foregoing banks and keeping their savings—often in the form of gold— within their homes (Vigil, 2002b). Youth gangs, often relying on a tip or inside information, target a Vietnamese home and survey it for several days. After obtaining sufficient information, they invade the home and force the victims to reveal the hidden location of their savings and valuables. During these crimes, the gang employs lookout drivers equipped with cellular phones. In the rare event that police arrive at the scene, the lookouts alert the robbers and distract the police.

Home invasion robberies can be highly lucrative. The gang splits the profits, and many times the money is used to purchase cars (some youths claimed they bought a new car each week), expensive *GQ*-like clothing, weapons, drugs, and food and drink at fancy restaurants and bars. Sometimes youth use the money to gamble. In addition to these invasions, organized crime rings, such as "the Frogmen," engage in extortion, prostitution, and illegal gambling. These groups provide guns, money, and other support for the street gangs.

Complicating the notion of a "model minority" typology—that is, Asians characterized as American success stories—our discussion reflects the effects of street socialization and racism on marginalized Vietnamese youth. Our subject for this chapter's portraiture, Jared G., the son of Vietnamese refugees, attends the University of California full-time. Attending junior college for 5 years before his transfer to the University, despite spending time in jail for a felony conviction, he is one quarter away from graduation and determined to finish. Though Jared never became an official gang member, he continues to associate with friends and acquaintances who do claim membership. Jared's life is a constant struggle between loss and liberation.

A LIFE WOVEN FROM TRAUMA, LOSS, AND DISCIPLINE

Jared was born on July 23, 1985, in Santa Ana, California, the second child and first son of immigrants from war-ravaged Vietnam. Prior to their arrival in the United States, his parents spent 2 years in a refugee camp in the Philippines. Jared's father, Duc, met Jared's mother, Nhu, in the camp and used his influence to help her gain admission into the camp, a necessary step to gain a chance to immigrate to the United States. The memories of Jared's parents diverged as they told their respective accounts of events that took place in Vietnam.

Both parents agree that Jared's father, Duc, one of nine children, was born into a privileged family. Duc finished high school and joined the Army of South Vietnam. Captured during the war by the North Vietnamese, he spent 8 or 9 years (he wasn't sure) in a North Vietnamese Communist prison. His parents and four of his brothers died in these prisons. Of his family, he was the only survivor. When Nhu immigrated, she left 11 siblings and her parents behind, but at least they were all alive. The couple made it to the United States in 1980.

They immigrated with the second wave of Vietnamese refugees, taking to the sea in tiny, overcrowded boats. Finding their way onto these rickety boats, they had no formal immigration papers, which would have allowed them to enter the United States. Instead, they hoped to make it to one of the refugee camps in Malaysia, the Philippines, Hong Kong, Thailand, or

Indonesia. If they made it to a camp, they would have to apply for asylum and wait—sometimes for years. The lucky ones, like Jared's parents, made it to the United States with the outside shells of their bodies intact.

Losing a Father, Losing a Place

Jared's mother remembered her husband as alcoholic, physically abusive, and lacking all ambition. Duc saw himself as a once-gifted student who, if he only had received guidance, could have thrived in America. Jared wasn't sure who to believe. He knew that the horror of the civil war brutalized its victims and their children, even as they immigrated to foreign havens. But he also knew his father. He described Duc as "an abusive man who has never worked a day in his life here [in the United States] and has only lived to extort money from his ex-wife and children." Jared leaned toward his mother's view.

When Jared was 2, his father walked out the door, taking his cruelty with him. Jared's mother and the children were physically safer. But the absence of a parent takes away many things. For a family like Jared's, as its memories, identity, and culture disintegrated in the offal of a brutal war, the loss of their father added to the trauma. Jared didn't have a chance to grow to see his father in more than one light.

As cruel as his father was, maybe there was a time, before he was imprisoned by the Communists, when his father had viewed himself as a young man with a future of possibilities. Maybe the gifted student once walked down red-dusted lanes bordered by pineapple fields and rice paddies, proud to be respected as an educated person, secure in his place in his family, one of many sons. Secure in his community. Maybe he heard distant music at night, the clicking, chiming sound of the *sientienh*, a centuries-old instrument, and, as he listened, never guessed that the sound would become foreign and dusty to him one day, reachable only in his dreams. He thought he would always be able to look up at the Southern Cross and dream of being *vuongdao*—a noble man. Maybe there was a time that he took for granted when he was a man—a respectable man.

Jared never heard any such memories . . . of belonging to land and people. Maybe if his father had stayed, he would have initiated his son into manhood by sharing such intimacies—fragile intimacies—treasured but lost to time. To share these would expose the fact that there was no way to return to those times, but perhaps it would have given Jared pride in his ancestors . . . an inheritance based on 4,000 years of Vietnamese history and his own heavily populated family tree. His people had endured the rule of the Chinese Han Dynasty, colonization by the French, Japanese occupation, and, finally, Uncle Ho Chi Minh. Instead, Jared heard nothing and the only thing inside him was a sense that he must endure and push—a vague echo from the Buddhist traditions of the place that would have been his country. From the time he was little, he remembered his mother telling him that he should strive to give back—that it is a true sign of love for him to live beyond himself and his selfish desires.

Maybe Jared's father would never have shared anything of goodness anyway. Maybe he was ever and always a limited person—a mean boy and a mean man. In every country, surely there are such men. But Vietnamese culture values extended family and community. In prewar Vietnam, someone would have had the heart and resources to help with Jared—an uncle or a grandfather . . . someone. Jared, born in the United States, didn't have a stable community around him to show him that his face was the face of a good man. He only knew what his mother told him. She told Jared that he looked just like his father.

Jared thought, *So be it, that is the father I had, the hand I was dealt . . . I use that to push myself further and try harder.*

Vietnamese, Koreans, Caucasians, and "Mexicans with Indian Strength"

After his father left the home, Jared's mother moved her small family to Garden Grove. The city was close to Little Saigon, an enclave for Vietnamese immigrants located in Westminster, California. Their Garden Grove neighborhood was of mixed race and ethnicity. There were Koreans, Mexicans, and Vietnamese, with a few pockets of Caucasians. By the time of the family's arrival, several more relatives from Vietnam had arrived—Jared's aunt and uncle and several cousins. They chipped in to help Jared's mother with child care. But the little family lived in poverty. Forced to depend on welfare and food stamps, speaking no English, Jared's mother clothed the children with castoffs. A photo from the time shows 3-year-old Jared wearing toddler girls' clothing.

Jared's mother finally got a job working the graveyard shift at a hospital. Every night, she lifted Jared and his sister out of bed and carried them to their aunt's nearby home, running across the grass and through the sprinklers. The children slept at their aunt's house on a pullout sofa. Nhu wore damp shoes and clothing to work.

And she worked hard. But there still wasn't enough money to do laundry on a regular basis. His mother told Jared and his sister to wear their clothes over and over. She taught them to wipe their hands on their shirts so that they could keep their hands clean.

When he reached school age, Jared began to attend elementary school in Garden Grove. The school was as diverse as the surrounding community. When students enrolled, they were all assessed for English proficiency. Jared was not fluent in English. One day, Jared's sister tried to teach him a new word. She pulled out an electrical appliance and showed it to the small boy. She said, slowly, "Vaaacuumm. . . . Now, you say it." The little boy's face lit up as he pointed to the appliance and answered proudly and quite correctly, "*Chan khong!*" He knew the correct name! She tried again: "Vacuum!" He answered once more, triumphantly: "*Chan khong!*" Because of his lag in English proficiency, the school placed Jared in remedial English classes. His sister quickly became proficient in English and soon transferred to a school for gifted children. Jared did not become proficient in English until 3rd grade, assisted by patient teachers and hours spent parked in front of the television set.

His mother shopped at the local Korean supermarket, where she faced the disdainful glares of the shopkeepers, who made no attempt to hide their dislike of the fact that Vietnamese lived so close to them.

Jared had his own problems. The Latino and Vietnamese children didn't get along at school. Many Vietnamese kids didn't get along. Jared had to fight other Vietnamese kids at school and sometimes the Vietnamese kids would join together to fight the Latinos.

Every day, Jared and his cousin Lanh walked home from school together. They often cut through a back alley where Mexican children congregated. One day, while walking home, Jared asked him in Vietnamese, "Do you want to rumble with these Mexicans?" Lanh responded, "Are you crazy? Mexicans have Indian strength!" Jason took Lanh at his word and the two boys walked peacefully home.

When he was 7, when all the adults in the apartment were out work-ing, a man molested Jared in the living room of his aunt's house. For many years, Jared thought the man was his father. But later, he became convinced that the man was their "creepy" landlord, who had grabbed at Jared and his cousins as they rode their bikes through the neighborhood.

The Rise of Anger in a "Dirty Asian"

About this time, Jared's mother met his stepfather, who had three children of his own. All the children seemed to get along well and Jared's mother and stepfather married in 1992. The blended family included Jared and his sister plus three older teenagers—two stepbrothers and one stepsister. The three stepchildren were all Vietnam-born. Their mother had died when they were young but no one ever talked about it. The family relocated to Westminster, California.

Jared started to fight with neighborhood kids and even with family members. One time, he fought his friend, Trong, and Jared's family took Trong's side against Jared. Another time, Jared fought his cousin Robert. This time, one of Jared's uncles held him and let another older cousin, Phuoc, punch Jared. Jared chased his sister with screwdrivers and chased his cousin with knives. His mother told him that Jared's father used to chase her with knives, too. Jared's family often sided against him. He figured he deserved it because of his violent nature.

The family moved to a three-bedroom home in Westminster. Part of the kitchen was set aside as a sleeping area. Here, Jared bonded with his 18-year-old stepbrother Sinh. Sinh let Jared tag along to his basketball games at the park. He bought Jared a foot-tall stuffed Ninja Turtle, introduced him as his little brother, and told him that he was his favorite brother. Sinh was known as a fighter, tough and respected. But one night the police arrested him for burglarizing a home in Westminster and he was gone—incarcerated for 2 years.

Soon, Jared's stepfather got an opportunity to go to Ohio to take advantage of a business opportunity. A friend there was opening a nail salon and there was a chance to make money. Jared's stepfather moved to Ohio. Soon, Nhu joined him. Then Jared's aunt left. Whenever an adult guardian left, the family arranged for the children to stay with another relative. The adults in the family told the kids that everyone had to put aside selfishness so that the whole family could do well.

By 4th grade, Jared spoke English well, began to excel in school, and became popular with his classmates. He and some friends started a little no-name club for themselves. There were designated roles for members. Jared was co-captain. They assigned some older children to be enforcers. Sometimes, while they were kicking it, they would get into fights with the FOBs—"Fresh Off the Boats." These were newly arrived Vietnamese children who didn't speak English at all. Jared thought it was fun.

One day, Jared's mother sent word that she was returning to California. The nail salon in Ohio was making a killing, but Nhu had discovered that Jared's stepdad had been spending "too much time" with prostitutes in visits back to Vietnam. Nhu filed for divorce, lived briefly with her children, and then moved away without them once more, this time to San Jose. Jared and his sister moved in with their aunt to Huntington Beach.

Jared didn't have any friends in Huntington and he wasn't quick to make new ones. It took time for him to trust people. One day at school, a girl asked him, "What kind of Asian are you?" He answered her: "Vietnamese." She made a face—"Ewww, you're the dirty Asian!" One day a Mexican, one of his ancient enemies, called him a "gook."

Making Money with the Viet Family

Jared rebelled and began to distance himself from his remaining family members—his sister, his aunt, and his cousins. He started hanging out on the street and drinking. In 10th grade, when he was 15, a Vietnamese friend came to him with a proposition. The friend's sister was dating a White guy, who was a member of a Vietnamese gang, the Viet Family (VF). The gang members called this white guy "Mi Chang" ("White" in Vietnamese). Mi Chang, who Jared laughingly called "OG Heeny," had some gang connections up the street in Westminster He said that Jared could start selling drugs in Huntington Beach—coke, meth, weed, ecstasy.

Jared and a partner started selling out of his friend's house, including mushrooms. They hit up all the White kids. Members from different gangs showed up at the house—from the V, one of the most sophisticated Orange County Vietnamese gangs, to the Viet Family, along with the Dragon Family, the Nip Family, the Nip Family Juniors, and the Viet Family Juniors. With this volatile mix came violence, and one day a gang member named Monkey from VF showed up at the house with OG Heeny. Someone had shot at them and a .22 round had grazed Monkey's scalp. As no adult was present, no one got into trouble. Business continued as usual.

At 15, Jared started to make a lot of money. By now, he had developed a habit of obsessive cleanliness—immaculate nails and clothing, smooth-shaven face, hair perfectly cut and spiked. Jared started giving his father money. One time, he trusted his father to sell a car for him. His father sold it and kept the money. Jared vowed to never be like his father.

You Can No Longer Call Me Mother

His mother made an announcement. She was going to become a Buddhist nun. Long a Buddhist, Nhu wanted to take the next step. Her children were almost adults. She chose to renounce her former way of living. She committed herself to mindfulness and to meditation, sometimes sitting motionless for 6 hours or more. She told Jared that although she would visit him, he could no longer address her as "Mother." That was a rule. Jared accepted this change. One more change.

About this time, Jared started to use some of his product and by the time he was 16, he was a full-fledged "tweaker"—a meth user. Jared's partner started buying some guns for intimidation and protection and they soon added the buying and selling of guns to their enterprise.

No Time for Feelings in Jail and in Rehab

Jared graduated from high school in 2005—but just barely. He had gotten into trouble with the administration for painting graffiti in a room. After graduation, he was in a car with a friend when the friend threw something from the moving vehicle. A policeman saw this and the two were charged with battery. Jared spent 2 weeks in jail. He stopped using drugs for 5 months and moved out of his aunt's house into an apartment. He was making enough money to pay 6 months of rent in advance.

He kept the business rolling, enrolled in a community college, and obtained a job at a retail telecom store. He started a little side business there. People came to the telecom store with information culled from stolen identities. Jared would set them up, using the stolen information, with 6 months' free use of a "burnout" phone—a phone with no bill, no contract, no deposit, and unlimited use of all its features. After 6 months, the phone would burn out and become unusable. In return for providing these phones, Jared got a flat rate in cash or drugs. A Long Beach detective opened an investigation into one of the stolen identity cases, but no charges were ever filed.

Jared started using meth again. In early 2005, the cops raided him and arrested him for selling weed. They also found some knives and brass knuckles on him, so Jared got hit with two felonies, receiving a sentence of 120 days in jail, 45 days of Cal Trans labor, and 3 years' probation. Two years later, he was busted for a DUI in San Diego. While he was on probation, his drug use escalated. He added prescription drugs—Xanax and OxyContin—to the meth, weed, and other drugs he was taking. His probation officer forced him to take a drug test and the results were dirty. After failing a Proposition 36 program, part of the Substance Abuse and Crime Prevention Act of 2000 (California Proposition 36), Jared was ordered into rehab—1 month inpatient followed by 6 months outpatient. It worked for a while.

In rehab, they tried to get Jared to open up about his feelings. Jared didn't know about feelings. The only big feeling he remembered having in his life was anger. Any other emotions—he knew he probably felt them when he was a little kid, a long time ago, but he couldn't remember feelings of being afraid or abandoned or rejected. He couldn't remember being happy. The drugs accounted for part of the blank spots in his memory, but not all. He was blank about things that happened before the drugs. He couldn't explain. It was as if the things that happened to him happened to a different person.

The University Schoolboy

He got sober and joined Alcoholics Anonymous. He had a sponsor and for a year and a half, he succeeded. He even sponsored younger kids. Still attending community college, his grades rose from a GPA of 1.3 to about 3.0. During this time, he applied for admission to the University of California, Irvine. He was accepted and started attending in 2006. His grade point average at UC Irvine was over 3.0. Although he achieved good grades, Jared started to slip up with drugs again. He discovered a quasi-society of drug users at the university. He was amazed at how many students used drugs.

He relapsed. He started using anything he could get his hands on—all the drugs he had used before, plus heroin. In 2009, he and a gang friend robbed a drug dealer. Jared was surprised how easy it was to force someone to do what you want. You just take stuff from people using force—they get scared—and most of them won't do anything about it. Jared also, with another friend, robbed a house. They took marijuana plants and made two grand, but Jared "started to feel karma, probably due to my Buddhist upbringing. From then on, I wasn't going to steal or do criminal acts. I was going to stop doing drugs."

Jared weaned off the heroin by substituting coke. Then he weaned off the coke. He continued to use drugs, but not as many hard ones and not as often. By the time he reached his final year at UC Irvine, he had maintained an average GPA of 3.28. He was enjoying school and learning. When the summer of 2010 came around, Jared only had one more quarter to go. The LSAT was straight ahead. And then he ran into a girl—a girl who liked drugs. The cycle started again.

Jared's Plan to Succeed

Three months after his girlfriend survived an overdose, Jared stuck to his plan. He graduated and, in his final quarter, received two A's and one C-. But he hadn't stopped using drugs—just yet. He planned to stop in time to concentrate on his prep course for the LSAT, scheduled for June 2011. If he passed, he would apply to a law school, preferably in the Bay Area. His sister and an uncle offered to take him in—they knew about the drugs and wanted Jared to get completely clean. But Jared didn't want to be dependent on them. He wanted to move only when he had a purpose, not just to sleep on someone's couch.

Jared wouldn't say that he was "quitting" drugs just yet. But he planned to be completely sober by age 30. He wanted to marry and father children and not be a drug-using parent. One thing at a time. Every day, he concentrated on waking up at 8:00 a.m. and going to bed by 1:00 a.m. He thought, "I've got to work the plan. I want to make my mother happy and be a success to pay back all her years of hard work . . . and I want to achieve success for me."

CONCLUSION

Like the Mexican immigrants, the Vietnamese community, upon arrival in Orange County, encountered various forces disrupting their adjustment to life in America. These are similar to the disruptions experienced by African Americans as they migrated from the South to the North in the early part of the 20th century. The historical features of Vietnamese immigration and assimilation have posed singular—and perhaps uniquely severe—challenges to Vietnamese people. Among them, the experience of the boat people stands out in terms of sheer misery and trauma suffered, which has further complicated the adaptation processes of many refugees. In addition to the boat people experience, other forces faced by Vietnamese refugees and their children greatly impact the acculturation processes. Often, they have witnessed the atrocities of war (violence and imprisonment), resulting in post-traumatic stress. Torn from culture and community in a way that has no transnational sense (different from travelers throughout the Southwest), they face unique difficulties. It is with an appreciation for these difficulties and the context in which they arise that we can begin to form a descriptive account of the youth gangs in Little Saigon and its surrounding pockets. We can examine the distinct sets of actors and infractions that give context to that region's criminal traditions.

Jared embodies the contradictions and complexities that shape or circumvent gang formation and involvement among immigrant youth. In his quest to acculturate to American life, Jared received little support from institutions, except financial aid for college and rehabilitation through Prop 36. He could have greatly benefited from in-school and out-of-school programs that could mitigate the impact on not only the families of Vietnamese refugees, but refugees of war from other countries.

The Southeast Asian Health Project in Long Beach, California, for instance, launched the Light of the Cambodian Family Initiative in the early 1990s to prevent refugee youth from joining gangs. The program focused on early-elementary school children of the Khmer community, an ethnic enclave that was experiencing a serious gang problem with adolescent youths. It was a preventive effort, targeting 6-year-olds—1st-graders—and their adult caretakers or parents. The program took into account several human development factors and specifically targeted youth's self-esteem. Policy and practice should embrace promising early prevention programs, in order to assist the sons of immigrants and refugees like Jared, who struggle to adjust and cope in a new land.

Chapter 3

A Second Chance

A Portrait of A Mixed-Race
African American Man

*The trouble with Black boys is that too often they are assumed to be at
risk because they are too aggressive, too loud, too violent, too dumb,
too hard to control, too streetwise, and too focused on sports. . . .
The trouble with Black boys is that most never have a chance to be
thought of as potentially smart and talented or to demonstrate talents
in science, music, or literature. The trouble with Black boys is that
too often they are placed in schools where their needs for nurturing,
support, and loving discipline are not met.*

—Pedro A. Noguera,
"The Trouble with Black Boys"

Social historian and biographer Taylor Branch (1989), in his Pulitzer Prize
winning book, *Parting the Waters,* asserts that "race shapes the cultural
eye." The statement captured the challenge facing those who, like Martin
Luther King Jr., advocate for policy change for people of color. This quote
also suggests the necessary path to successful advocacy during times of
social and economic struggle. The groundwork for policy change must
acknowledge and address existing racial perceptions in the quest to gain
equality and justice.

This chapter includes an in-depth case study that includes an overarching summary of relatively recent economic and historical forces impacting
African Americans—the Great Migration, the Watts Riots, the rise of the
Crips and Bloods, and the increase in the rate of unemployment. In this
context, there has been a rise in African American youth gang membership and an increase in juvenile delinquency. The forces impacting young
African Americans shape their options and carve racial perceptions in the
mind of the public. Realistic proposals for policy change need to address
the necessary transformation of the "cultural eye." This chapter serves as
an effort in that direction.

THE RISE OF AFRICAN AMERICAN GANGS

The African American immigrants who came by the hundreds of thousands via the "Great Migration" of 1915-1929 constitute the first critical mass in the movement of mostly unskilled urban workers and farmers from the poor South (Wheeler, 1993). Fleeing racism, they sought jobs in industrial cities, but were largely restricted to a few isolated areas that constituted a spatial ghetto (Vigil, 2002b). After the Great Depression, a new wave of westward African American movement turned the state of California into a primary destination.

African American Los Angeles gangs are relatively recent, emerging around the 1950s (Vigil, 2007). Racial incidents were the primary catalyst for the emergence of Los Angeles' first African American street gangs, which emerged as a defensive response to White violence in the schools and streets during the late 1940s (Alonso, 2004). Additionally, they can be linked to a reaction to European American car clubs in the 1950s and the effects of the civil rights movement in the 1960s. African American gangs have since become increasingly well-organized groups, focusing on business-like activities (Sanchez-Jankowski, 2008). Unlike Chicano gangs in Los Angeles, which are traditional neighborhood gangs that value their neighborhood's identity, African American gangs are often entrepreneurial; most are drug business operations motivated by desire for profit and control of the drug market (Vigil, 2002b).

In the mid-1950s South Central gangs such as the Businessmen, Slausons, Farmers, Parks, Outlaws, Watts, Boot Hill, Roman Twenties, and later the Gladiators and Rebel Rousers served as the architects of social space in new and usually hostile settings (Vigil, 2002b). During this time serious juvenile delinquency became a widespread problem for Black youth (Simpson & Pearlman, 2005). Recreational opportunities and playgrounds for children in overcrowded environments were scarce.

The tendency toward juvenile delinquency encouraged by such conditions was perhaps augmented by the fact that 44.1% of the African American workforce in 1940 was female and the corresponding figure for White females was 35.8% (Wilson, 1996). This prolonged separation from children on the part of the working mother may have played a role in fostering such delinquency. By the end of the 1950s, more than one-third of Black residents lived in public housing (Vigil, 2007). On the streets, homicides, stabbings, shootings, and fistfights became more common.

The Watts Riots and Beyond

Following the Watts revolt of August 1965, there was a period of 3 to 4 years when rival gang hostilities were put aside to some degree. Many street gang members, males and females, focusing on their shared hostility toward the police, started speaking of the 1965 disturbances as the "Great Rumble." African American street youth immersed themselves in the Black

Power Revolution. The Black Panthers were especially popular among street youth (Anderson, 1990). The abrupt destruction of the Panthers and the cutbacks in War on Poverty programs undoubtedly contributed to the acceleration of membership in street gangs in the early 1970s (Alonso, 2004).

Crips and Bloods

The first Crips gang was formed in 1969 and soon caught the attention of the authorities and the media. Media attention on the group's activities generated new members and rival gangs for the Crips, such that by 1972, 3 years after the first Crip gang was formed, there were 18 Crip and Blood gangs in Los Angeles (Vigil, 2002b). In the context of problems at home, in schools, and with law enforcement, it is not surprising that gangs have been embraced by many youths as the buffer to help them negotiate through adolescence and street life in the absence of occupational training and employment opportunities (Vigil, 2010).

In the half-century from 1940 to 1990, the Black population in the city of L.A. had mushroomed to close to 1 million, and a larger critical number of gang-age youth found themselves in the streets. By the 1970s "Crippin'" (i.e., taking part in Crips activities) had spread through the city as Crip "sets" were established (Vigil, 2002b). Under the incessant pressure of the dominant Crips, a number of independent gangs (some descended from the pre-Watts generation) such as the Brims, Bounty Hunters, Denver Lanes, Athens Park Gang, the Bishops, and the Pirus became federated as the Bloods. In response to pressure from the Crips gangs (identified with the color blue), the Bloods (red, obviously) formed and became particularly strong in the Black communities in South Central but especially on its periphery, in places like Compton, Pacoima, Pasadena, and Pomona.

Unemployment and Escalation

The situation only worsened in the 1980s. The unemployment rate for African American youth was a staggering 45% (Wilson, 1996). It should perhaps not be surprising that the underground economy, particularly the illicit drug industry, became a major problem in these circumstances (Sanchez-Jankowski, 2008).

From the 1980s to the beginning of the 1990s, the Bloods and the Crips escalated their violence. They started to expand their business to include narcotics trafficking, which resulted in the migration of gangs across the United States (Valdez, 2007). During this period of gang escalation, Los Angeles experienced a high gang homicide rate, which peaked in the early 1990s. Los Angeles always had a higher rate of gang homicide compared to the whole of California (Tita & Abrahamse, 2004). Due to this expansion into narcotics trafficking, gangs started to fight one another in order to gain more territory, resulting in more wealth and power for the gangs.

The Bloods and Crips gained notoriety through gang violence and illegal ventures, primarily drug and gun trafficking (Cureton, 2000). Steve Cureton explains Jack Katz's (1988) street elite theory and what it implies. Katz's theory states that potential gangsters are those who have been rejected or denied access to legitimate life chances. As a result, "these potential street elites become humiliated or humbled by the lack of prospects for participating in conventional society" (Cureton, 2002, p. 86). Gang members who were interviewed by Cureton solidified Katz's street elite theory. All four gang members interviewed agreed that access to legitimate opportunities is blocked. Their responses suggest that they are confident in their abilities to be successful in conventional society but believe that legitimate opportunities to fulfill the American Dream are not open to them. This is a major theme witnessed in Samuel's perplexing portrait.

FINDING THE FACE IN THE MIRROR
OF A MIXED-IDENTITY BLACK MAN

"Do you want to be part of the hood?" Samuel didn't know what the big boy meant. So Samuel didn't answer—just poked a stick in the gutter, mixing dust and trash. The big boy, standing with other boys and looking down at Samuel, spoke again—"Our hood! Shelley Street Pie-Roo!"

Samuel had just moved to the Santa Ana, California, neighborhood from Oklahoma and he knew a little bit about Shelley Street. His mother, Sharon, a Native American, once told him that Shelley Street used to be a mountain and that Shelley, a Native American queen, lived on the mountain. But Samuel didn't tell the big boy the queen story. He said nothing, even when the boys pulled him to his feet, punching and kicking him. He covered his face with his hands. After a while, the punches stopped and turned into pats on the back. The boys who "jumped" Samuel into the gang were not yet members of the Bloods. They were only 8- and 9-year-olds, copying their elders. One of the boys told Samuel, "Now you our homeboy." Samuel was 4.

Growing up in the Piru Gang

Samuel was born in 1972, in Oklahoma. Half African American and half Native American, he remembered that 1976 day as the beginning of his membership in the Shelley Street Piru Blood gang, an offshoot of the first group of Bloods in the United States, named for Piru Street in Compton.

As the years went by, Samuel continued as a member of the Piru gang. His mother worked long hours and the children of the family were unsupervised for much of the day. Except for telling him the story about the queen of Shelley Street, his mother, for unknown reasons, refused to teach Samuel about his Native American roots. "You're Black," she insisted.

Samuel hung out with the homies and played sports at school. He excelled in football and could play any position, but his favorites were tight end and running back. The coaches, in an effort to keep him working hard, put him into the games in all situations. A couple of years into high school, a business opportunity presented itself.

He started selling drugs. At first, he only sold small amounts. Pocket money. But something changed when he turned 16: "I started to sell more drugs because it was the only thing for me to do, you know . . . " He started with rock cocaine and then grew to specialize in cocaine, PCP, and a little weed. He said that he could make $20,000 in a day, sometimes $25,000, but that he had to put a lot of the money back into the business. He was so busy he didn't have much time to be scared of getting caught. But there was one night he remembered—a night of jumpy uneasiness. He remembered going for a nighttime drive with his homies. Samuel had just turned 16.

A Close Call

One of his gang associates, Lil AK, had called Samuel, his voice hard, the words dropping out quiet and smooth. Even over the phone, it sounded like Lil AK was insane and relaxed at the same time—a bad combination. It was "BLATT" time, and Lil AK told Samuel that he had to get over to the neighborhood in Santa Ana. BLATT stands for "Blood Love All the Time," and Lil AK was calling Samuel to duty. Someone from another gang had messed around with one of the Piru Blood girlfriends.

Samuel remembered meeting up with his gang brothers at a house. He remembered the guns tucked into the fronts of pants and the slow, easy methodical walk to the car and the drive to the other gang's neighborhood. The Pirus had heard that the other gang was having a party that night. As Samuel and his gang brothers drove up a residential street, the driver suddenly slowed the car—it was barely rolling—and Samuel saw the right shoulder of the guy in the front passenger seat rise as he pulled the gun from his waistband. They were almost at the house. He saw the shadow of a gun, right in front of his eyes, pointing out of the car, but the house was dark. He heard the sound of the safety being released on the gun . . . then suddenly the driver called out—"They ain't there!" And the driver accelerated away. It was over. That was all. Samuel was back at school the next day, practicing with his football team. Just like normal.

A Rise and Fall in Fortune

As months went by, Samuel's sales increased and he began to skip school to make drug runs. He made enough money to rent an apartment in Buena Park, where he stayed sporadically. Samuel set goals for himself. He wanted a big mansion. If he could be successful in football, he could get a house and any cars that he wanted—maybe even a limo. Samuel bought an El Camino and then, later, he spent $20,000 on a new Toyota Supra. Then he was arrested . . . and convicted on drug-related charges. The state sent the teenager to the Nelles Youth Correctional Facility. He should have been finishing up high school.

During an interview, Samuel sat on a plastic orange chair, denim-clad, in the visiting area of the Youth Correctional Facility in Whittier, California. The facility, dedicated in 1890, originally opened as a reform school for both girls and boys. In 1916, the California Youth Authority (CYA), a division of California's Department of Corrections, transferred the girls out and allowed only boys to reside in the facility. A strapping, 215-pound, 6- foot-tall, muscular 17-year-old, with no visible tattoos and a café au lait complexion, Samuel told his visitor, who wore a special yellow badge, that he was no longer a gang member. Soon to be paroled, he had been living in Ford Cottage, a cozy name for a dwelling in a place of incarceration. A favorite of the guards, he reported that his mother was talking to someone who would help get Samuel into "a school or something, but not right now, 'cause it's summer." He planned to play football in college and the NFL. In terms of what he wanted to study in college, he replied, "Nothing. I just want to get a better education . . . When I go, I'll study engineering, and so if I don't make it to pro football, I can fall back on something. I want to be a successful person."

He handed over a questionnaire that he had filled out before the visit. Along with basic questions about his family (he had one brother, two sisters, and his mother—Samuel is the youngest), the questionnaire includes other inquiries about gang life. One question: "How did your school's administrative staff react to the gang?" Samuel's answer: "Thay [sic] didn't really mined [sic] until fights started." Another question: "How did your folks react to the gang?" Answer: "Thay [sic] really didn't no to [sic] much about but thay now [sic] about the colors that I dressed in." Samuel reported that he had a B average. His file at the Youth Authority classified him as a "slow learner" and, as such, he had taken special classes during his time there.

Samuel reflected on the situation between the Crips and Bloods. He knew they would continue fighting, but he pointed out, "there's another war, between the Blacks and Whites. Everybody wants to be on top of things in America." Samuel acknowledged his own internal war—a war between doing right and doing wrong. Samuel knew it wasn't over, just like the war between the Crips and Bloods. He said, "I still got to fight with it."

Another Chance

Samuel was released when he was still 17-years-old. He was assigned a parole officer, who was going to monitor him and write up reports. On the day he was scheduled to get out, he sat in a waiting area for his mother to arrive. His mother walked in the door, with her long thick shiny hair barely laced with silver strands. Samuel used to play with her hair when she tucked him into bed. Samuel stood up as she silently walked over and hugged him tightly, holding on for several seconds. They walked out.

They barely spoke until his mother's Toyota cleared the gates. Then she smiled. She told Samuel that she was proud of him for finishing his time and that even though he had done wrong, he had followed the rules in the CYA. That was something to start on, she told him—everyone can be stupid from time to time. They stopped at a Coco's restaurant and as they sat in the booth eating burgers, his mom gave him the ultimatum.

She promised to help Samuel get started on the right path. She would take care of him until he was 18, but if he messed up again after he was 18, that was it. It was on him. If he flew straight, she would find someone to tutor him for the GED, to help him to find a job. She would give him room and board for a few more years. But he had to come with her to Pomona—she had moved from Santa Ana a couple of years earlier. She told him that he had to stop hanging out with the Piru Bloods. No more of that life, she said. After she finished speaking, Samuel said nothing.

When they arrived at the small house in Pomona, Samuel went straight to bed and stared at the ceiling. He saw a Bible on the nightstand next to the bed. His mother must have become a holy roller. He didn't want to hear about it because he didn't need another voice in his head. He hadn't called any of his homies from the Bloods, but they would soon hear that he was out. If they thought that he was trying to get out of the Bloods—what would they do? Blood in, blood out. That's what he had always heard and he had witnessed enough to be wary. As Samuel continued to struggle with his thoughts as he lay on the bed, there was another thought tickling his brain, behind the fear. What about all the money? Cash . . . all the time . . . that's the way it had been for him. Thinking about all his time as an associate in the gang, Samuel knew that he wasn't any kind of relative to any of the Bloods. Hell, Samuel wasn't even a relative to most of his blood relatives. He hadn't been back to Oklahoma since his mom had brought him to California. All that he had of his Native American inheritance was one story—a fantasy fed to him as a child, just to make him accept the move to California. Now that he was older, he still liked to remember when the story was real to him. He liked thinking about how, a long time ago, the Native Americans were everywhere in the land. Samuel only knew one Native American—his mother. She was always there.

Waiting for Darkness to Fall

Staying awake all night, the morning arrived and Samuel finally made up his mind. He walked into the kitchen where Sharon was making him breakfast and he told her that he had decided to leave the gang. He said that maybe his juvenile record could be sealed and he could have a chance to play football in junior college. He could tell that his mom was trying not to look too excited but that she was happy. She told Samuel that it wasn't too late for him to do something good.

Samuel waited to see what would happen next. As expected, he began to receive calls from the Piru Bloods . . . calls of expectation and demands. Samuel started saying that he was going to try to go to school for a while; he could barely say the words out of fear. The Bloods knew where he lived. Now, instead of being in the car with the shooter, he would be the person in the house, waiting to hear a car slow down and knowing what would happen next. But after he took a few calls, a week went by and the calls came more infrequently. Late at night, he listened as cars rolled by on the street that fronted their house. But nothing happened. One week turned into 2 and then into 3. Pretty soon, if the Bloods called, he told his mom to say that he wasn't home. Nothing happened. He knew that it would have been different if he were still living in Santa Ana. He was grateful for being so many miles away in Pomona.

Samuel missed the money but he didn't miss the constant dread. He didn't want to be on the wrong end of the deal . . . always watching and waiting. Once he turned 18, if he messed up it would mean prison. He slowly discovered that he liked waking up and having a simple life. Because of his mom's support, he didn't have to worry about food or a roof over his head. But he knew he couldn't just sit around.

The GED and the Mountain to Climb

Samuel's mom was working at a nearby grocery market as a checker. A week after Samuel got home, he asked his mom if she could help him sign up to take the GED. Samuel had never done well with tests. After agreeing to help him, Samuel's mom took him to the Pomona Library so that they could get a study guide. Even with the guide, Samuel struggled. He spent hours and only covered two pages of the guide. He just couldn't learn.

When Samuel was in elementary school, during the 1970s, scientists and doctors were struggling to find a consensus as to what constituted a learning disability. But right about the time that Samuel entered kindergarten, in 1975, the U.S. Congress passed the Education for All Handicapped Children Act. This act gave learning disabilities official status within the government. But recognition did not mean that the government formed viable, effective programs to help those with learning disabilities. Often, the only accommodation to these students' needs was to place them with other children of the same ability—"the low-ability group." There were few distinctions and understanding of the different categories of learning disabilities. And there was much argument over the definition of "learning disability"—was it of neurological origin or could it also be born of social and emotional disturbance (Hehir, 2005)?

Additionally, there has been much concern over why minorities are overrepresented in special education classes. Considering that African American and Hispanic groups are minority populations, they are overrepresented in the ranks of the learning-disabled. Some have argued that this overrepresentation is caused by tests that are racially biased, or by diminished access to health care or specialized educational programs. Samuel had never received a learning disability diagnosis, but his records, including his writing samples, suggest that he should have received testing. But he didn't, and as he tried to prepare for the GED, he felt like a failure. He considered going back to Santa Ana, but if he went back to the Pirus, Samuel felt like he would never get out.

Help Found in an Unlikely Place

His mother remembered somebody from the grocery store—a little old Italian American man, Mr. DiGiovanni, who shopped with a cane in hand. He always dressed neatly, with a cardigan, a fedora, a button-down shirt, and trousers. Over the course of time, she discovered that he was a retired teacher.

She soon arranged for him to tutor Samuel.

Samuel was willing to meet with Mr. DiGiovanni. At their first session, he listened to Samuel read and dictated a short paragraph to the boy. Then he looked Samuel in the eye and told him that almost every person can read and write. He asked Samuel if he thought that he was a smart fellow. Samuel said yes, but not at school. Mr. DiGiovanni said that Samuel could learn school things but that he was going to have to work hard. No complaining. They arranged to meet weekly.

Pouring Patios

Now Samuel wanted a job. A relative knew a Mexican American guy in Alta Loma—a guy in his late thirties. This guy had been in some legal trouble when he was young, but now he had a small business pouring concrete. He owned two trucks and some equipment and he needed someone to help. Samuel still thought that he was going to play football, once he got through the GED thing, and he figured that this kind of job would be good to stay in shape. Samuel was hired and soon was rising early to drive out to job sites. They poured a lot of concrete patios and Samuel learned how to build forms around the area they were going to be pouring, how to put rebar down, and how to pour and level the concrete. It was hard, exacting work and Samuel's boss was quick to yell at him during his first few weeks. But little by little, Samuel figured things out. And he wasn't making bad money.

His lessons with Mr. DiGiovanni continued. If Samuel balked at having to repeat sections of the book, Mr. Digi (that's what Samuel started calling him) told him, "If you don't have time to do it right, you don't have time to do it twice." They worked through the book, paragraph by paragraph. Mr. Digi taught him that there were some "tricks" to taking these kind of tests. "If you work, you are going to pass," he told Samuel. Samuel hoped that was true. In order to pass, he had to get better scores than 30% of the nation's high school seniors. That calculated out to getting more than half of the answers of each subtest right.

Test Day Arrives

The first day of the test arrived and Samuel arrived at the test center early. He was kind of nervous, but he figured that he had studied so hard that he would probably do okay. He followed the tricks Mr. Digi had taught him. He made sure he answered every question. He went home that night feeling confident at first and then, as the hours passed, old fears settled down in his stomach.

Over the next few days, he returned to the test center to finish the rest of the subtests and then it was time to wait. Samuel had some extra time on his hands. He hadn't been hanging out with anyone and life was boring. He almost called one of his former friends, but he didn't. Instead, he started hanging out with some of his co-workers and some friends of the family. They played pool and basketball. Some of them already had wives and children and Samuel started going to their family events. Even though he was underage, they handed him beers. Nobody used drugs, except for an occasional joint, but Samuel hadn't ever been into taking drugs—just selling them.

One day, at one of the picnics he attended, he met a young woman his own age. Her name was Royce and she was half White and half Latina. By the end of the day, they both knew that they were going to see each other again. Royce wanted to go to school to be a respiratory therapist. She had been an excellent student in high school. Samuel didn't mention anything about the GED to her.

A few days later, Samuel learned the results of the GED. He had passed! Samuel wondered whether he should invite Royce to the dinner celebration. He called her and told her that he had just obtained his GED. He asked her if she wanted to come to the dinner at his house. Royce accepted the invitation. All evening, Samuel kept thinking, *I don't have to take the test again. I did it. I don't have to take it again.*

Samuel Moves Forward

In 2010, Samuel was 39 years old and had been married to Royce for twenty years, living in Diamond Bar, California. They have three children, all sons—ages 18, 17, and 9. Both parents worked. Samuel owned his own concrete-pouring business and Royce worked in a doctor's office doing administrative work. She and Samuel ended up wanting to have children early in their marriage, so she put her plan to be a respiratory therapist on hold. She wanted to go back to school to fulfill her dream once their youngest reached high school age.

As Samuel started making good money from working in concrete, he slowly left the dream of football and college behind. Getting married young matured him, and he and Royce started saving money so that he could get his own business. When the time came, his boss from Alta Loma, who had been immensely successful, gave Samuel his blessing to start a concrete-pouring business as long as he didn't compete for the same territory. Samuel and Royce started feeling financial stability.

For a long time, Samuel didn't call anyone from the old neighborhood even though he was curious to find out what had happened to some of his old cohorts from the Piru Bloods. But one day, Samuel picked up the phone and called one of his old friends. He didn't even know if the number would work. But the phone number hadn't changed and a familiar voice answered. It took a minute for the man to remember Samuel, but once he did, he updated Samuel on a few of the others from the old days. Two or three were dead and even more were in prison. Samuel didn't say much—just told the man that he hoped everything was going well for him. And that was it. Samuel never called again.

Samuel filled his days with work and coaching his sons. The oldest one liked football. Samuel didn't know if he'd go far with it, but that was okay with Samuel. It was a different time. The schools had special programs for learning disabilities and they worked with his kids, who were showing progress. Samuel tells his sons that they are smart—they just have to find the right way to learn.

CONCLUSION

Similar to Vietnamese and Chicano youth, Samuel's life reflects the effects of poverty, street socialization, and racism over time. But he inherited these effects, not from transnational currents or the imported impact of a distant war, but from homegrown racism dating back to our nation's founding. Marginalization played a factor in where his parents lived, what school he attended, and whether he would be able to leave a life of extreme poverty. He also struggled with his mother's refusal to acknowledge his mixed ethnic heritage. She constantly reminded him of his African American heritage and discounted his Native American background. His mother, the greatest influence in his life, did not instill pride in Samuel for his Native American heritage and culture. Instead, she only allowed Samuel's father, whom he had never known, to classify Samuel's identity through his DNA and skin color. This along with poverty further complicated his life. Fortunately, he managed to do well despite the odds.

Samuel has been able to totally understand how he sees an African American face in the mirror, yet feels his strongest connection to identity in his Native American mother. But what does he know about Native Americans? He was ripped from any connection to that background, except for her. So his Native American background is still cloaked, only revealed in the swing of his mother's still thick, but now gray, curtain of hair. When he sees that hair swing, as she hugs one of her grandsons, he remembers how, when he was little, she and her thick hair were what he held most tightly.

Samuel's portrait captures the complexities of growing up poor and conflicted about his ethnic identity. He had been street-socialized at an early age and lived a gang life, experiencing time in the custody of the California Youth Authority. However, he managed to overcome the odds. With the assistance of a retired schoolteacher, Samuel obtained his GED and positioned himself to start a family and eventually own a business. Samuel deserves credit for his perseverance and effort. However, he had help from more than one person. Because of his mother, he was able to move away from Piru Street. Despite probable learning disabilities, he received one-on-one tutoring to obtain his GED. And, equally important, he was able to obtain a job and make a living wage.

Early on, Samuel, like many other young men in the streets, could have been benefited from community programs like the Big Brothers/Big Sisters of America. This organization has been shown to address poor self-esteem and limited hope for the future among low-income youth. Big Brothers/Big Sisters is focused largely on mentoring, but an integral aspect of the program involves a responsible adult volunteer taking his or her little brother or sister to enriching and interesting places for exposure to a world outside the neighborhood. This program has benefited many children and helped to take them off the streets. Ultimately, unlike many Black men in society who were not as fortunate, Samuel was given a second chance.

Chapter 4

Never Let Go

A Portrait of a Chicano Living
in and out of the Margins

*It is essential to recognize and acknowledge that we can no longer
remain silent about this growing epidemic. We believe that for Latino
males to succeed in the varied academic pathways, researchers,
policy makers, public officials, private sector leaders, and Latino
families and communities have to embrace this social justice agenda.
The sobering statistics are a clarion call for proactive action. We are
compelled to raise awareness of this issue at all levels of education,
K–12, postsecondary, and workforce development. There is a
pressing need to address this issue because Latino males represent
an untapped resource in our intellectual marketplace. We need to
illuminate the importance of educational policies that assist and
support Latino males in the educational system.*
—Victor B. Saenz & Luis Ponjuan,
"The Vanishing Latino Male in Higher Education"

The idea of movement conveys change. A river carries silt and minerals
as it churns to the sea, its final destination in stark contrast to its snow-
packed genesis. The movement of Latino immigrants is no different, with
the cultural, legal, economic, and linguistic changes faced in their new
environments often more jarring than the physical journeys they have
endured. But a paradox exists. So many have traveled far for better lives,
enduring change and wanting more change; yet their children often end
up in static positions, finding it difficult to utilize the avenues to success.
Latino immigration in the Southwest ebbs and flows, which differs from
other immigrant groups. This chapter, which includes a narrative portrait, will trace the rise of Latino street gangs and the criminalization of
Latino youth, which continues to limit their opportunities. We end the
chapter by suggesting strategies to open paths of upward mobility for
Latino youth.

THE EMERGENCE OF CHICANO YOUTH GANGS

Chicano gangs emerged in the mid-20th-century in American barrios and have become a major source of discontent in cities throughout the United States (Vigil, 2002b). The oldest street gangs stemmed from the first decades of Mexican immigration, and by the 1940s they were fixtures in many urban and rural neighborhoods. El Hoyo Maravilla and White Fence are examples of two of the oldest in East Los Angeles that later became active in forming prison gangs such as the Mexican Mafia (Rafael, 2007). Revolving around the dynamics of immigration and adaptation to American culture, gangs were comprised primarily of second-generation youth, who became marginalized as a collateral effect of their elders' problems adapting to mainstream American society.

As immigrant families—-similar to Vietnamese immigrants and others—encountered problems in their adjustments to life in a new setting (due to poverty, lack of education, low-paying jobs, and discrimination), youth often sought respite in the streets from problems at home (Conchas & Vigil, 2010). Many of these street groups began as a small number of disaffected youth, usually undergoing the "storm and stress" of adolescence, whose street socialization and behavior over time evolved from a pattern of malicious mischief into a deadly and violent lifestyle. For example, at its height, gang homicides in Los Angeles alone reached a high close to 1,000 per year in the mid-1990s (Vigil, 2010). Nonetheless, the resulting Chicano gangs usually comprised a relatively small percentage of the total population in their neighborhoods, anywhere from 4 to 15%, and of that percentage, the number of females was a small segment (Vigil, 2007).

The effect of gangs on society has been significant, particularly in the criminal justice system. Aggression and group conflict have always been a part of the Chicano gang experience. With the spread of illicit drugs and weaponry in the contemporary era, intergroup violence and homicides have at times seemed to spiral out of control, affecting even bystanders. Confined to mostly low-income areas initially, gangs have spilled over into working-class suburbs and, through the help of media, have begun to influence White youth (Vigil, 2007).

As noted in Chapter 1, culture shock and conflict accompanied street socialization during the social control transformations. The change from a Spanish-speaking background and a Latino/a culture to an English-speaking, Anglo culture had profound repercussions on the children of immigrants (Valencia, 2010). Away from home and school, both language influences became attenuated, and a street patois materialized. Dramatized in the Mexican case, this led to a decidedly *cholo* (i.e., marginal; stemming from early Spanish and Mexican usage of this word for racial or cultural marginals) fragmented cultural adaptation with both Mexican and Anglo-American traits and habits mixed together (the language some call "Spanglish"). Street socialization shapes and solidifies a street identity. A youth with a street identity often ascribes a higher value to the geographical boundaries of his neighborhood. Protection of barrio territory frequently generates and ignites the gang conflict, including drive-by shootings and other violence, which pits barrio against barrio and gang against gang (Vigil, 2003). One can arguably attribute the aggressive tendencies of gang youth to the effects of systemic suppression of the Chicano peoples and the generalized aura of violence and aggression that pervades pressure-cooker poverty enclaves. The gang provides a protective role for disaffected Chicano youth, a type of fictive kinship and friendship network, which we will see through this chapter's narrative portrait on Pedro, who was raised in a gang neighborhood in South Gate, California.

The city of South Gate, where Pedro grew up, has a singular history when it comes to race and ethnicity. During the 1920s and 1930s, the city, which incorporated in 1923, saw an influx of blue-collar Whites. Many of these migrants came from the Dust Bowl, the central prairie region of the United States, which was plagued at the time by drought and dust storms. By the 1940s and 1950s, South Gate was almost 100 percent White and shared a border with the 100 percent Black community of Watts, which was part of Los Angeles. Young White youth in South Gate formed a gang, the "Spook Hunters," to ensure that their city remained segregated (Alonso, 2004). In 1965, the Watts Riots, which didn't spill over into South Gate, nevertheless caused the beginning of white flight from the city. As the number of Whites declined, the number of immigrant Mexicans and working-class Mexican-Americans increased. By 2010, South Gate was 94.8% Latino (U.S. Census Bureau, 2010).

Pedro's life history will illuminate the touchstone situations and conditions that marginalized Chicano youth in poverty circumstances must deal with on a daily basis. These situations and conditions help determine whether youth win or lose the battle for their identities and whether they will be lost to the streets. The pressures and forces that produce gangs and gang members in some poor neighborhoods are sometimes overwhelming, as we witness in Pedro's life journey.

A PORTRAIT OF PEDRO, THE OPPORTUNIST

Born in 1979 to Mexican immigrants, Pedro, the eldest of three children, spoke Spanish as his first language. His parents barely spoke English, so they couldn't help him when he began to struggle in school, even though he attended regularly. From the beginning, even as he learned English, Pedro seemed unable to concentrate. His parents—mother Deborah, a home health care provider, and father Luís, a carpenter—worked night and day.

Excepting his parents, most of the males in his extended family were members of gangs, many living in the same South Gate apartment complex as Pedro's family, which was managed by Deborah. Out of 12 units, non-gang families occupied only 1 or 2 units.

Plastic Badges and Handcuffs

It was outside, playing in the streets, that Pedro found a place to belong. He didn't participate in any community after-school programs. Whenever his friends played cops and robbers, he became the head cop. Pedro saw a lot of police in South Gate. The cops, with the handles of their guns peeking out of their gun belts and their gleaming badges and shoes, could give orders and nobody said no to them.

Pedro found an old suitcase and begged his mother to let him use it. He spent hours writing in small booklets—imaginary clues, lists of suspects and pretend evidence. He needed plastic badges and handcuffs, which, after a good amount of nagging, his mother purchased. When he and his friends played, he referenced his notebooks frequently, making sure that they witnessed his attention to detail, as he soberly carried out his duty to protect and to lead his "men."

Joining Southside Nuthood Watts

When Pedro was 9, everything changed. Southside Nuthood Watts, a gang, took him into their fold. He put away his badges and briefcase and started smoking weed and getting into trouble. He wrestled kids in class and liked to mess with the teachers. Sometimes he moved the teacher's things and hid them, waiting with the class for a look of confusion to take over her face as she searched for her books and records, opening and closing drawers, breathing hard, putting her hands on her hips, and finally giving up. The other kids smiled.

His mother and father had, years before, forbade Pedro's uncles from bringing him into their gangs and his uncles had honored the order. Pedro's uncles were highly respected members of Ghetto Boyz, 27th Street and 18th Street. But his parents had no sway over Southside Nuthood.

During junior high, Pedro was expelled multiple times and ended up attending four different middle schools. Pedro bullied others and destroyed property—writing on walls and writing on books. South Gate Middle School expelled him for pushing a counselor down the stairs. He and a friend grabbed a kid walking down the hall and threw him into a crowd. Pedro felt a hand on his shoulder pulling him back. Without looking, he turned and shoved the person. He watched in horror as a counselor tumbled down the stairs. Pedro reached out to stop the fall, but it was too late. He

ran out of the school. The school authorities found his mother. That afternoon, his mom told him that he wasn't going to that school anymore. She
was disappointed, but it didn't stop Pedro. The same behavior kept happen-
ing . . . over and over.

After 4 years of witnessing gang attitudes seep into Pedro and watching
him, seemingly remorseless, getting into trouble repeatedly, Pedro's parents
figured Pedro wasn't going to make it. When he was 13, they bought him a
casket. Pedro didn't care.

The Fall of Big Alex

Death was familiar to the family. When Pedro was 13, he watched his uncle,
in the middle of the day, die on the street. Pedro was at home when the
phone rang. The caller alerted the family that Big Alex, a dope dealer from
Ghetto Boyz 27th and Pedro's uncle, had been shot two or three blocks
away. It was a drug deal gone wrong. Pedro and a couple of his uncles found
Big Alex on the ground. At first, his uncle was conscious and talking, but
during the 45 minutes it took for the ambulance to arrive, his uncle grew
quiet, unresponsive, and, finally, cold. Big Alex was dead on arrival at St.
Francis Medical Center, which was in the nearby city of Lynwood. It was a
shot to the lung—a point-blank shot.

Pedro and his uncles scoured the neighborhoods so that they might
avenge the death, but they never found the shooter. Pedro knew that you
did what you could do and that was all. The gang retaliated whenever they
could pull it off. Pedro already knew how to carry himself. He kept his face
placid and unreadable, no matter the circumstances. He could die any day.
Many of his cohorts were going to die young or die in prison. He accepted
that. But he wasn't going to go easily. He started carrying a gun and watching over his shoulder.

During his high school years, as with junior high, Pedro attended four
different schools, due to his behavior. On a typical morning, at 6:00 a.m.,
standing in the dawn light at the bus stop, he was already high on pot.
On days when his gang had no plans for an incursion into neighboring
gang territory, Pedro chilled with the gang and chatted up girls. One of
Pedro's homeboys had parents who owned a hall that they rented out for
parties. Whenever the hall wasn't rented out, it became, according to Pedro,
"our DPDA—Ditching Party Designated Area." Here, they cranked up the
DJ system, drank, and took drugs. The drugs were free, due to the kids'
close relationship with the neighborhood drug dealers, who were family
members. Pedro tried meth, cocaine, LSD, everything except "slamming"
(heroin). He didn't really like any drugs except his old faithful, marijuana:
"Meth alters you—you're jittery . . . It deprived me of sleep. I wasn't able to
eat. What kind of drug is that? I stuck with pot."

A Secret Dream

Yet somewhere deep inside, Pedro secretly harbored a long-hidden hope. Though his suitcase and badges were long gone and he reveled in wrong-doing, he still, paradoxically, dreamed of becoming a policeman and getting respect—not just from his homies, but from all kinds of people. One day, when he was 15, his mother told him about the South Gate Police Explorer program. Pedro wrangled an interview and filled out all the forms. Determined to finish every assignment, Pedro graduated second in the class. A lieutenant from the police department took Pedro under his wing and invited him into his home, gave him haircuts, and fed him.

Police Explorers is a program in which young people from ages 14 to 20, many hoping for careers in law enforcement, delve into different facets of police work. They perform police-related community service, such as assisting with traffic control and leading tours of the police station. They learn about radio procedures, crisis negotiation, arrest control, search and rescue, and high-risk car stops, among other topics. They have weapons training (batons, pepper spray, electronic control devices, and, under supervision, firearms training) ("Law Enforcement," 2011). Pedro excelled at every task before him. He, along with other members of the South Gate Explorer group, competed in tournaments against Explorer teams from other jurisdictions. As long as the program lasted, Pedro excelled. The real test came after graduation.

The South Gate detectives had warned Pedro that in order to maintain his status with the program, he was going to have to stringently follow a standard of high moral character. They knew he had grown up in a gang neighborhood and that he had gang associates. He could no longer hang out with them or do drugs. That life was over. Except that it wasn't. Pedro had his habits and he had his ties. It was almost impossible to become a ghost to his own past in the neighborhood—invisible to gang associates, invisible to his friends. Everyone in the neighborhood knew what he had been up to with the Explorers, and as a result of his involvement with the police, he experienced friction and faced retribution.

More than a few former friends wanted to kill him. What stopped them was the reputation of Pedro's uncles, who were still respected *"veteranos"* in the neighborhood. If anyone took out Pedro, he would have to deal with them. So Pedro got to live, but to most of his past friends he became a cipher, no longer existing in their time and place. They believed that Pedro had rejected them in favor of the police. A few friends continued to endure Pedro's presence and grudgingly acknowledged his new life. They figured that Pedro was just trying to do something for himself. Pedro remembered what the police had told him, but he thought he knew how to stay out of trouble. That strategy worked . . . for a while.

Kicked Out, Becoming a Father

One night, shortly after his graduation from the program, Pedro and some neighborhood friends headed to a party in Long Beach. They passed through South Gate. The boys were "hot-boxing," smoking weed with the windows closed. Someone in the car saw a cop's patrol car and the boys, in their panic, instantly opened all the windows. The thick plumes of smoke rose into the air, immediately catching the cop's eye. The rookie cop stopped the car and, while searching each boy, found a paper in Pedro's pocket, which listed his locker number at the Police Department. The policeman asked him, disdainfully, "What's YOUR affiliation with the South Gate Police Department?" Pedro thought, *Should I tell him? . . . Aw, he has my license anyway and he's going to find out.* So Pedro answered: "I'm a Police Explorer."

The officer phoned Pedro's lieutenant from Explorers, who showed up shortly. The lieutenant's face, once friendly, showed no humor or warmth. Pedro wasn't anybody special anymore—just another problem. The officer asked, "What the hell are you doing hanging out with these guys?" Pedro didn't answer, and the lieutenant kicked Pedro out of the Explorers.

When Pedro was seventeen, his first child, Carlos, was born. The mother of the baby was Pedro's junior high sweetheart. Pedro looked down with pride at the little face but fatherhood didn't seem real. It was as if Pedro could only see the baby as an accessory to his otherwise wild life.

Swerving and Rolling

One of the more crazy activities that Pedro participated in was "swerving," a driving technique. Also known as "drifting," this skill first gained attention in mid-1970s Japanese road racing, when drivers used it to maintain speed during turns. When swerving, the driver makes a hard, fast turn—oversteering and creating slippage of the wheels. The rear wheels slide more than the front wheels, with the front wheels ending up pointing in the opposite direction of the turn. When done correctly, it looks very cool.

Sometimes the Nutwood gangsters lined up five or more cars and staggered their drifting starts, so that the synchronized tailgates resembled an undulating snake writhing down the street, accompanied by the sound and smell of skidding tires. In December 1999, 18-year-old Pedro was driving his brand-new SUV, an all-wheel Mitsubishi Montero. Carrying half a pound of weed and stoned, he was making deliveries when he recognized a girlfriend. Stopping to say hi, he found out she was going to a party. Pedro decided to go, too. She got into the Montero, which joined two other cars filled with friends.

One car in front and one car behind, Pedro decided to do some swerving, right down the middle of a residential street, going 50 miles an hour. Going into a turn, he lost control and the Montero rolled, coming to rest on its side with the driver's door down. Both Pedro and his passenger jumped out of a window, the girl scraping and bloodying her leg.

The other two cars took off and the neighborhood was coming alive at the sound of the crash. People approached the couple.

"Are you guys okay? The ambulance is on its way."

In a moment of astringent clarity, Pedro focused his faculties on the real problem. It wasn't his wrecked Montero. He thought, *I have dope in my car. A lot of dope.*

He raced back to the SUV and climbed in, frantically reaching behind and under the seats, opening and closing the glove compartment, shoving his hand in crevices, shaking jackets, and throwing things around. *Where was it?* Breathing hard, he could hear sirens in the distance. *Oh man, oh man. . . .* He gave up and decided to run. He climbed out and dashed down the street with his ex, past the bewildered residents of the neighborhood. Diving into some bushes, his ex disappeared into another hiding place just as the cops arrived.

"Come out or we're sending in the dogs."

Pedro stayed put and watched as his ex walked out of the shadows with her hands up. Pedro thought, *Aww . . . it's over now'* He surrendered.

Arrested and taken to jail, he was eventually charged and convicted of a misdemeanor DUI. The police never found the pot. For Pedro, the crash and the DUI were wake-up calls—he could have died. His son was barely 2 years old. Pedro lost his license for a while and gained his first and only arraignment and conviction. But he had been arrested and locked up several times before this event.

Guilty by Association

Like other minority youth, Pedro, because of his gang affiliation, stood a much higher chance of arrest during any encounter involving police. A study by Tapia (2011) considered a sample of 8,984 youth in order to determine whether gang membership alone is a risk factor for increased arrest. In order to isolate the effect of gang membership, it makes sense to consider previous delinquency and criminal history. If a youth has already committed a serious crime, it is no surprise to find that he has an increased arrest rate. But what if a youth has never committed a serious crime and doesn't have a history of delinquency? What if he just happens to be in a car, or walking with friends from his gang neighborhood? Does that youth, solely on the basis of affiliating with gang members, have an increased risk of arrest? The study found this to be the case.

Controlling for prior delinquency and criminal acts, the analysis found that gang membership "increases the number of expected arrests by 45 percent for Hispanic youth." In contrast, if you are a White youth, gang membership alone *decreases* your risk of arrest by 38 percent. As a matter of fact, the study showed that White youth not affiliated with gangs had an increased risk of arrest compared to White gang members (Tapia, 2011). What this means is that if you're a White gang member, you don't have to worry about being stopped just for how you look or for how your friends look. White gang members are not profiled and targeted for extra attention. Pedro estimated that he had been arrested, in total, 8 to 10 times. All but one resulted in nothing more than a 72-hour hold. But every time Pedro filled out a job application, he had to list all of his arrests, not just his DUI conviction. When asked, he wrote the truth.

Growing Up, Gaining a *Compadre*

After the DUI, Pedro started to grow up. He met his future wife, Adriana, in a high school where Pedro was fulfilling community service hours related to his DUI. When he met the slender, dark-haired, talkative Adriana, Pedro wasn't into her and she wasn't into him. But they exchanged numbers and Pedro called her. After several long phone conversations, their feelings changed and soon they were dating. When Pedro was 19, he and Adriana had a son—Daniel—his second child and her first.

Pedro had been working since high school graduation in a factory for the Hon Company, a furniture manufacturer. Pedro started out working on the assembly line, building chairs. But, slowly, Pedro's attitude and outlook started to change for the better. He wanted more. Now that he had two children, Pedro finally felt a dawning pressure to be a better father. He started to think about the future. And he met a man who would help him move forward. He met his "*compadre*"—his friend, his mentor, and the future godfather to his children—Prasert.

One day at the factory, a team of six engineers passed by Pedro's line. The engineers were down on the factory floor that day because the Hon Company utilized a process based on the Japanese concept of "*kaizen.*" In the United States, this concept is known as "Rapid Continuous Improvement." The idea is to bring together workers who perform different functions and usually don't interact. The hope is that this unlikely team will generate ideas that solve problems and make processes run more smoothly.

Pedro listened carefully as the engineers gave a short presentation on fabrication—the design and implementation necessary to manufacture office furniture. When the presentation ended, the engineers turned to leave and the workers returned to the line. Except for Pedro. He stepped forward and stopped one of the engineers, telling him, "Hey, I'm interested in participating with what you guys are doing." The engineer, Prasert, took Pedro at his word. Prasert, born in Thailand, is an engineer and professor at Webster University, a private Missouri institution.

Prasert saw something in Pedro. Right away, he saw that Pedro was smart, and as he spoke with him, he saw a person with a good heart. Looking at him, he thought that the young man just needed some guidance. Prasert began to mentor Pedro. He helped him to get work as a fabricator and started advising him to consider going to college. Pedro performed well on the job. Pedro listened. His little family had grown to include a daughter, Denise Sunshine, born when Pedro was 21. He began to invite Prasert to join his family barbecues. Prasert became godfather to Pedro's two youngest children.

With his drive and his *compadre's* encouragement, Pedro continued to learn and to grow at Hon. But Pedro still lived in the Southside Nuthood neighborhood. He straddled two worlds—his Southgate neighborhood and his work. Although he spent 40 hours a week at work and had just decided to sign up for college, he still smoked pot daily. If he could walk that line, for just a few more years, everything in his life, everything for his family, would improve.

A Chance Meeting in Court

More years went by and things seemed even more stable. That is, until the day Pedro attended the trial of yet another uncle. Sitting in the courtroom that day in South Gate, Pedro noticed some familiar faces standing up front. The police leaders from his Explorer days were there and they recognized Pedro.

Before his arrest, Pedro's uncle, a big-time Los Angeles dope dealer, had been making $15,000 or $20,000 a day. Now that he was busted, the police were looking for the person likely to inherit the dope sales. During the hearing, Pedro could see that the police were appraising him, staring and whispering. He was right. They raided him a few weeks later, rolling a flash-bang grenade into his apartment as his wife stood behind him, her arms around his three children—his son from his first relationship and the two they had together. The raid yielded only a tiny amount of marijuana. The police never found the cocaine in the ceiling or the $200,000 in cash that Pedro was holding to use for his uncle's attorneys' fees.

After the raid, the cops held Pedro until 4:00 a.m., but since they didn't have enough evidence to hold him longer, they had to release him. He arrived at his job at Hon at 5:00 a.m., exhausted and still a little high from smoking weed the night before. One of his first jobs for the day was to move a large stack of files with a forklift. He tried to carefully pick up the files, but they weren't lined up evenly and they wobbled and dropped to the floor, important papers sliding out of their proper folders and shuffling themselves into jumbled, incomprehensible piles. Pedro thought, *That's it for me.* He knew what would happen next.

Whenever someone damaged anything worth more than $1,000 at Hon, he had to immediately go to the office and get drug-tested. And this was Pedro's second offense. He had once accidentally driven the forklift off a dock. In that instance, his boss gave him a second chance. But that wasn't going to happen today. He was drug-tested and the results came back dirty. After 7 years working at Hon, he was fired. Pedro went home to face his angry wife. The cops never filed charges, but Pedro lost his job. Pedro and his family went on welfare.

Trying on the Dream—One More Time

In 2007, Pedro decided to take a chance on his long-time dream of becoming a peace officer. Filling out the application to be a Los Angeles County Sheriff, Pedro decided to tell the truth. He detailed each and every arrest, including the details of his teenage DUI conviction. He passed all the preliminary tests—the civil service exam, the physical testing, and the physical exam. Then it was time for the background check.

The background investigator was, as Pedro described him, a "super gringo." He told Pedro that he had failed the background check. With all his arrests, plus his DUI, he was out. Pedro tried not to show disappointment as he walked away. The cop must have noticed something strong in Pedro, something unbent and unbroken. When Pedro was almost out the door, the investigator called him back. His voice was soft: "Come back here." Had he changed his mind? Pedro slowly walked back to the desk. The officer paused and, looking Pedro in the eyes, he told him, "I just want you to know that you will never be a cop. It's never going to happen for you, so don't walk out of here thinking that you will." Recounting this event, Pedro's voice cracked ever so slightly.

After the rejection by the Sheriff's Department, Pedro worked for his *compadre*, Prasert, as manager of a furniture store in Valencia. Prasert trusted him completely, often leaving him alone and in charge. Pedro lived up to his trust, but the business eventually folded. So, in 2007, Pedro finally went to college.

Pedro Becomes a Catalyst for Change

When Pedro first began attending Los Angeles Community College, he discovered that the campus offered work-study programs, but only for on-campus jobs, which were all taken. Pedro convinced the coordinator to change the policy to include off-campus jobs, and he became the first student in a pilot program. His efforts led to the Work Study in Public Agencies program, which offers student internships at public agencies. The advisors told him that he was the first and that he'd better not mess up the chance.

In 2011, Pedro continued to attend Los Angeles Community College, where he had made the Dean's List, studying Criminology. He planned to transfer to one of the University of California campuses the following year.

Pedro has succeeded in every work-study job since—dealing with seniors and disabled people, drawing sketches of aerial property drawings, and now working full-time for the Community Development Commission in Los Angeles. In 2007, he was featured in an article in the *Los Angeles County Digest,* where he is described by one of his superiors as "dedicated . . . hard-working . . . an invaluable asset . . . punctual and professional in all aspects." Pedro now lives with his family in East Los Angeles. He doesn't see any of his former friends from South Gate. Pedro makes spending time with his children a priority. All three of the kids are doing well—two of them are in Gifted and Talented Education (GATE) programs at school. Adriana also attends college—she wants to be a psychologist. The couple has a tight schedule, but they seem to be pulling it off.

Pedro knows the facts. He will never be a cop. He's letting go of that dream but grasping at others. He's aiming to become Area Director. When Pedro first heard about this book project, he thought: *Dude, I've been waiting for someone to recognize this forever 'cause I've always felt like I've walked that good and bad path.* But he is thankful that "I've always been able to weasel my way to better things."

CONCLUSION

As witnessed through Pedro's portrait, the barrios that spawned gangs endure, as do poverty, stressed families, inadequate schooling, and cultural identity problems. The children of the newest immigrant families are pulled into the subculture of the streets at a faster rate than that of previous generations. One can safely state that the pressure cooker of poor communities has accelerated the acculturation process. As in earlier decades, crowded housing and troubled familial conditions continue to push children into the streets. As we have observed from the Vietnamese case, as immigration continues, the marginalization process in cities will ensure that Chicano gangs endure.

In recent decades, Latino gangs have become a global phenomenon. Through diffusion, immigrant youth who return to their home countries export gang culture. In this vein, U.S. immigration authorities have deported Salvadoran gang members and have unwittingly exported gang culture to their home country, which had never experienced this destructive youth subculture. The repercussions of globalization have had great impact in Latin America and the Caribbean. A major effect of this process has been increased migration from rural areas to cities, both within nations and across international boundaries. The effects of time, people, and place travel with the movement of transnationals. Even thousands of miles away, in El Salvador, a youth and his community cannot escape the marginalization experienced in Los Angeles.

Pedro was fortunate. Even though he is an American citizen, if he had not been able to find a way out of his neighborhood, he would have struggled to steer clear of its effects. He chose to cut off all contact with his former cohorts. He found a dream—being a policeman—that placed him, in his mind's eye, outside of the gang one day, giving him hope. The Explorers program provided Pedro with a different identity. His mentor at the Hon Company girded the scaffolding of Pedro's burgeoning maturity. Finally, Pedro benefited from funding for the federal work study program, which enabled him to developed advanced skills in his work for the Community Development Commission.

In addition to the limited resources Pedro gained, he, and others like him, could have benefited from programs that institutionalize academic success and encourage high college and career aspirations. One such example is AVID (as discussed in Chapter 1). AVID places students with high potential of doing well but whose circumstances place them at risk of school failure into college-track classes. Mehan et al. (1996) demonstrate how de-tracking low-income students into a college-going culture and the social scaffolding in the AVID structure mediate student agency and positive dispositions toward school success. The program also helps whole neighborhoods by helping kids stay in school and away from gangs, making them realize that higher education is an attainable goal. Teens with college attendance as a goal are motivated to stay focused in school and to stay away from the pressure to join a gang or to become involved in any activity that might hamper their future success. Similar to Jarod in Chapter 2 and Samuel in Chapter 3, Pedro is a resilient person, but factors of time, people, and place figure in their array of choices that boosted their foray into eventually productive adulthoods.

Chapter 5

I Call Myself Chicano

Multiple and Shifting
Mexican American Identities

*Large-scale immigration is one of the most important social
developments of our time. It is a transformational process affecting
families and their children. Once immigrants are settled, they
send for their loved ones or form new families. Hence, the story of
today's immigrants is also a saga of their children: a fascinating and
critical—but often forgotten—chapter of the immigrant experience.
The children of immigrants, who make up 20 percent of all youth in
the United States, are an integral part of the American fabric.*
—Suárez-Orozco & Suárez-Orozco, *Children of Immigration*

The children of immigrants will have a significant impact on American
society. As constituents, students, future parents, and participants in
the economy, these young people, their families, and their environments
together present unique profiles worthy of exploration. One of the greatest areas of concern is their educational plight. This chapter concentrates
on the educational experiences of Latino youth, from recent immigrants
to those whose families have been in the United States for generations.
As a case study for this book, this chapter seeks to unravel the relationship between acculturation and school success by offering a holistic and
longitudinal approach to three time periods.

By doing so, we are able to devise policy and practice designed to
impact the largest ethnic minority group in the United States, a population constantly facing changes. As new waves of Latino immigrant labor
enter the United States to meet the enormous demands of a global economy, we suggest that an examination of the Latino experience carries profound implications, which will address issues of acculturation and school
achievement among all ethnic immigrant and migrant populations in the
contemporary United States.

Factoring into this analysis is the framework of time, people, and place. The dynamics of Latino acculturation and adaptation differ across the three time periods studied and across environmental settings, as well as among different populations. The diversity of cultural styles, languages, and ethnic identities within the Latino American population needs to be recognized within such an analysis. As mentioned, similar contrasts and variations exist within other ethnic groups.

SOCIAL FORCES, DEMOGRAPHIC CHANGES, AND RACIAL POLITICS

Educational practices in the United States directed toward Latino American students have often been paternalistic and racist, reflecting the secondary status accorded Latino Americans in the country (Chávez, 2008; Gándara, 1995). This treatment persisted throughout the 20th century, as immigration from Mexico brought millions of settlers to the Southwest in search of better living standards. Many Americans believed that the only way for Latinos to achieve social mobility was via acculturation to Anglo American standards of speaking and behaving. This theory dominated educational practices through the late 1930s. Educators argued that minority students needed to learn English and assimilate as rapidly as possible. This policy was carried to an extreme, however, as teachers often demeaned the native culture of minority students.

This approach was often the only alternative to the more egregious practice of outright segregation, which offered separate, inferior, or even nonexistent school facilities for minorities (Valencia, 2010); see Taylor (1934) for such contrasts between blacks and Chicanos in Texas. The policies of Americanization and segregation combined to ensure problems in school for Latino American students—damned completely by segregation and daunted by a learning program based on a premise of cultural deficiency (Gándara, 1995; Gonzales, 1990; Gutiérrez, 2008).

Latino people in the United States resisted blatant forms of racism and discrimination from the onset and regularly struggled for equality on numerous fronts. Outright segregation was eventually struck down, but the cultural deficiency perspective endured. In the aftermath of World War II, the Mendez v. Westminster case in 1947 struck down separate and unequal schools in California (Donato, Menchaca, & Valencia, 1991). However, as recently as 1968, Latino American children (and blacks) who tested low in the San Diego School District were labeled Educable Mentally Retarded (EMR) and placed in special classes. Many of these students spoke little English or were out of touch with the dominant Anglo culture on which the test was based. Thus, the cultural deficit philosophy still existed, but was hidden under the cloak of inadequate, biased tests. Only after this practice was challenged by a coalition of leaders from the NAACP and the Latino American Political Association (LAPA) was the EMR policy changed.

The Civil Rights Movement of the 1960s included various protests and rallies that represented a challenge to the orthodoxy of the established, Anglo-dominated system. The Chicano Movement of the 1960s grew from this earlier movement. During the Blowouts of 1968, more than 7,000 from three East Side Los Angeles high schools left their campuses to stage public protests (García, 2010). This student activism achieved various educational reforms, including the introduction of bilingual education and an increase in college enrollment and activism of Latino youth.

Despite the fact that the protests were quickly conceived and hastily organized, improvements began to appear. By 1974, student and community activism began to break down the monolithic cultural barriers that impeded adjustments to Latino students' needs; a cultural accommodation promised in Article XXI of the Treaty of Guadalupe Hidalgo of 1848 states that in the event of differences between Mexicans in the newly acquired Southwest and the government of the United States, there should be "no reprisals, aggression, or hostility of any kind." However, this was not the case.

This period marked the beginning of a shift from the Anglo promotion of Americanization to one advocating ethnic pluralism or cultural democracy (Vigil, 1997). The Chicano movement encouraged barrio youth to retain cultural distinctiveness and not to assimilate, regardless of one's generation or cultural orientation. This was a dramatic reversal; even up to the mid-1960s, it was still common for Chicano students to seek a trajectory to Anglo customs. Up to this time, Anglos often degraded Spanish-speaking students by referring to them as "T.J.s" ("*Tijuaneros*"—a derogatory slang term for new immigrants from Mexico, or more specifically, Tijuana), even if they were born in the United States. Many students, particularly from the more Anglo-oriented third and fourth generations, found themselves in a quandary. As they pushed to fit in with Anglos, the rules in their neighborhoods reversed back toward a Latino orientation.

The 1970s to the present saw a significant increase in immigration from Mexico, which has broadened the Mexicanization process. The increase in the number of Mexicans, and Latinos in general, in the United States creates a critical mass, which affirms and further invigorates political and cultural awareness efforts (Chávez, 2008). This presence has made it more palatable and acceptable to be "Mexican" (Gonzales, 1990). Mexicanization often guides the ethnic self-identification process among adolescents and youth (Vigil, 2002).

But while this Mexicanization process gained ground in the 1980s, a political backlash also began to form. The conservative Reagan administration proved particularly difficult for many minority groups in the United

States. Poverty increased in response to funding cutbacks, and the government cast a blind eye to persistent socioeconomic problems. Government funding for low-income and ethnic minority communities dropped significantly from the late-1960s levels of the Great Society era (Katz, 1986; Quadagno, 1994). Special education and Head Start lost funding. Paradoxically, bilingual education expanded during this time, due to lobbying efforts initiated by a coalition of ethnic organizations.

As cultural assertiveness grew among Latino opinion-makers, government leaders regressed and reintroduced Americanization policies. For example, the "English Only" language movement, led by outraged nativist Americans, became popular during this time. Consequently, significant tension began to develop among educators who disagreed on the direction of future educational policy initiatives (Moran, 1987; Valencia, 1991).

Political pressures to counter the effects of massive immigration continued and took a turn for the worse. The English Only movement, anti-immigration initiatives, and antipathy toward Latinos are still present (Chávez, 2008). Elected political leaders, at both the federal and state levels, use the demographic and multicultural changes to appeal to the worst fears of the public. The passage of Proposition 187 in 1994 in California stands as an example (Ono & Stoop, 2002). More recently, the signing of Arizona's SB 1070, which orders all immigrants to carry their legal identification papers at all times, generated a furor across the country. In some quarters, there exists a push to generate laws that would prevent "anchor" babies, children born in the United States of undocumented parents, from being granted citizenship (Chavez, 2008). These governmental and political forces shape the communities, school climates, and lives of those in their path.

NEIGHBORHOODS AND SCHOOLS
IN A CHANGING SOCIETY

Two schools in the Los Angeles area were sampled and studied, one in an urban area and the other in a suburban locale, over three time periods to understand the relationship between acculturation and engagement.[1] In 1974, a sample of 39 students was chosen from each of the two schools by randomly drawing equal numbers of students of Latino descent at each grade level (10th, 11th, and 12th). In 1988, a similar design was employed. In 2004, we administered surveys to 460 students and conducted formal intensive interviews with 50 students representing both schools and, additionally, continued to offer AVID workshops on at least a yearly basis.

The urban location is a largely low-income Latino American community in East Los Angeles. The homes and infrastructure here date from as early as the first decades of the 20th century (Diaz, 1993). The suburban neighborhood is located approximately 14 miles southeast of East Los Angeles. In this area, the well-maintained school and neat rows of tract home developments exemplify the suburban explosion that characterized greater Los Angeles in the 1950s.

There are many differences between the two communities sampled in this study, both location differences (urban barrio vs. suburban working and middle-class) as well as differences over time. During the initial study in 1974, the urban barrio in East Los Angeles, composed of Mexican immigrants and Mexican Americans, had a population of more than 102,000, of whom 85% were of Latino descent. Residents were generally poor. The average annual household income was only $7,526, and 18% of the households were receiving some sort of public assistance. Adults in the urban barrio had an average of 8.8 years of education, and 7.4% had no formal education whatsoever.

In contrast, the suburban area, in 1974, had a population of approximately 15,500, 48% of whom were of Latino descent. The suburban residents were generally middle- and working-class with household heads in blue-collar occupations. The average annual income was $11,478, and only 4% of the households received public assistance. Adults in the suburban area had an average of 12 years of education, and only 1.5% had no formal education whatsoever. By 2004 the Mexican population had mushroomed in both locales, with urban income increasing to about $31,022 and suburban to $43,223 and public assistance remaining about the same over time.

By 1988, an erosion of the economic infrastructure had occurred, which was caused by a statewide recession that affected jobs and social habits in both areas (Moore & Pinderhughes-Rivera, 1993). Socioeconomic experiences play a particularly important role in determining an individual's access, exposure, and identification with the dominant culture (Darder & Torres, 2004).

Demographic shifts showed a general increase in poverty, with an alarming emphasis on the feminization of this poverty (Bauman, 2008). A steady rise in crime and related gang behavior materialized (Vigil, 2007). The urban barrio had grown in population, as had the proportion of residents of Mexican descent. The total population in the suburban area had not changed significantly, but the populace was much more Mexicanized.

Significantly, in 2004, gang and street youth activities became more prominent in the suburban neighborhood, as school officials and law enforcement emphasized suppression tactics to stem the tide. Suburban areas by then had become sufficiently urbanized that marginalization had taken its toll. In large part, older classic gangs characterized the urban area, and as the Mexican population moved to other places, the gang problem followed them.

MEXICANIZATION AS A SOURCE OF PRIDE

Communities in both the urban and suburban areas produced a new generation of youth and families who were proud of their cultural background. For example, the urban field site experienced a large influx of recent Mexican immigrants (as well as other Latinos, especially Central Americans). In the suburban field site, there were high numbers of immigrants who had been in America for many years, many coming as young children. Asserting a cultural allegiance to their "home country," the immigrants of this "1.5 generation" (Feliciano, 2006a) were unlike either first- or second-generation immigrants of the past.

South Central and Southeast Los Angeles and Pico Union (west of downtown) replaced East Los Angeles as the primary port of entry for immigrants. New arrivals gravitated to older, cheaper housing and neighborhoods that were closer to the downtown garment and sweatshop factories. Some newcomers displaced the Chicano residents of older, traditional barrios. Consequently, third- and fourth-generation Chicano families, some gang-oriented, moved to suburbia, filling the void left by white flight.

In the suburban area, the remaining Anglo residents often met the Mexicanization phenomenon with resentment. Clinging to their notion of privilege, many Anglos, including teachers and other public employees, struggled to maintain an aura of control and dominance.

The high schools sampled in the three time periods reflected their respective environments. The urban high school, built in the 1920s, sits on relatively little acreage. The suburban school, built in 1955, sits on a sprawling, green campus. In 1974, the urban high school's population primarily included students of Latino descent: 32% of the students were born in Mexico and 92% of the students were of Mexican heritage. In the suburban high school, 35% of the students were Mexican American, and only 5% had been born in Mexico. Despite having a similar total number of students and average schoolwide grade point average (GPA), the urban high school had a significantly higher percentage of dropouts than the suburban school—official rates of 24% versus 14%, respectively. In the new millennium, as noted, a tremendous wave of immigration increased the Mexican percentage to close to 100% in the inner-city area and near 90% in suburbia. Urbanization had overwhelmed the suburban environs of Los Angeles in the previous 40 years. Today, the new suburbia is located in the outskirts of Orange County.

In 1974 the two high schools and their respective communities reflected contrasting populations in terms of culture, class, and social issues. Place plays an important role in this study, but the dynamic of time is also significant. By 1988, the high schools had experienced dramatic changes. The urban high school student body was now composed almost entirely of students of Mexican descent, and it had grown in total student population by more than 50%. In the suburban high school, the proportion of Latino American students in the total student population had nearly doubled. The local population, quite obviously, was mirrored by the school population, which by 2004 was increasingly majority Latino in both the urban and suburban contexts. The few Anglos who remained were the elderly whose children had matured and moved out to the new Orange County suburbs.

In addition, there was a Mexicanization of the political and academic landscape. By 1988, there were several Latinos on the school boards of both schools, and the number of Latino faculty and administrators had also increased from the time of the first study. Parent-teacher meetings were sometimes conducted in Spanish.

From 1974 to 1988, schools developed strategies to "discourage" gang members and other "incorrigibles" from attending. As a result, more gang members were in the streets than in classrooms. Both the suburban and urban high school, in 1988, appeared to be "gang-free." The only students allowed in school were those with clean records and the proper appearance. To some degree, the proliferation of street gangs in the years between the studies can be traced to the failure of schools to reach out and address the special circumstances and learning difficulties of "choloized" youth (Conchas & Vigil, 2010).

For the modern era, the introduction of new learning strategies like AVID (Advancement via Individual Determination) made a strong impact in the urban school. The latter program was tailor-made for the neglected inner-city students who were identified as bright and capable of rigorous study despite spotty, mostly poor, past academic records.

In addition, a school counselor/psychologist initiated a special group therapy workshop for students, which stressed deeper counseling and emotional attention. This group of about 25–30 students, mostly females, met weekly and, in round-table style, voiced their feelings about personal and family problems. Sessions like this brought out some of the hidden secrets of their lives—tales of molestations and incest—and appeared to have a healthy, cleansing quality. Students were enthusiastic about this workshop and how it helped them work through their problems.

School district officials put a stop to this practice, however, for they thought the counselor/psychologist should stick to safe, traditional test and measurement routines. The motivation for this administrative fiat was the avoidance of any legal entanglement. A row ensued between teachers, who were willing to take risks when students would benefit, and administrators and school hierarchies, who wanted to play it safe. Part of the fallout was that the counselor ended up suing the school district. Experimental strategies, like the unique group counseling example, are often frowned upon by school districts for legal concerns and more subtle reasons, despite their potential for positive impact on students in need.

Suburban students also benefited from AVID but had an additional program of AP (Academic Advancement) courses to accelerate their educational trajectories. There was a special, rigorous accelerated history class for each grade level. It included many speakers and outside enrichment outings, during which students heard lectures by experts and visited institutions and historical sites. Teachers in both schools also were recruited on the basis of their ethnic background. The urban school employed about 60 Latino teachers—some were even graduates of that school.

In addition, institutional changes related to gender tensions evolved as a result of the growing awareness of differences in how males and females receive their education (Noguera, Hurtado, & Fergus, 2011). Many teachers and school officials coordinated their efforts to meet the needs of female students. By 2004, the educational paths of females had opened to the point that they were a sizeable majority of graduates going on to higher education, even if only to local community colleges.

With an increased Mexican and Latino presence, school officials in the urban locale made progressive changes to meet the demands of their student population. For example, the school strengthened its bilingual education approach in order to soften the culture shock for immigrant or Spanish-speaking children. Moreover, as noted, the recruitment of more sensitive and culturally aware teachers, adding to the core of those from the 1970s, and an increase in a significant number of Latino and Latina instructors contributed to a more accommodative learning climate.

Other developments countered these improvements. A "back to the basics" education curriculum led to the appointment of school principals who took no-nonsense, quasi-military approaches to campus life and operations. The urban school, in particular, had a short period during which a former military officer became principal and operated the school like a "tight ship." However, to pull this off, he had to cater primarily to well-behaved and academically motivated students. He generally ignored the other students and, in fact, eliminated any street-socialized students, including gang members, by sending them to a nearby school. Overall, on the surface, this window dressing provided an attractive façade, but a large percentage of the local school-age population was underserved and shunted aside. After a few years of this, some of the parents persuaded the board of education offices that this type of arrangement was elitist, especially for a low-income, ethnic-minority school.

ADDITIONAL COMPARATIVE FEATURES

Various other factors besides structural ones influenced educational performance. These were often culturally based. By comparing students with higher GPAs against those with lower GPAs, factors such as immigrant aspirations, lower economic status, family stability, gender, and ethnic identity were found to affect academic success. Those students with an adequate socioeconomic status, active parental involvement and support, a secure family environment, successful role models, and a stable ethnic identity seemed to do very well at school. Although many students were familiar with streetsmart rules and regulations, they often preferred schoolsmart routines and rhythms. For example, there were always a few role-shifters in the urban school, balancing their daytime learning activities with nighttime entertainments and adventures on the street. The effect and degree that these roles play in determining educational success is still unclear. Research does suggest that these factors are interconnected and that no single factor, present on its own, ensures academic success (Carter, 2005).

Socioeconomic Status and Immigrant Aspirations

Socioeconomic status and immigrant aspirations can be strong factors affecting educational success. Those students with high aspirations were motivated to succeed in school, and this motivation, in turn, helped drive their academic success. Recent immigrants tended to have the highest aspirations. Comparatively, many third- and fourth-generation Latino Americans lowered their level of expectations (Suárez-Orozco & Suárez-Orozco, 1995). This was due to a diminishing "newcomer" effect—the excitement and energy applied to a fresh arena. Some immigrants to the urban locale had experienced setbacks in the United States, and had, over time, lost momentum and motivation. In contrast, some immigrants in suburbia felt a sense of relative affluence compared to their urban relatives. As a result, some did not strive for a higher socioeconomic status than their parents and were satisfied living a de facto blue-collar lifestyle.

The socioeconomic status of immigrant families both before and after entering the United States also affected educational performance and acculturation (Feliciano, 2006b). Some immigrants who came from educated and fairly affluent backgrounds were able to do well in America within the first few years of migration. Others had faced poverty both in Mexico and in the United States, which dampened their aspirations and hopes. A recent study reported that because of an increase in undocumented children, mostly in the urban area but also in suburbia, there were additional hardships that dampened their educational trajectories (López & López, 2010). Simply put, because parents feared apprehension and deportation, they were unable to fully participate in school affairs, parent-teacher conferences, and other school events. Along with the many obstacles outlined in this chapter, legal status problems add to the difficulties in the modern period.

Family Stability and Support

Family stability and parental support are recurrent themes in the students' life histories. A functional family, headed by parents with high expectations, clearly helped the students in this sample to start and sustain a positive school career. The active participation and involvement of parents, adults, and older siblings in school-related activities was also beneficial (Delgado-Gaitan, 1991).

Family stability alone was not a predictor of academic success. Several students from relatively stable families had parents who had no strategy or interest in helping their children perform well in school. They were preoccupied with work and other concerns, thus depriving their children of time and attention.

Unfortunately, for several students, tension and instability were characteristics of their family life. This had a negative consequence on their performance at school. Positive home dynamics provide a crucial foundation for success in school. Young people need encouragement and support, a secure family environment, and a climate conducive to learning. To reiterate, in the new millennium, the tremendous rise in undocumented workers and their school-age children has affected family integration and survival strategies. Large, extended families that provide social capital are much less common in the United States. The lack of established familial networks adds another burden to the equation for hundreds of thousands of children educated in the nation.

School, Classrooms, and Teacher Culture

The environment or "culture" that a school fosters is a significant factor to consider when analyzing academic success. Classroom dynamics and teacher-student interactions are especially significant (Conchas, 2001, 2006). Despite many obstacles, several students in this study were performing well at school; they often attributed much of their success to the efforts of their teachers. Teachers can be very influential role models for students. They can motivate students to realize their full potential and provide nurturing learning environments.

Just as teachers can bring about positive changes in their students, their actions can also be detrimental. The teachers in the 1974 study were found, in general, to have lower academic expectations for their students; negative attitudes and racist comments were also more common among them. Discrimination, however, still existed in the 1988 and 2004 studies. In 1988, some students expressed resentment at such treatment, but their responses were subtle. In 2004, conversely, students were more vocal about the racism they experienced in and out of schools.

The 1970s saw an increase in hostility and friction in the urban high school employees, mainly between the Chicano principal and the teachers, who were mostly middle-class whites. The Chicano movement had played a role in getting the principal appointed, against the wishes of most of the teachers in the school, who resented this imposition. The subsequent tensions led to a negative climate for students in the school. Frequent gang fights also contributed to creating this negative atmosphere. As a result, two youth lost their lives during the study year.

After a heated political struggle that involved teachers and many community and school officials, the school district replaced the Chicano principal of the urban high school in the mid-1970s with an Anglo male. A series of administrators, at the behest of Los Angeles Unified School District officials, reintroduced a traditional educational curriculum, avoiding some of the more culturally experimental learning programs. Meanwhile, new teachers, many of them Chicanas and Chicanos, joined the faculty. Together with more established Latino teachers, they collectively made a difference despite the opposition of some top administrators.

The ESL program of that time period is one example. This program proved pivotal to the participating students' academic success. It created a learning environment of cultural accommodation for Mexican-oriented students, which eased their acculturation stress. In recent decades, such programs have become more established and have made their mark in the urban setting, even though controversy continues to swirl around them (Colvin, 1995).

In the suburban high school, the Expanded Horizons program helped students mediate the acculturation process. When the program was launched in the mid-1960s, it was considered innovative but somewhat safe—Latinos were a minority at the time. In the late 1970s and 1980s, when the district, school, teachers, and officials began to become increasingly Latino, some people began to consider such programs a threat. Fortunately, cooler heads prevailed and school district leaders made adequate adjustments to the program in lieu of its elimination. The program became institutionalized district-wide and renamed New Horizons. It expanded to include working-class Whites, similar to the previously mentioned AVID initiative that was not ethnic-specific.

Administrators introduced additional learning approaches. For example, and as noted, the Advancement via Individual Determination (AVID) program is a daring, innovative strategy for low-income or mediocre students who are identified as "bright" on the basis of subjective criteria, not standardized test results. These students are placed in academically oriented classes that address their potential and special learning needs. Research shows that the AVID program has been successful and makes a difference among its students (Mehan et al., 1996).

The suburban school did not escape the onset of tensions between principal and staff. In her attempts to adjust to the tide of Mexicanization, the suburban principal resisted strengthening the multicultural learning environment. Nevertheless, with the persistence and help of certain district officials and a group of committed and dedicated teachers and parents, most of the students were still able to gain a good education and, at the same time, develop pride in their Latino heritage.

By the turn of the 21st century, both schools had Latino principals and key school counselors and teachers who openly embraced some of the learning strategies developed earlier that were now being carried out in a more systematic way. For example, the suburban director of New Horizons was a Chicana activist who went beyond clerical office duties and took risks on a daily basis, including instructing students to boycott the school during a regional and statewide "Day Without Mexicans" protest. Unlike many other teachers and midlevel administrators who toe the party line, she proudly and calmly declared for the principles of the Chicano movement and provided an example for students.

Racism and Ethnic Cultural Identity

Another recurrent theme influencing academic achievement is ethnic and cultural identity. Strong educational pursuits are associated with a stable and relatively stress-free ethnic identity. Those students in the study who exhibited the greatest confidence in their ethnic identification were the Mexican-oriented students. Their stable ethnic identity, coupled with a supportive family environment, resulted in a better academic record at school. The ESL program deserves the credit. In addition to easing the students' acquisition of English, the program prevented serious identity anxiety when difficulties did occur; students' problems largely stemmed from socioeconomic forces.

Ethnic identity formation varies significantly across time, people, and place. Unlike their suburban counterparts, the 1974 urban Anglo-oriented students did not have much access or exposure to Anglo-American culture, as they lived in a predominantly Latino barrio. Suburbia, on the other hand, brought with it a greater exposure to Anglo culture. Anglo-oriented Latino students felt little discomfort in denying their ethnic identity.

However, even if a unidirectional Anglo acculturation was enhanced in the suburban locale, there were feelings of anxiety and ambivalence associated with the process, especially for some of the Mexican-oriented students. The elements necessary for retention of Latino culture and practice of the Spanish language were limited. Nevertheless, despite the absence of a large Latino ethnic population base such as East Los Angeles, several students were still strongly Latino-oriented. For these students, the Expanded Horizons program helped to mediate the acculturation process. The program helped instill a sense of ethnic pride in several students, even if they could not speak Spanish and knew little about their heritage. Thus, the Expanded Horizons program helped students regain a sense of identity and stability.

A parent's influence affects a child's sense of ethnic and cultural identity. Several students in the 1974 suburban sample were explicitly told by their parents to change their ethnicity. Some parents did this to spare their children the racism the parents had experienced when they were young. Other parents' motives were based on their own prejudices and, perhaps, even shame of their ethnicity. Parents thus socialized their children toward the dominant culture. These parental strategies of denial were, to a large degree, successful in forcing acculturation because their children were in an Anglo suburban environment.

Some of the 1974 suburban parents, on the other hand, based on their own experiences of racism, told their children to be wary of Anglos and often passed on their resentment. Racial appearance, in fact, is a significant mediating factor in acculturation and is found to greatly affect ethnic identity formation (López, 2003, 2011). The fact that many of these parents and their children had dark skin, with a mixed-race appearance, adds weight to these beliefs. These students' strategy of acculturation was thus often stressful and produced, at best, mixed results.

By 1988, different forces were in place to affect the process of the students' ethnic identity formation in dynamic ways. The influx of newcomers strengthened existing programs, such as bilingual education, and resulted in a trend of Mexicanization. Latino American youth were now reclaiming their heritage; students were no longer ashamed of publicly labeling themselves as Latino or Chicano. A sound, solid ethnic (and personal) identity in this context enabled students to succeed and achieve. Even some of the third- and fourth-generation students and the mixed-race students in the sample were now claiming their Latino heritage; some of the lighter-skinned students refrained from calling themselves White. Unable to speak Spanish, they still sought to affirm their identity by following traditions and customs such as eating Latino foods, maintaining an interest in their native history, and associating with other Latinos. Being "ethnic" became fashionable, but it also brought challenges. Some of the mixed-race students hinted at difficulties with the White aspect of their identities.

The range of the acculturation spectrum in 1988 had, in fact, narrowed. Students were clustered in the middle. A resilient bilingual-bicultural experience seemed to be the trend now and, perhaps, in the future (Gutiérrez, 2008; Hurtado & Gurin, 1995). Most of the 2004 sample—from both urban and suburban areas—was adamantly and clearly embarked on a path of "no assimilation at any cost," espoused by the Chicano movement. This only meant, however, that Spanish language retention and pride in their Mexican heritage would remain constant as they became equally proficient in the language and traditions of their new adopted country.

As noted, the urban area and school became proportionally more first-generation Mexican. Suburbia, to reiterate, was swallowed by urban sprawl and marginalization and also turned in a strong Mexican direction generationally and culturally. The spatial separation between the areas remained the same but the social and cultural worlds were much closer and blended. One sign of this change is the spate of new Mexican restaurants in the suburban area, some challenging the exquisite cuisine and dishes once dominated by the East Side Los Angeles of the Chicano world. Of course, in this context of conflict and change produced over time, it was fairly clear that being Mexican was something to either be proud of or, more commonly, something to tacitly accept and take for granted. There were still a few students who struggled with self-identity, but now their struggle was based on whether they were Mexican enough.

Pre-Acculturation and Pre-Immigration Backgrounds

Pre-acculturation experiences in Mexico affect the tone and rate of acculturation of Mexicans in the United States, as well as educational performance (Feliciano, 2006a). Some parents familiar with and acclimated to American culture were better able to achieve their socioeconomic goals once they found themselves in the States.

The distinct regional and socioeconomic differences among migrants also affect the acculturation process. As mentioned before, those who had a relatively high socioeconomic status in Mexico, as well as a strong educational background, had an accelerated head start once in the United States.

Differences in places of origin add another significant dimension to acculturation patterns. The population of Mexican descent in the United States has a very diverse background. There are people from rural areas, towns, and cities; there are those who are from the south, center, north, and border areas of Mexico; and there are those who are indigenous, mestizo, and White. Each of these place or people characteristics strongly affects the nature of acculturation. For example, many indigenous Mexican peoples (i.e., Zapotec, Maya, Mixtec) have to acculturate to Mexican as well as to Anglo lifestyles if they, upon their arrival in the United States, settle in predominantly Latino-populated regions.

Since the 1980s, more immigrants have arrived from large town or city backgrounds, with many of these less peasant-based in their orientation (Chávez, 1992). (Nevertheless, a sizeable number of them are peasants, especially among the tens of thousands who claim an indigenous heritage.)

These immigrants are familiar with modernized mass media and are relatively more prepared for a life in a modern urbanized area such as Southern California. Directly linked to the pre-acculturation dynamic addressed earlier, these immigrant families and their children get a "kick-start" in their acculturation to Anglo-American lifeways and customs (Feliciano, 2006b). This trend became more pronounced in the modern era, as downtown Los Angeles, unlike other cities and regions of the United States, acquired a large indigenous Mexican population. Being Mexican was more popular, and the idea of being Indian within being Mexican was also growing in strength and meaning to many.

A FINAL CONTEMPORARY PERSPECTIVE ON THE TWO SETTINGS

The 2004 follow-up to these two settings clarifies that places and peoples have changed over the decades. We visited often over the years and kept a steady eye on broader social and cultural developments in these schools and communities. Through the 1990s and early 2000s, we spoke regularly at the two schools and observed and interviewed students along the dimensions of this chapter's topic, that is, acculturation levels, and ecological contrasts of urban and suburban transformations. In addition, we conducted a survey in 2004. As a way of summary, what briefly follows are some of the developments that we observed.

Mexicanization has deepened and expanded, but there is an important difference to note about this expansion. The students are now mostly second-generation, as East Los Angeles and suburban Southeast Los Angeles are no longer the main entry points for Latino immigrants. As a result, many students are comfortably bilingual and embrace a bicultural life, evincing a linguistic and cultural fluidity that was nonexistent in previous times. After the Civil Rights Movement and the uphill struggle for bilingual-bicultural education, all things Latino are au courant. Academic achievement has not necessarily blossomed in this context, as class and structural barriers still dominate the process.

Significantly, both schools have a high percentage of Latino students, as even the suburban school has seen its Latino percentage rise such that it is approaching 90% of the student body (a marked increase from 30% in 1974 and 70% in 1988). As noted earlier, there is no longer a stigma or embarrassment associated with their ethnic background. Racial appearance, however, as a carryover from Mexico, has persisted. Indigenous, darker-appearing students are more likely to experience disparagement from both fellow Latinos and from members of the dominant race (López, 2011).

REASSESSING EDUCATIONAL ENGAGEMENT OVER TIME

Both sizeable and seemingly insignificant factors influence educational performance. As noted, a secure socioeconomic status, a solid family environment, positive and influential role models, and a stable ethnic identity contribute to enhance school achievement and behavior. In contrast and as carefully outlined by the multiple marginality framework, when each sector is marginalized and weakened, the end result favors a *streetsmart* orientation. This chapter illustrates how the individual within the family is nested in the social, the structural, and the cultural milieu of his time and place. All sectors need to come together when analyzing educational success: social (family stability and support), cultural (clear strategy, embracing a multicultural orientation), economic (stable SES, even in working poor), and psychological (self-esteem, stable ethnic identity, role models). Thus, as we suggest in Chapter 1, both cultural and structural conditions must be part of the equation.

Instead of counter posing these perspectives in a this-or-that rivalry, we must begin to reconceptualize them in a this-and-that-and-that combinative manner. This approach will synthesize and build rather than segment and isolate. This chapter has shown how culture and structure can, in fact, be used in complementary ways within the same analysis. Also, it reiterates how the sometimes delicate balance between *schoolsmart* and *streetsmart* quickly unravels when weighted or voided on either side.

CONCLUSION

A multilingual and multicultural strategy is the best acculturation route and one on which to build other significant elements (Banks, 2001). It is a path of adding and combining, giving recognition and respect to various cultural influences that enrich individuals' personas (or "*personas mexicanas*," which denotes a multilingual and multicultural heritage). Academics have referred to it as additive (nativist) rather than subtractive (unidirectional or assimilational) acculturation, as a pathway to adaptation and integration into America.

Students who are bilingual and bicultural can also be good students, as evidenced by the studies in this chapter. A unidirectional assimilation path is no longer the only route to academic success. Especially important in this regard is how unidirectional acculturation can be reexamined and rethought to include an almost definitive multicultural strategy—one that teaches respect and interest in cultures other than one's own (Banks, 2001). Cultural and linguistic accommodation and integration is thus the one area where public institutions and political leaders can readily make a difference, because control is in their hands to make schools effective and productive experiences for the culturally different, politically underrepresented, and economically powerless.

In light of the vehement backlash to multiculturalism and, in particular, to the waves of immigrants and Latino culture, we must emphasize that multiculturalism does not signify anti-Americanism. Indeed, a multicultural strategy can benefit Americans of all backgrounds (Banks, 2008). Milton Gordon (1964) long ago pointed out that we could learn and maintain primary (American) ethnic customs, practices, attitudes, and relationships and simultaneously cultivate the dexterity to hold secondary (other culture) ones; this is known as ethnic pluralism or cultural democracy. Switching back and forth as the occasion warrants, showing a cosmopolitanism that places us in the world culture, is beneficial because it encourages resiliency and openness instead of rigidity and myopia.

Latinos are poised for major contributions to the United States in the 21st century. In particular, the example of a bilingual-bicultural American identity will help steer the United States away from a monolithic-centered language and cultural orientation to one that connects Americans to a global society and economy. It can also make a major difference in steering youth away from a *streetsmart* path and help develop and firm up a self-identity foundation that bodes well for pursuing *schoolsmart* lifestyles.

Chapter 6

They Make Me Feel Like I Am Somebody

Empowering Urban Youth Through Community-Based Action

As we look around the housing development we see a sea of Black and Latino faces. We observe many kids running around, young people hanging out on staircases, and a group of young boys playing basketball on a court in the distance. The president honks the van's horn and waves at various people outside their apartments. Suddenly the van stops . . . Up to this point, we were uncertain about the president's actual face-to-face relationship with low-income people of color in these neighborhoods. This night however exuded a climate of respect and trust between a white middle class man and a community of low-income urban residents of color.

— Researcher observation

"The Club" was a weekly gathering for youth at a community center located in the central part of a large city on the East Coast. Most youth either walked to the program's headquarters or got picked up at their doorstep by the vans. The purpose of the weekly meeting was to provide a space for young people to feel safe—treated as important citizens of the community— through community-building and critical thinking activities.

According to the program leaders, this space contributed to "young people having the social, critical, and academic skills necessary to create positive changes in their lives, community, and society as a whole." The president of the organization believed that youths needed support to realize their strengths, which they could build on for future success. Young people needed to "move" away from alienation and failure. To do that, they had to be engaged in every aspect of life. The weekly Club meeting nurtured that engagement, and participants began to realize their goals and aspirations.

79

This type of critical space increases self-esteem, maturity, and confidence, allowing young people to find and pursue a positive purpose in schools, communities, and society.

This chapter provides a specific case study of a community-based organization. School and community partnerships promote the social mobility of urban youth. These meaningful relationships, as observed in previous chapters, have the potential to address inequality and the achievement gap. Often, community-based organizations are more equipped than schools to combat inequality at its roots—poverty, racism, and neighborhood context issues. We suggest that schools are not immune from the social ecology of poverty, but we need to tackle neighborhood factors that generate the alarming dropout rate among urban youth. What follows is a community-based organization's attempt to reengage youth in school and to chart productive paths toward adulthood.

COMMUNITY-BASED ORGANIZATIONS AND
THE NEED TO ADDRESS TRUANCY

This chapter revolves around social capital and four youth-identified initiatives that significantly influenced participants' social and academic engagement. The connection among truancy, learning disengagement, and dropouts is all too familiar when studying urban youth and schools. The term "dropping out" is too broadly applied. It is true that some students leave for individual reasons—boredom or gang involvement—but others are pushed or kicked out of school because they need to work to support family or care for younger siblings or ill or elderly adults. Struggles outside the schoolyard walls seep into the academic partnership between students, parents, and school, affecting academic achievement and retention, but schools are not adequately equipped to deal with these struggles. The effects of truancy on the academic and social outcomes of youth are highly interrelated. For example, correcting for low expectations and poor grades, truancy is the most common determinant related to students dropping out of school (Wehlage & Rutter, 1986).

Truancy often leads to destructive social effects for young people, such as run-ins with the criminal justice system through crimes related to drugs, alcohol abuse, and violence. When youth are truant, many congregate on the streets and attend ditch parties. To prevent these negative consequences, authorities have increased the police presence in inner-city schools (Advancement Project, 2006).

Truancy leads to the ultimate forms of school exclusion—dropping out and getting pushed or kicked out. Research shows that these exclusions are hyperconcentrated in racially segregated central cities (Orfield,

2004). Programs, practices, and policies should be concentrated on contexts that fit these racially segregated profiles. Dropout rates among large inner-city school districts are consistent with the national average of approximately 25%; however, the rates of Hispanic and African American children are much higher, 39.1% for Hispanics and 46.5% for African Americans (Orfield, 2004).

Combating truancy via community-based intervention is imperative and requires immediate action. A systemic response to reengage truant youth and to prioritize school success and college preparation can serve as a possible pathway out of poverty. The first step is to combat truancy. External agencies, such as community-based organizations, have executed meaningful approaches in attempts to reduce truancy and dropout rates.

The research on after-school programs and community-based programs is promising (Rodríguez & Conchas, 2009). Such initiatives often commit to utilizing rigorous and proactive strategies to engage youth. Some are adamant about making critical linkages between communities/programs and schools for the purposes of building an expansive network of support for students (Noguera, 2001). The school and community dimensions to truancy and dropout intervention empower students, while also boosting achievement and engagement.

The idea of deliberately bridging institutions, such as community-based organizations and schools, is rooted, in part, in social capital theory (Putnam, 2000). In order to effectively build capacity among people across various institutions around any issue, such institutions need to make connections, partnerships, and meaningful relationships with one another. In the case of urban young people, community-based organizations and schools are two of the many stakeholders that show the most promise in collaboratively addressing the needs of truant youth.

Bridging institutions is particularly critical because while institutional processes within schools matter (Conchas, 2006), school systems are overwhelmed. Schools build networks of support between teachers and students (Stanton-Salazar, 2001), but overcrowding and large classes challenge their ability to provide students with adequate opportunities and resources. Schools should not be blamed or left alone to deal with issues of inequality. As a result, there is a need to bridge institutions, such as community-based organizations and schools. These links are essential to combat truancy and dropout.

The Truancy Project in Atlanta, Georgia, addresses truancy by matching volunteer lawyers with young people in the community. The idea is to intervene at an early age by advocating on behalf of the students while mentoring them. Program evaluation results show that over 50% of students once failing and truant reengaged with school and successfully completed the academic school year (Gullatt & Lemoine, 1997). Another community-based organization that addresses truancy is Young People Visions. This organization works on developing social and leadership skills among marginalized young people. The founders of the program planned to empower young people by giving them direct responsibility for handling teen problems. The program was based upon the principle that youth should have a space to talk with other youth—in their own language—in order to support each other and manage the difficulties of school, home and society. Program developers believed that adolescents occupying the same social space needed the opportunity to work together and identify issues (Roth & Hendrickson, 1991).

These practices and programs show how intervention-based programs can effectively mediate student truancy and dropout rates by investing in key sources of support that students may be lacking. These include providing rigorous, engaging, and supportive academic environments; pairing youth with caring adults and advocates; and, most importantly, investing in the belief that youth bring experiential, intellectual, and community cultural wealth (Yosso, 2005). This approach seeks to find ways that institutions are positioned to recognize the "funds of knowledge" (Moll et al., 1992) that urban young people bring and to challenge the deficit myths typically associated with this population. The young people's experiences and perspectives below suggest that effective practices across multiple institutions can adequately respond to resist student truancy and to promote student success.

RESEARCH ON THE URBAN YOUTH CENTER AND COLLEGE SUCCESS

A case study approach was used to empirically assess Black and Latino youths' experiences in an after-school college success program. Youth interviews were used to illuminate the impact of the various program components on their experiences in school and beyond. That is, an examination of student (dis)engagement—particularly through the experiences and understandings of student participants—was conducted (Maxwell, 1996), primarily to arrive at how and why the youth were truant and the degree to which the program shaped their experiences and redirection to school.

The Urban Youth Center (UYC) is a community-based organization that seeks to prepare socially and academically disadvantaged Black and Latina/o youth for college and successful futures. The program's central mission is "to help young people develop spiritually, emotionally, academically, and economically" (UYC Mission Statement). The organizational structure and programs revolve around key social and educational scaffolds, which engage and empower low-income disadvantaged urban young people toward promising educational practices. As a result of being in the program, participants once considered truant find themselves, over time, attending school and developing an orientation toward academic achievement. Most significantly, program graduates matriculate into 2- and 4-year colleges.

UYC has several initiatives. It specifically has three central programs under its Building Futures Educational Initiative: 1) the School Success program, 2) the Academic Enrichment Center (AEC), and 3) the College Vision program. UYC believes in providing a variety of social scaffolds that include one-on-one counseling, motivational activities, and tracking student engagement and progress.

The objective of Building Futures is to improve educational opportunities for low-income urban young people. The initiative specifically seeks to increase attendance and performance among truant students, to reengage them in school, and to get them prepared for college. The program has four major objectives: 1) decrease truancy by 70%; 2) improve academic skills and grades; 3) prepare youth to enter and complete college; and 4) overcome the digital divide that affects urban youth. This chapter concentrates on the specific strategies within the School Success program that aim to decrease truancy by 70%.

These features empower marginalized youth and provide them with extensive outreach opportunities throughout the year. A major component of the School Success program is the Academic Enrichment Center. The center provides academic skill-building, which includes the improvement of reading and math skills, study skills, computer training, and self-esteem exercises. These serve to build the self-esteem of students so that they can focus on their educational goals. In an interview with us, the president of UYC defines truancy as "young people who are continuously late to class or who do not present themselves in class at all for long periods of time." In these cases, the student is often not showing up to class for more than 3 days of unexcused abscesses. Truancy, therefore, is the root of the problem that School Success targets by focusing on school attendance and performance and by creating strategies that enhance community mobilization and increase institutional capacity, which help to prevent and overcome truancy among chronically truant adolescents.

All three components work to advance the participant to the next level. The College Visions program focuses on older program participants and seeks to improve grades and prepare young people for the SAT and college. For example, all students are able to receive tutoring at the Academic Enrichment Center. The School Success program focuses on reengaging middle and high school students. The Building Futures Educational Initiative serves as a truancy intervention and prevention program that seeks to foster optimism among urban young people.

Demographics of the Youth Served and Their Community

The program serves 500 youth from ages 11 to 16 and has since expanded its services to approximately 800 youth in the community. Most young people come from several low-income communities in a large city in the East Coast. Female participants, at the time of writing, accounted for 51% of the students served. Seventy-two percent of the students were African American, including many Haitian youth, with the remaining students being Latina/o. Students learned about the program through various institutional partners: one of the three partner middle schools, the courts, the Department of Youth Services, or the local grass-roots network of police, churches, and local agencies. UYC staff conducts extensive fieldwork throughout the community, recruiting young people to join the program.

UYC staff define "at-risk" youth as adolescents who live in impoverished urban communities. Many are young people of color who lack structured guidance and support. Most UYC participants are "more at-risk than average due to the multiple family and personal problems that they experience of which include violence, substance abuse, drug trafficking, gang involvement, court involvement, and/or school failure or dropping out" (UYC Profile, 2005). The staff suggests that since program participants are street-oriented, many face extreme odds of surviving socially, economically, and academically.

While truancy is the entry point into the lives of youth, the program chooses to address many of the social and psychological stressors dealt with on a daily basis. Through capacity-building across community institutions and schools, a solid commitment by program staff, and a firm belief that "it doesn't have to be this way," the efforts of the UYC program show promise in mediating truancy and preventing dropouts in the urban context.

Building Futures Educational Initiative

The foundation of the School Success program is the comprehensive network of community-based case managers. Case managers work closely with students through middle school and high school; once in high school, students are also eligible to join the College Visions program. Students work with case managers at least twice a week. These managers provide program participants with one-on-one counseling and family and school advocacy. Case managers also make home visits, visit schools twice a week, and build strong relationships with religious organizations. In addition, UYC sponsors a weekly Breakfast Club that aims to motivate young people to attend school.

In addition to case managers who address the social and academic needs of students broadly, the program also builds the academic skills of its participants. Serving all program participants daily between the hours of 3:00 and

6:30 p.m., the after-school program provides comprehensive academic assessment tools provided by a local university, tutorial/homework skill-building, computer training, group discussions, planning and organizational skill development, service learning, field trips, and access to the weekly "Club" hosted every Monday night. Students enthusiastically signed up for the after-school program, eager to access its tutors and opportunities.

The program also provides activities that promote pro-social values in a large peer group context. The aim is to increase self-esteem and to emphasize achievement over street values. Young people experience peer group relationships through club meetings, college tours, job training, youth enterprises, service learning projects, and field trips such as camping and rock climbing.

Another major component of the program is its commitment to recruit, train, and utilize local young people as mentors, with the hope of influencing new patterns of school involvement. Program mentors work with young people one-on-one and help to mobilize a network of support for each participant across institutions. At the time of data collection, the program was in the process of expanding its provision of mentors. The idea was to train mentors in youth development, effective mentoring, supporting and accessing community resources, and helping students with setting goals.

The final program feature, vision casting, encourages program participants to set and pursue realistic long-term goals and to connect positively with peers, parents, and others. Program staff and participants discuss what each young person wants to achieve, what obstacles stand in the way, and what can be done in the future. They develop a plan for family and peer relationships, school success, career development, recreation, and community involvement. Case managers and program participants develop each plan mutually and update them periodically. Most importantly, the participant must "own" the plan in order for it to succeed. Parents, peers, teachers, probation officers, and mentors all have roles, coordinated by the case manager, but the program participant has the most important responsibility. Each plan is unique, but all plans are structured around clearly outlined, attainable objectives. Program participants gradually but steadily progress toward improved, self-motivated educational performance.

UNEARTHING URBAN YOUTH EXPERIENCES OF SUCCESS

Following is a presentation of key elements that the program participants believed to be critical to the its effectiveness. Utilizing student voices, we place their experiences and perspectives at the center of our analysis. The responses suggest that the School Success program critically motivated once-truant youth to engage in school and to eventually become productive young adults in society. The themes that emerged are based on extensive field data and interviews with the young people and adults. Participants deemed UYC important because it provided: 1) space promoting peer relations, 2) incentive structures within programs, 3) social networks, and 4) youth advocacy from caring adults.

The Role of Space

Social space is a tangible, created, and delicate artifact to social life. Some argue that space consists of sites where identity, culture, and resistance are built and fostered (Lauria & Miron, 2005). In many countries, there is a constant fight over land and territories. In states, politicians often redistrict particular communities for political gain and cities frequently enact zoning laws to protect spaces for development or investment. In urban contexts, people socially congregate in churches, community centers, and on street corners. They gather on sidewalks in front of businesses or close to their residences. Urban youth take ownership of any space they can—on basketball courts, in parks, or outside public transportation areas. Even in schools, some students socially organize based on definitive identities that range from racial/ethnic to gender distinctions. Others' style of dress depends on trends generated by the hip-hop or rocker crowds (Warakoo, 2011).

In school, because of various structural and cultural restrictions, students often lack opportunities to engage in safe social spaces that promote positive community-building. Under the UYC programs, students identified space as a significant factor in promoting positive peer relations. Student interviews and participant observations revealed that space was viewed as a structured location, created for the purpose of empowering young people through a dialectical process, which gives young people opportunities to co-construct one another's knowledge and truth through dialogue. Within UYC, space is a location where learning and teaching occurs among the young people. One African American student talks about the benefits of participating in the program: "It [the program] is fun because you all know what [we] have been through and just having conversation all the time . . . so we can talk to each other so we won't be absent and missing out and missing school." Not only does this student value the space to engage in dialogue, but he also conveys a collective experience that many of the program participants seem to share. He recognizes that such space is related to engagement in school, another key intention of the program's overall mission. Similarly, a Latino participant expressed the value of the opportunity to engage in a special space: "It [the program] is better than staying at my house all day and listening to the radio." These reflections indicate that attending the program gives young people something to do and helps forge a degree of belonging to a social group.

For many young people, the program provided a place where they felt comfortable and part of a friendship network distinct from street life. One student felt that if she were not in the program, she would probably be getting into trouble " . . . on the streets hanging out, not going to school." Another student agrees, "Okay, school is just like the Club, but . . . it's just like you go to school to learn . . . you go to the Club to have fun and meet people." This student defines his participation in the program with his attending Club on Monday nights rather than his bi-weekly check with his case worker at school. He clearly experiences a degree of belonging to the program—perhaps due to the positive climate created by the weekly Club sessions.

While anywhere from 40 to 70 youth are in attendance each week at Club, these sessions are quite personal. Program staff members do their best to exchange words and acknowledge each student throughout the meeting. Staff members make genuine efforts to show each student that they are valued. According to students and program staff, attending these weekly sessions keeps young people off the streets and in a protected space, where stimulating discussion revolves around themes that were particularly pressing to urban youth. In one interview, one student was asked what the purpose of the program was and quickly answered, "To keep kids off the streets, try to keep them somewhere productive and keep them somewhere safe. Give them another home to go when they are in trouble." This participant acknowledged the multiple dimensions of effectiveness provided by the program—a safe space that promotes a sense of belonging, but also a place that is an outlet of support for youth caught up with street drama.

Space also helps redress damaged peer relations so frequent among urban youth. We found that positive peer relations helped reinforce healthy friendships and a pro-school ethic. A Latino student states, "It's my friend, Joann, that encourages me by going to the program and doing this and that. That was good for me." The program allows young people the space to interact with peers about many issues that impact their lives. In addition to peers, older mentors, typically program alumni who participated in weekly activities, also frequently attended sessions. These home-grown role models often served as critical sources of support for the program participants. The program capitalized on these mentors by encouraging them to mentor and visit with younger program participants in these deliberately structured spaces.

These opportunities forged intimate, meaningful interactions. They forged relationships among young people who shared a collective experience—one of struggle. Most importantly, such spaces helped to create a climate whereby young people helped one another navigate school and develop a pro-future orientation. The created space for young people promoted healthy relationships between the program participants and the program staff, alumni, and mentors, while also addressing some of the school and social struggles that many of the students shared.

Club sessions enabled us to observe the advantages present in a space co-created by students and adults. Every Monday night, we listened to students' perspectives and observed that the club served as a powerful and seemingly effective medium to communicate with program participants. Young people spoke their minds in front of their peers on issues directly pertinent to their lives. These culturally relevant spaces encouraged participants to express themselves and to be critical about the reality of living in low-income urban communities. Such spaces relayed to students that not only were their experiences valued and affirmed, but that such opportunities were provided by a supportive network of peers and caring adults who understood and legitimized their realities—an occurrence that rarely gets played out in the traditional school system.

The Role of Program Incentive Structures

During hours of observation, researchers had the privilege to witness how program youth and staff interacted on an interpersonal and programmatic level. Program staff seemed to harbor a "whatever it takes" approach to engaging the program participants, who were particularly initially resistant youth. Creatively, and with the help of generous donations from community organizations in the local area, program staff were able to provide relatively meaningful incentive structures for program participants. Incentives were as simple as a ride to the subway station or home, food in the after-school program, or all-expenses-paid overnight college visits. To encourage youth to attend the tutoring sessions, staff often purchased pizza and soda for the students.

Providing food served a dual purpose—to tantalize and to help fill empty stomachs. Some kids felt an extra pull to attend because they loved pizza. Others didn't know where their next meal was coming from. Such incentive structures served as mechanisms to motivate young people to take positive action through investment and participation—the kind that can lead to short- and long-term benefits. We found that, ultimately, incentives helped to achieve positive academic, personal, and social results.

Many students voiced their enthusiasm for the incentive structures provided by the program. One African American student shared that going to colleges and sleeping over is something all students really want to do: "I really, really, really want to go!" Another student shared the same convictions about the program, stating, "It was like you know, they go places. You know, they go to see colleges and stuff. To see how kids start in college. Stuff that they [college students] did and stuff." Once students persistently engage in program activities such as Club, case workers set individual goals. When progress is made, program participants become eligible to attend field trips.

For most youth, exposure to different surroundings and leaving the city for the first time was an eye-opening experience. Program staff tell students over and over that the purpose of such opportunities is to give them more than aspirations. They want students to mark a goal that will be realized in the future. Exposure to distinct communities greatly mediated students' desires to reach for new goals and to experience positive dimensions of life. Reflecting upon a college field trip, one student stated:

> Yes, it [field trips] helps me a lot. It shows me about what life is about. I went to this trip, I think it was last month, with Amy and Geoff [program staff] and them. We went to this college. There was something about the college. I really do want to go to college. I am going to school. I am doing good in school.

The college tour trip was particularly influential for the above student. The student not only recognized the possibilities of attending college, but acknowledged the role of positive engagement with school in making that dream a reality.

Because many of the program participants often come from home and community realities that are unpredictable, many students entered the program without any vision beyond their immediate context. Many students, given their social and economic struggles, directed all their energies toward survival. They had to strategically navigate their neighborhoods, avoiding certain streets or hot spots that were correlated with violence or trouble. For these participants, exposing them to visions of college imprinted a new reality and an alternate possibility in life.

Program staff believed that exposure to field trips opened doors to new possibilities. The college field trips enlightened many participants because they helped forge new identities as possible college students. Such incentive structures gave youth a sense of hope and helped to build and relay the high expectations set out by program staff—expectations that constantly pushed students to set and meet goals.

Students had to meet a minimum standard to participate. In order to go on field trips, students had to show improvement in attendance and grades. They had to demonstrate active and consistent participation with the different program components (i.e., attending Club). Once the student made progress and exhibited effort in transforming his or her decisions and actions, he or she was rewarded with other program incentives (i.e., field trips).

Fortunately, the program had the financial and human resources to accommodate and oversee incentives such as overnight college visits. But the more practical message and logic behind the college visits was communicating the relevance of college to the participants' lives. The program not only encouraged young people to stay in school and do well academically, but also planted a seed of possibility in the minds of the young people—"You can attend and thrive in college and this is how you are going to get there." So the incentive structure not only rewards students for their immediate transformation of behavior, but also provides them with the opportunity to think and to plan ahead, making a connection between their current actions and life's possibilities, including the opportunity to go to college.

The Role of Youth Advocacy and Institutional Accountability

United States youth, in general, often feel powerless. They have no say in who their parents are and have little to no legitimized power to elect politicians or to devise policies and practices that serve them across various institutions. In addition, urban youth are less likely to have health insurance, more likely to have antagonistic relationships with community authorities (i.e., police), and more likely to come from families that are struggling economically. Low-income youth of color are also more likely to attend overcrowded and underresourced schools. Given these realities, urban youth often get lost in this nation's social institutions, which are meant to serve as safety nets.

The program staff recognized the marginalization that urban youth experience. Thus, the program made it a priority to deliberately create opportunities to advocate for the students, both within the family and in the school setting. Such advocacy was meant to facilitate opportunities for students to positively engage in these various contexts. The program affirmed the voices of young people, who are often institutionally marginalized and powerless in their families, schools, and communities. According to the program staff, advocating for students empowers the participants to become better students and citizens in society.

Many of the students in the program believed that one of the most positive aspects of the program was the case management approach. Every student was assigned a case worker. Case workers checked in with program participants twice a week via school visits. They encouraged them to attend after-school tutoring. Students began to feel that an adult cared about their well-being. One student said that he really enjoyed working with the case worker because " . . . when [I] needed something, [the case worker] calls home to see if [he] can come." Being able to call an adult for help is a rare luxury for urban youth in overcrowded schools. Because of large classrooms and the policies and procedures that often dictate school life, school authorities either run out of time or burn out.

In addition, parents or guardians are often disconnected to school issues because they are busy working or have unpleasant memories of their own schooling experiences. This reality of urban schooling therefore makes the case worker approach particularly valuable for program participants. Over time, trust is built between participants and case workers. Participants begin to rely on case workers and view them as positive adults in their lives. One student stated, " . . . [my case worker] encourages us to go more to school. And she tells me like if I don't go to school to call her and let her know why I didn't go to school and stuff like that." Young people appreciate and understand the importance of having an adult advocate for their concerns in school, at home, and in their community.

Case workers provided in-school advocacy that was another degree of support particularly meaningful to program participants. Based upon several interviews, we found that case workers were able to influence various dimensions of the student's in-school experience, adding another level of accountability on the student's behalf. For example, because of case worker advocacy, teachers and school administrators reconfigured a student's place within the school's programmatic offerings. Case workers advocated for placing students in appropriate courses. They collaborated with teachers and administrators to create strategies and goals for the student.

During the advocacy process, teachers seem to invest more once they realize that students are making a concerted effort to improve their attendance and school performance. A male student confirms this observation when he states that:

> They don't know I am in the program, but they know that I am changing a little bit, so I think the teachers try to listen to me a little more than they did before . . . they was listening to me, but I was trying to act stupid and say stupid answers and stuff, and they didn't have time to listen to me, because you are playing and not taking serious, until my [case worker] came along and helped me.

While the student believed that his teachers were not aware of his participation in the program, his teachers observed a transformation in him as a student. Because of his participation in the program, according to the student, he believed that the case worker, serving as an advocate, had a positive effect on his life in school.

In addition to advocates helping students navigate the various trials of urban school life, many students also believed that case workers kept them safe from forms of institutional violence. Students felt at ease knowing that they had someone looking out for them in their communities and in their schools. One student stated, " . . . how the [program staff] tell you that nothing is going to happen or they watch your back and watch over you." These students, who often live in violent environments, believe that feeling safe is a major factor in their engagement and motivation to do well in school and life. Adult advocacy mediates the violence that students perceive or experience and helps build a network of multi-institutional advocates who influence urban youth to reengage in school and succeed. This community-school connection demonstrates the power behind the notion of capitalizing on the social capital. By building bridges across institutions, we can facilitate the success of the community's most vulnerable children. This form of community advocacy has important institutional implications, as the process begins to soften the rigid structures of the school.

The Role of Social Networks

It is well documented in educational literature that low-income youth, and racial minorities specifically, are far less likely to acquire the social and cultural capital that is traditionally valued and legitimized by the school culture (Oseguera et al., 2010). Recognizing this struggle, program staff prioritized access to role models and mentors who could forge opportunities and deliver information to marginalized urban youth. In fact, program participants identified the power behind the social networks that, according to students, operated to foster a pro-school ideology, one that shows how social capital operates through social networks to provide the information necessary for school success.

Within the program, social networks comprised of family, school, and community partnerships validated, nurtured, and functioned to empower young people around a matrix of healthy relationships. The program leveraged and utilized social networks in its initiatives and in its practices. For example, at Club, students had access to program alumni and older program mentors. During the after-school program, students had access to college-level tutors. During field trips, participants developed critical connections with college students and garnered necessary information to help them make college a reality in their futures.

Students believed that the program capitalized upon peer-peer forms of social networking. Reflecting on his experiences and responding to whether he felt the program was helping him, one student noted, "Yeah, 'cause I got a whole bunch of people that I am friends with and I got older adults that I have to take care of me." Many of the students reflected upon how adults formed meaningful relationships with the young people—relationships that generated a strong sense of support.

For many of the young people, case workers functioned as mediators to positive social relationships. The following student explains how his case worker mentored him over time:

Yeah, 'cause, I was gonna get involved, I was involved with this like. . . .
Okay, let me say. Mike, which is the counselor [case worker] I have,
told me about a couple of things with girls and stuff, like girls like you
can have sex and be sexually active with girls and stuff . . . but he told
me to . . . keep safe and because I have a girl now but I want to take it
slow 'cause all the advice he gave me like he, like Mike is like a father
telling me advice and stuff and I take it to the head [listen] and just
use it in a way that helps me with my social life and personal life and
everything.

Because of the case worker, this student has been able to gain some insight
on life and interpersonal relationships. The case worker validates the student's
desire to be in a relationship with a female but nurtures his decision-making
and empowers the student to question the decision to have sexual relations
prematurely. Based on the student's reflection, he reconsidered the nature of his
relationship with his girlfriend and is now "taking it slow." Social networks
embedded within the program provide important sources of information,
encouragement, and support to empower program participants in personal
and academic spheres.

THE TRANSFORMATIVE POWER OF
COMMUNITY-BASED SUPPORT

While a significant amount of time can be spent on assessing various outcome measures (i.e., grades, attendance, and tardiness data) to determine
the program's effectiveness, we believe a more qualitative, humanistic
understanding of the program's impact on students' lives yields a useful
understanding of the program's impact. Upon a rigorous analysis of the
interview and observation data, it became clear that over time, the program by ways of its various initiatives, transformed the lives of its program
participants. Students, for instance, began to transform their once-negative
perceptions about school and society into positive dispositions toward life
and the future. In their own words, program participants began to discuss
how they changed the way they behaved in school and how they were better
disposed toward their family and their community. This process of change
makes students active agents in the transformation of their lives. They begin
to feel like healthy and productive members of their communities.

One student, for instance, disclosed positive views toward school
several times in an interview: "It is good for me to stay in school" and
"for us to stay in school, all of us. Get good grades and stuff." When
asked to share thoughts about the purpose of school, this student continued, "To get a good education and stuff. And get the point that school

is important." The student also commented on identity formation—how other students could benefit from knowing about the schooling process. Prior to participating in the program, this student, like many others, was unaware of her role in creating her future. She was unaware of the promise associated with going to school and getting an education. She even suggests that others do not quite "get it" the way she does, as a result of participating in the program.

Coming from urban youth once at the brink of dropping out of school, such stories are significant. Many of these students have navigated various community issues, moved through foster homes, and dealt with various family and relationship problems. The program promoted a pro-education ideology that often led to student engagement and motivation to succeed. For example, one student stated, "[The program] encourages [the student] more, like for the next year to try to do all of my homework." This motivation for future effort links what participants do *now* with their opportunities to attend college *later*. The program uses college visits and connections with college students and program alumni to generate such enthusiasm. Another student's words echo a similar sentiment: "Yes, it [the program] helps me a lot. It shows me about what life is about." This response is liberating, suggesting that the student was, before the program, unaware of college and career opportunities.

Another once habitually truant participant talked about the transformation of his disposition toward school and the nature of his peer relationships. The student stated, "Like today, in the morning, my friends were telling me to get with them [skip school]. But I said no, I had to go to school. Plus I had to take the Stanford Nine. I told them no, it is not cool." Later in the interview the student remarked, "Yes, I go to school every day. Never be late, like I used to before. Wake up in the morning and be lazy. I am not lazy any more because I know school is important." Such reflections came from a student who rarely attended school and frequently engaged in physical fights with other students. The program empowered him and others to recognize the value of education and its implications for the future. In addition to academic transformation in identity and behavior, the program also influenced the social awareness of its participants. The program helped youth to realize the importance of pro-social behavior that could help keep them clear of getting into trouble.

Through the program's various initiatives, its processes and practices operated to influence the participants' sense of identity and their actions in school and community. Students learned to take action to empower one another as they confronted many social and academic challenges daily. Program participants realized that school is more important than they had previously thought. They began to be more positive about attending and succeeding in school and aspiring for college success.

CONCLUSION

The students' comments demonstrate how institutional bridging and the beliefs and practices driving the work of the program provided various opportunities to transform participants' perceptions and actions in the quest to reengage them in school. The program also provided hope for a more promising future. The program is committed to providing a safe space, incentive structures, institutional advocacy, and social networks. This comprehensive approach around social capital contributed to personal transformations.

Understanding the connection between schools and communities allows for a deeper understanding of the issues urban young people confront. The students' experiences demonstrate that a program's commitment to bridging the gap between the community and the school can be an effective approach to curbing truancy and dropping out—reengaging young people in school. In other words, schools are not immune to their surrounding environments. The partner schools demonstrated their commitment to program youth by enabling access to the school sites so that case workers could communicate with teachers and access student records. Program leaders knew the academic status of each participant. At the same time, school authorities recognized the additional support the community-based program provided to teachers and students. Building this bridge between community-based organization and school proved to be a powerful lesson on the possibilities provided when relationships, resources, and will are capitalized through partnership.

Given that urban schools struggle to meet the needs of all their students, especially the most vulnerable, community-school partnerships provide a dimension of accountability in order to meet the needs of each student. In many cases, school authorities became more responsive to students' needs after discerning that those students had advocates. This community-school connection influenced schools to hold off on resorting to disciplinary action as a first response in the event that a student was in trouble.

The program deliberately created safe spaces for meaningful student engagement. During Club, during the after-school academic enrichment program, during one-on-one engagement with caseworkers, and during the rides to and from various activities, participants connected with peers and adults in safe spaces of engagement. Many participants indicated that such spaces were absent within their school experiences, so the opportunities created and information exchanged in such spaces was highly influential to students. Schools should forge ways to create such spaces so that students have opportunities to engage with adults and peers in similar ways.

The practices and processes contributed to the effectiveness of the program and its impact on the students. Students' perspectives demonstrated the importance of having access to peer mentors who shared similar backgrounds. They found it particularly meaningful to see other young people

from their community thrive in the program, succeed in school, and matriculate in and graduate from college. The constant positive messages, melded
with consistent, sustained, and personalized support, relayed genuine interest and action that encouraged the success of all participants. The impact
of the program, as measured by the transformation of the participants' dispositions and comportment in school and in the community, showed the
impact of the program's efforts. Their experiences demonstrate that when
given the opportunity to succeed, young people will exercise their agency to
participate, to believe, and to transform their lives despite their marginalized status in society.

Chapter 7

Education *Is* Key for People of Color

Career Academies and Youth Hopefulness

Investments in career-related experiences during high school can produce substantial and sustained improvements in the labor market prospects and transitions to adulthood of youth. In fact, Career Academies are one of the few youth-focused interventions that have been found to improve the labor market prospects of young men.
—James J. Kemple & Cynthia J. Willner, "Career Academies"

I think it's the work. . . . When you get hit with a problem, Black, White, Mexican or Asian, you can go ask them, ask them if you think they know it . . . It's not about racial things; it's about getting your work done.
—Tyrone, Career Academy student

Within urban California high schools, places rife with violence and low performance, many ethnic minority students remain optimistic. As a low-income urban high school student, Tyrone plans to succeed in school and become a medical doctor. While others are dropping out of school, he perseveres.

Tyrone is not alone in his quest for education and social mobility. Many other students are performing well, helping one another out, and planning to enroll in college. These students are part of California Career Academies, small learning communities that embrace them, challenge them intellectually, and prepare them for college and career. They are part of a learning environment that mediates their sense of optimism toward success and future mobility.

This chapter provides an example of a high school initiative that attempts to combat the alarming opportunity gap and high dropout rates in inner-city schools. Through the Asian, African American, and Latino student perspectives,[1] this chapter explores how and why Career Academies promote a sense of optimism and success among urban minority students. The chapter specifically illuminates the components and processes that contribute to school success among youth in two Career Academies found within the same urban high school. Finally, while acknowledging limitations, this chapter suggests that Career Academies are a significant and potentially successful high school reform strategy around college and career success.

CALIFORNIA CAREER ACADEMIES

In the early 1980s, Career Academies in California grew out of the need to retain potential dropouts and to prepare students whose circumstances place them "at risk" (Stern, Raby, & Dayton, 1992). To date, the number of Career Academies and other forms of college-to-career pathways in California has increased dramatically; it is estimated that there are over 500 Academies in California alone and have reached about 7,000 academies nationwide (Stern, Dayton, & Raby, 2010). Career Academies include three common core features.

First, they are small learning communities. An academy comprises a cluster of students who have some of the same teachers for at least 2 years and who share several classes each year. Program administrators schedule teachers, from academic as well as vocational disciplines, to lead classes made up of predominately Academy students. Teachers meet with one another on a regular basis and share in decision-making related to administrative policies, curriculum content, and instruction. One faculty member assumes responsibility for administrative tasks and usually serves as a liaison between the teachers and school authorities—the principal, the building administrators, the school district officials, and the employer partners.

Second, Academies organize college preparatory curriculum with a career theme. Examples of common themes are health care, business and finance, communications, media, and transportation technology. The program links academic courses that meet high school graduation and college entrance requirements with vocational courses that focus on the academy's fieldwork. Teachers sometimes share planning time in order to coordinate course content and instructional strategies. Courses include issues related to employment and job readiness. Work-based learning opportunities for students tie classroom activities to internships with local employers. College and career counseling informs students about options and planning for employment and further education.

Third, they have external partnerships and employer support. An advisory group for the Academy includes employment representatives from the local community, academic faculty, and district-wide administrators. Employer representatives give advice on curriculum, appear as guest speakers in classes, supervise student internships, provide financial or in-kind support, and sometimes serve as mentors for individual students (Stern et al., 2010).

Because of their emphasis on dropout prevention, some Career Academies have been viewed as vocational programs for low-achieving high school youth. Strong postsecondary outcomes of students in Career Academies, however, indicate the contrary. An evolving key ingredient in the Career Academy model is its determination for low- to high-achieving students to enroll in higher education. For students to become professionals, such as lawyers and doctors, they must seek baccalaureate and graduate degrees. The model also recognizes that in a global knowledge-based economy, all students need to engage in a "thinking curriculum," wherein they are held to rigorous standards. Most Career Academies foster student interest in various professional endeavors and strongly encourage students to pursue and prepare for both college *and* careers (Conchas & Clark, 2002; Stern et al., 2010).

A SOLID RESEARCH BASE

Research shows that the Career Academy model has a long tradition of promoting academic excellence. Evaluations have shown that students in Career Academies have a lower dropout rate, perform better, receive more high school diplomas, and are more likely to enroll in postsecondary education than students in comparison groups (Stern et al., 2010). In addition, Career Academies reflect principles present in recent high-school reform proposals, such as small learning communities and college-preparatory curriculum that is focused on a work-related theme (Kemple & Snipes, 2000).

Although research points to the benefits of the Career Academy model for youth whose circumstances place them at risk, a certain amount of caution is still in order. Stern et al. (1992) emphasized the ability of Career Academies to improve student achievement, but also called for more systematic studies in order to isolate the specific aspects of Career Academies that contribute to positive student outcomes.

In the late 1990s, using a comparative approach between Academy and non-Academy students, Maxwell and Rubin (1997) supported the finding that academies positively affect students, but also suggested that not all students benefit equally from the Academy experience. Their data showed that many students acquire higher grades, score higher on exams, and are more content within the Academy. Yet outcomes for some Academy students are not as positive. Although most Academy students are able to engage in and benefit from the Academy structure, some do not show much improvement. These students, compared to non-Academy students, may not benefit substantially from enrollment in the program. Maxwell and Rubin acknowledged that their quantitative analysis was unable to explain why this was so, although they did call for further exploration to assess the within-and-between academy processes, which may explain differences in school engagement.

In 2000, a study by Manpower Demonstration Research Corporation (MDRC) began the process of systematically addressing the disparity present among Career Academies (Kemple & Snipes, 2000). The study found that Career Academies that link career-based curriculum and work-based learning activities with strong interpersonal and academic support are more likely to increase school engagement. Kemple and Snipes (2000) specifically stated that a "highly structured school-within-a-school organization can create a necessary set of conditions for providing these supports" (p. 3). A less structured Career Academy, on the other hand, runs the danger of reducing school engagement among some students. Moreover, the study strongly recommended that student populations in Career Academies should be of varied academic ability, because of the significance of peer relations for both low-performing and highly engaged students.

Most recently, Kemple and Willner's (2008) experimental study found significant social and economic gains for Career Academy students compared with non-Academy students. The gains were especially pronounced for boys of color. Specifically, they found that 1) Career Academies produced sustained earnings gains that averaged 11% (or $2,088) more per year for Academy group members than for individuals in the non-Academy group, 2) this earning gain greatly impacted young men, who have as a group experienced a severe decline in real earnings in recent years, 3) Career Academies served as viable pathways to a range of postsecondary education opportunities, but they do not appear to have been more effective than options available to the non-Academy group, and 4) Career Academies generated an increase in the percentage of young people that were living independently with children and/ or a spouse or a partner. Young men also experienced positive impacts on their marriages and their success as custodial parents. Indeed, these findings are promising, to say the least.

The findings suggest improved labor market prospects and healthier transitions to adulthood for boys and men of color. This important finding comes at a time when boys and men of color face a crisis in higher education and labor force mobility. Stern et al. (2010) state:

> Career academies aim to provide the kind of academic preparation that will give as many students as possible the option of attending college. But the fact is that only about 30 percent of all 25–29 year-olds in the U.S. actually have completed bachelor's degrees. . . . Career academies respect and encourage students' college aspirations and—whether or not these aspirations are fulfilled—the career academy also gives students some practical knowledge and skill to earn a living. (p. 22)

The Career Academy structure and culture inspire both college and career aspirations. In so doing, Academy students are better prepared with 21st-century skills to compete in a dynamic world market.

THE TWO CAREER ACADEMIES SIDE-BY-SIDE

The large comprehensive high school is located in a large urban city in Northern California. The population of the city is mixed, with ethnic minorities comprising the majority, similar to many large urban cities in the United States. Although a full curriculum was offered at the high school, ranging from general classes to Advanced Placement (AP), student access to the various academic niches was not always equitable. The high school housed a Medical Academy for students who were interested in pursuing health-related occupations, a Graphics Academy, a Teacher Academy, a Transportation Academy, an English Language Learners program (ELL), and a well established Advanced Placement (AP) Program. The college pre-paratory curriculum was composed of standard college prep courses as well as 12 AP and honors courses.

The Medical Academy

The Medical Academy began as an experimental program bridging class-room lessons with real-life experiences. An English teacher at the high school founded the program and was involved in its implementation for 15 years. She and a devoted team of teachers spent countless hours working to increase the number of inner-city students pursuing careers in health, medicine, life sciences, and biotechnology. Since its inception, the focus of the Medical Academy has been to serve all students, but especially those with high potential. The goal of the Academy has been to interest students in health and bioscience careers and to provide them with the breadth of educational experience they need to be well prepared for careers in health or the biosciences, for postsecondary education, and for active and healthy citizenship.

Medical Academy teachers have made a strong effort to recruit a racially heterogeneous student population. The 267 students enrolled in the Medical Academy during 1996–1997 more closely reflected the racial makeup of the overall student population at the high school than did those enrolled in the Graphics Academy.

The Medical Academy's racial makeup was 55% Black, 32% Asian, 10% Latino, and 3% White. The Academy was more than two-thirds female (69% vs. 31%), which was usual over the years. In addition, the academy encouraged low-, middle-, and high-achieving students to partici-pate in the program.

For 3 or 4 years, Medical Academy students took interrelated academic and lab classes during 80% of their classroom time. Students typically joined the program in the 9th or 10th grade. The Medical Academy relied heavily on team teaching to link curriculum along interdisciplinary lines. All academy students participated in related worksite learning, including volunteer experience, career explorations, clinical rotations, summer and senior year internships, career portfolios, senior projects, and demonstrations of mastery. In addition, the program provided career mentors and postsecondary student coaches, frequent contact between school and home, tutors and workshop support services, and special social and awards activities highlighting students' success. A sense of community was a major emphasis of the program.

The graduating class of 1997 was remarkably successful: 93% of the 267 students graduated (the remaining 7% left the school district or enrolled in another high school). Of those who graduated, 98% enrolled in college—79% in 4-year universities and 19% in 2-year community colleges. Two students chose not to attend college due to personal reasons.

The Graphics Academy

The Graphics Academy specialized in computer-assisted graphics technology and had a reputation for catering to students with a strong math and science background. The Academy sought to prepare students for careers in computer technology and for success in college. During their 3 years in the Graphics Academy, students took a variety of classes in physics, calculus, and chemistry. In the summer following their junior year, they participated in paid internships linked to their studies.

The Graphics Academy enrollment fluctuated from 100 to 150 students. During the 1996–1997 academic year, the academy enrolled 127 students; these students were 56% Asian, 25% African American, 10% White, and 9% Latino. The racial and ethnic makeup of the academy did not reflect the larger school profile where African Americans were the majority. Although program recruitment occasionally took place at other schools in the district, most students were recruited within the ninth-grade AP pathway. These students were predominantly Asian and middle-class African American and White students. Given the focus on students with prior strengths in math and physical sciences, it is notable that enrollment was nearly two-thirds male (63% male vs. 37% female). The academy director made a strong effort to recruit a more diverse student body, but still focused on enrolling high-achieving students. Neither the Medical Academy nor the Graphics Academy enrolled students classified as Limited English Proficiency (LEP), as the students were expected to read and write fluently in English. Graphics Academy students, like those in the Medical

Academy, continually showed high levels of success. The Academy had a 100% graduation rate during the 1996–1997 school year; nearly all graduates enrolled in selective 4-year universities.

CREATING ENGAGING AND SUPPORTIVE SCHOOL CULTURES

The smaller school climate and focus on a common theme enable teachers to concentrate on students and their individual needs, and helps to create an academic culture that actively engages students to succeed in school. As noted by an academy science teacher, students need to have a "culture that they share with their peers that validates doing well in school." A rich multicultural curriculum and pedagogy enrich the familial atmosphere. The academy teachers work long hours to provide this type of school climate.

Despite differences in demographics (the Medical Academy was more racially integrated than the Graphics Academy) and career focus, both Career Academies sought to treat students as important and valuable individuals. The academies engendered a close sense of community. Many students characterized their Career Academy as a "family." The high school's educational consultant spoke of the strong relationships formed:

> I really don't like and I am tired of the expression "It takes a village," but there is a village in the academy. It is much more like a family. And the school is too big to be a close family, but the academies are part of the family.

Teachers reported that students flourished within this setting.

The academic culture of these two programs influenced student engagement in school, creating a rich learning environment whereby students encouraged one another to excel. As one academy English teacher stated,

> These kids have a lot of classes together and they see the quality of work, that is good, [and] they are proud of it. The students like the projects. They tell other students, "I really like your project," "How did you do that?" They encourage one another. It's here. It's growing. It's happening.

Students felt comfortable in a setting where they belonged socially and academically. "Everyone feels good when there is a sense of belonging," reported another academy teacher. Likewise, the Graphics Academy director stated that the academic structure was so strong that even the lower-achieving students felt out of place and began to work harder. This process resulted in close friendship bonds. Unlike the general school setting, Academy teachers were key players in the creation of the academic environment.

The academic culture of Career Academies was linked to specific structural characteristics. For example, the majority of administrators, adults, and students interviewed expressed that the small academy setting was key to its culture. Reporting on how the smaller school-within-a-school structure encouraged a strong community of learners, the educational consultant reported that this structure also allowed for stronger social relationships among and between students and teachers.

Although both academy directors and teachers exhibited different styles in the activation of such relationships, the end product in both cases was a stronger sense of community than in the larger high school setting. In turn, this created a strong sense of optimism among Career Academy students.

HOW CAREER ACADEMIES GENERATE OPTIMISM AND SCHOOL SUCCESS

The academies enabled students to view themselves optimistically, as people with high potential. They felt close bonds with one another and their teachers. These relationships transcended race and ethnicity. As reported by academy teachers, academy students worked well with one another as they strove to succeed. Ana, an Academy junior, said that "The Medical Academy is like a group of people that are working together and if one is not doing good, the other helps to make it better, to make everything better."

Academy students expressed feelings of affinity and emphasized that students come together around common interests and as future professionals. "We are like a community," expressed an academy student, "because in the Medical Academy, they are always telling us to work together, and more things are going on for us to unite. We help each other to fulfill our goals in school and go into health." The Career Academies' various support systems create a community of youth united to achieve common career goals.

Academy students have suggested that school context is significant in the development of their optimism and motivation. Chica, a Graphics Academy student, stated that her motivation "comes from within, and then outside factors affect how your personality is." She further explained that the "school setting is the most important, because that is something that adults can control and the home life you can't really control." Students articulated an essential link between school context and academic engagement. They viewed the entire school context, including the teachers, the exposure to professions, and the college-preparatory curriculum, as essential to creating their sense of optimism.

The program exposed students to different careers through field trips, internships, and mentoring. This may have contributed to and solidified their desire to aspire to professional careers. Academy students agreed that internships helped them understand the path to becoming a professional in that field. Joe, for instance, stated that "summer internships are really helpful. The [Academy] gets you jobs in the career and that helps you out to understand the work better." Early exposure to careers, coupled with professional mentors, enabled students to observe firsthand what it takes to become a doctor or an engineer.

Early career exposure allowed some students to solidify their professional interests. For others, this exposure provided the opportunity to learn that a particular career was not right for them. Instead of spending many years studying for a career in medicine, Cass quickly concluded, after dissecting animals in class, that she would pursue a different route. "If you want to be in health," she comments, "the [Medical] Academy gives you many benefits, but since I've joined the Academy, I totally chose a different career. After dissecting and everything, I realized I really didn't want to be a doctor." Both outcomes are useful and positive. Whether students decide to pursue a Career Academy profession or not, they are exposed to networks, in and out of school, that are necessary for their social mobility.

Academy students expected to graduate from high school and go to college. They were informed and active agents in this process. Academy students recognized a relevant and rigorous curriculum as a prerequisite to postsecondary education. They also benefited from career-centered pedagogy in and out of the classroom. In this respect, Academy students, unlike those in the general school pathway, acquired a solid foundation to pursue their college and career goals. Despite ethnic variability, students affirmed their professional expectations and remained optimistic despite adversity.

ASIAN ACADEMY STUDENT PERSPECTIVES

Asian Academy students spoke of feelings of inclusion, based on relationships and high levels of camaraderie. They felt they belonged to an extended family in the school. Many perceived their peers as "brothers" and "sisters." "It can be like a family," Sandy, an Academy student, said. They recognized the importance of collaboration—not only for their social well-being, but also for school success.

The structural initiation of teamwork among Academy students helped reduce competition and increase racial tolerance. Sandy reported how students praised one another "when they get the right answer." She cheerfully commented, "I'd be, like, you go!" These students believed they were less competitive because they had a common goal. Kevin, another Academy student, said that in the Academy, "you know what direction you wanna go, you want to get in the health profession, and so then you focus on that with the other students and we help each other."

Although the Academy students preferred to work with their own ethnic group, the less competitive and more integrated setting facilitated the creation of a healthy social and racial climate. Kim noted that her experiences led to a greater level of racial bonding among students:

We still work with other Asians a lot, but you work with each other no matter what. . . . It's like, if your teacher wants you to, you get to know each other, like socialize, so I guess doing a project or research makes you, like . . . the stereotype that you thought about Blacks at first changed.

Similarly, Alex reported that he tends to work and "sit with his Asian friends in the Academy. . . . But I know Blacks and Latinos, too." Racial integration helped build relationships across groups and decreased social and academic tension. This was similar among the Black and Latino students as well.

AFRICAN AMERICAN ACADEMY STUDENT PERSPECTIVES

The Black males attending the academies reported that they experienced an intimate school-within-a-school community that created a spirit of camaraderie among students and teachers. The majority of the African American males interviewed for this study shared these views. "In the Academy," according to James, an African American student, "everybody wants to be friends . . . It's like a community where everybody wants to be your friends, so eventually everyone in the community are friends." In the words of Academy students, "we are like a family [where] everyone knows each other."

The structure of the Academy allows students and teachers to get to know one another well and to feel included as part of a team. Teachers also have more time to cater to individual concerns and needs, and this has a direct impact on students' experiences. For Martin, the difference between the Academy and regular classes is that in the Academy, one is "inside a school within a school, so, pretty much you get more attention than a regular teacher can give you. . . . Regular teachers have more kids than we have . . . basically block classes . . . and we get more attention and more things done in the Academy." This sentiment is echoed by another Academy student, who said: "The [Medical] Academy teachers give you more one-on-one and you have more time to focus on that teacher. . . . We never got that much in ninth grade, 'cause she have too many students who's coming to her and she can't teach the whole class. Here, they have more time."

The strong school-within-a-school community makes it possible to avoid or to lessen the racial and ethnic hostility found in the larger high school culture. This happens through the formation of strong interracial peer cultures. In contrast to the rest of the school, students in the Academy are exposed to individuals from a variety of racial and ethnic backgrounds. Black academy students report that they form genuine friendships with non-Black youths. These friendships make it possible for students to better understand each other and to learn to appreciate cultural differences. For example, Mike stated that: "Students here make a big difference. . . . Like in the ninth grade, I didn't have no real Asian friends . . . but now I have several of them in each class and I get to learn about their culture and stuff, like what they do and eat, what they like." The interview data revealed that Academy students thrive on strong and positive forms of peer and adult relationships that cut across racial and ethnic ties. Integration within a smaller learning community appears to be key to future academic success.

Given a more intimate learning community, effective pedagogy and career-related curriculum also help to further engage the students. The smaller Academy classes allow teachers to structure classes so students can work together on projects. Teachers view collaboration among students as essential and work long hours on pedagogical and curricular practices and activities. Teachers also want students to enjoy themselves. James described the work that teachers assign as both fun and educational: "You see, the work the teachers give is fun, and we group in a group way to get to know each other and everyone take care of each other 'cause we do stuff for health." James confirmed that the Academy structure encourages students to form positive social relationships.

The peer cultures in the academies create environments that appear to inspire and encourage hard work among the majority of students. While the peer culture stresses high achievement, students are not left to fend for themselves. They encourage and assist one another with their assignments and support one another in times of need. The caring and work-oriented learning environments seem to encourage most students to believe that they can overcome adversity—with the help of their peers.

For instance, Steve expressed this sentiment: "Peer tutoring is impor-tant. If there's anyone who needs tutoring, I'm willing to help. It's nice that most of the students in the Academy try to work above and beyond their potential." The caring and work-oriented learning environments seemed to encourage most students to tackle challenges.

LATINO ACADEMY STUDENT PERSPECTIVES

Latino students in the Academy also reported participating in a thriving school-within-a-school program where supportive institutional processes existed throughout. Academy students felt close bonds with one another and their teachers, and the Latino students also formed relationships with non-Latino youth. As Diego passionately explained, "We are like a family. We know each other well and get along."

The Academy also provided common visions and goals for Latino youth. Latino students in the Academy supported one another as they strove to succeed academically. Ana reported, "The . . . Academy is like a community of a group of people that are working together . . . and if one is not doing good, the other helps . . . to make it better, to make everything better." Marisol expressed similar feelings of affinity and emphasized that students united to meet common goals as future medical professionals: "We are like a community, because in the . . . Academy, they are always telling us to work together and more things are going on for us to unite. We help each other to fulfill our goals in school and go into health [professions]."

Latino students were actively engaged in their schooling and worked toward careers in the medical profession. Juan declared, "*Claro* (of course), we all help each other. *Todos queremos hacer bien* (We all want to do well). We want to be in health." These students linked their career goals with needs they witnessed on a daily basis; they observed poverty in their neighborhoods and acknowledged the great need for health care in their immediate families and in the lives of other neighbors. Consider these statements by a Latino student in the program:

> *Interviewer:* Why did you choose the medical career?
> *Diego:* I want to help other people. It's because what I see around me.
>   I've seen how in many cases Latinos don't have as much access
>   to health care. That's one of my priorities. Not just becoming a
>   doctor and forgetting about it, but thinking about my community.
>   I have also spent a lot of time in the hospital so I understand what
>   people go through. I think I can relate to people in need.

The cultural and institutional mechanisms in the Academy supported students' positive vision to do well in school and further enhanced Latino students' desires to become health professionals.

Additionally, the Academy community instilled principles of inclusion and teamwork within students as a way for them to form relationships. Competition was experienced as "healthy." "We are always happy for other students who do well and we help one another out," stated Diego, "but there is some healthy competition." Diego defined "healthy competition" as a form of competition that

> pushes you to work harder. It is not the kind of competition that
> makes you say, "Oh well, I'm the worst student and so and so always
> has the answer." And teachers encourage us to work in teams. . . .
> Like, I'm not worried about getting the best grades. I'm worried about
> getting good grades.

Latino students in the Academy were encouraged to work in teams and help each other in times of need. This form of peer relationships often resulted in higher levels of academic success. Latino students reported a strong and supportive academic program and participated in a high-achieving peer group.

CONCLUSION

Today, boys and men of color find themselves at a great disadvantage; they find themselves in an economic crisis where work is scarce. This is particularly the case for those young Black and Brown men with little education and especially true for high school dropouts. Many of these boys and men of color do not have the education and training to compete in a knowledge-based economy. In contrast, this chapter highlights an opportunity to provide optimism and academic success among high school youth enrolled in career-related academies. The Career Academy option is promising. Career Academies decrease the opportunity gap and prepare youth for a 21st-century world of work.

Career Academies offer young men different strategies to connect them to the labor market and to increase their aspirations. Research demonstrates how Career Academies encourage marginalized high school students to graduate, to foster contacts with future employers, and to go to college to succeed (Stern et al., 2010). The success of Career Academies rests in their ability to build connections between youth and local employers, resulting in students' making concrete plans to pursue certain careers and/or to enroll in college.[2] Furthermore, Kemple & Willner, (2008) found that Career Academies have raised employment rates and earnings for young men in comparison to non-Academy youth, even when they all grew up in similarly impoverished circumstances.

The finding of labor prospects is promising given our current state of economic uncertainty, which carries a disproportionate impact on poor inner-city communities and their populations. As we pointed out in the beginning of the book, William Julius Wilson (1996) reminded us in the 1990s of the devastating effects of joblessness on neighborhoods, families, and Black men. Most notably, his research showed how joblessness impacts the breakdown of communities and, specifically, the family. Regrettably, what Wilson observed back then continues to resonate today as we currently experience an economic recession. However, it appears that the Career Academy model might serve as a policy solution to educate and train youth for a 21st-century knowledge-based economy.[3]

The Career Academy structure can be viewed as one possible model for high school reform.[4] Career Academies induce youth into engaging learning environments with real-world experiences, which make sense in a changing global economy. Similar to the community-based organization discussed in Chapter 6, these high school strategies make strong headway in forging relationships outside of schools. In addition, they take into consideration how, where, and with whom young people spend their time. These academies promote the necessary networks that aid in the acquisition of intangible resources leading to engagement, optimism, and success among those students fortunate enough to be enrolled. Most importantly, Career Academies aim to promote the successful development of low-income urban youth as they mature into productive adults and active members of society. They encourage both college and career success.

Chapter 8

Obama Has Opened the Door

Understanding African American
High School Boys' Career Expectations
in an Era of Change

*Well . . . the stereotypical thing about Blacks and Mexicans is that
they grow up in the ghetto and especially Blacks. They say that
Blacks are always in the worst part, they're always in the ghetto, so
there is never going to be any successful Black guys, and we can see
that's not the truth because we have a Black President.*
                                        —Jarret, high school senior

*[What are your aspirations?] Hopefully go to the NFL. That's
the dream but if that doesn't work I was thinking of something
in real estate.*
                                        —Terrance, high school senior

African Americans have undergone a long and enduring history of oppression that infiltrates every aspect of their lives, including most notably their schooling experiences. Much attention focuses on understanding how African Americans continue to lag behind other ethnic groups, across all academic indicators. In 2008, many deemed the election of the first Black President to be a turning point for the African American community—a realization that their aspirations were limitless.

On the heels of this important historical accomplishment, we are particularly interested in understanding whether Black high school males, in the wake of Barack Obama's election, did experience an upward, broadening transformation in their career aspirations. Too often, over the past several decades, many Black youths' aspirations have focused on becoming a star in entertainment or professional sports. This chapter presents an examination of a diverse group of Black high school students' college and career aspirations and expectations in the Obama era.

The data presented are derived from a yearlong, 2008–2009, qualitative study of African American boys involved in an extracurricular social and academic male-identified academy. We sought to compare boys' perspectives on race, schooling, and academic engagement over time. Moreover, we hoped to unpack how students' experiences and perceptions of high school influenced their career aspirations and expectations. This is a compelling narrative given that our current time period represents, to many, a new era for African Americans under the leadership of an African American President.

THE IMPLICATIONS OF BARACK OBAMA'S PRESIDENCY

On November 4, 2008, Barack Obama was elected to the highest office of the United States. His triumph not only marked the meteoric rise of one African American, but also signaled a paradigm shift that many believed shattered the racial glass ceiling. Within minutes of President Obama's victory, the *New York Times* announced the breaking story with the headline, "Obama Elected President as Racial Barrier Falls." This aptly summed up the momentous impact of Obama's presidency and suggested the beginning of a new era: post-racial America (Nagourney, 2008). The *Times* story underscored the implication of Obama's presidency, which triggered what "amounted to a national catharsis" and symbolized an "evolution of the nation's fraught racial history" (Nagourney, 2008, p. 211). While the report explicated the importance of Obama's ability to rescue the nation from a deep economic recession and stagnant wars in the Middle East, the story was mainly concerned with the power of Obama's campaign to rally a record high voter turnout while signaling a "new kind of political idealism, inspiring citizens of a twenty-first-century multicultural America to believe in the impossible" (Nagourney, 2008, p. 211).

President Obama's campaign prevailed during a time of great distrust of the previous administration, demonstrated by President George W. Bush's 22% final approval rating—considered the worst ever for an outgoing president. The public needed Obama's leadership to restore the faith in the presidency. The *Times* story was one of many, including *Time* and *Newsweek* magazines, that celebrated the magnitude of Obama's election in altering the racial dynamics of society. While this news made headlines around the world, it is impossible to deny the historical impact still felt today, if not for a long time to come.

Obama's memorable inauguration came on the heels of a campaign that established new directions for the African American community. His *A More Perfect Union* speech proved to be a turning point:

For the African-American community, that path means embracing the burdens of our past without becoming victims of our past. It means continuing to insist on a full measure of justice in every aspect of American life. But it also means binding our particular grievances—for better health care, and better schools, and better jobs—to the larger aspirations of all Americans—the white woman struggling to break the glass ceiling, the white man whose been laid off, the immigrant trying to feed his family. (Obama, 2008)

Obama urged African Americans to shed the anger accumulated from the history of racial injustice. He encouraged them to seek a post-racial approach that perceived economic and class inequality as universal problem, one that strikes people of all races and ethnicities. In this speech, Obama promised that his presidency would advance this approach.

Obama's campaign themes of hope, change, and opportunity served to inspire African Americans to elevate their societal and economic positions. During his campaign, Obama exemplified persistence, and this, along with his welcomed vision for a transformed future, was crucial to his success in becoming the first African American to be elected President. Obama forged a pathway for African Americans to aspire toward their highest goals. Obama's trajectory—from Harvard Law School graduate to senator to President—is singularly remarkable in the history of Black Americans.

Given the relatively short time since the presidential election, the literature detailing the social and psychological impacts of this event has been rather sparse. However, Plant et al. (2009) conducted a study to discover whether Obama's presence in the White House positively affected non-Black college students and their levels of implicit prejudice regarding African Americans. During the 2008 presidential campaigns, Americans were heavily exposed to the "well-educated, motivated and articulate" Obama, who contradicted negative stereotypes of African Americans (p. 961). The participants, absorbing the mass media exposure of Obama's personal advertising (T-shirts and signs), displayed less prejudicial beliefs about African Americans, a change that was aptly dubbed the Obama Effect. Findings showed that when participants "had an increased activation of qualities associated with Obama as a political figure [and] primed with 'Black,'" they displayed lower levels of implicit prejudice (p. 963). Non-Black college students displayed less prejudicial beliefs about African Americans, as demonstrated during a lexical decision task in which students associated Obama, as a political figure, with various government-related words. Another study found that following a televised viewing of Obama's presidential acceptance speech, Black students took a test based on Graduate Record Examination (GRE) questions and improved their scores dramatically, rendering the White-Black test score gap "statistically insignificant" (Dillon, 2009). The implication of these studies is momentous.

Obama's rise to prominence caused people of all races to enhance their expectations of African Americans. We share interest in studying the Obama Effect and the extent of its impact beyond the time period directly after the election. Thus, we can see how Obama's portrayal of the counter-stereotypical African American male had a powerful effect in fundamentally changing the perception of the American public. But the lasting effects of this phenomenon have yet to be critically examined, especially among Black male youth.

The question remains: Have Black male students' perceptions of opportunity and life expectations changed, given the unprecedented presidential election of 2008? We posit that a complex relationship exists between the aspirations and achievements of African American students. This complexity is more pronounced among poor Black males who attend inner-city schools. These students typically express a desire to succeed in school and in professional careers, but also have considerable doubt that they will actually attain their goals (Carter, 2005; Conchas, 2006). Mickelson (1990) has attributed the apparent discrepancy between the aspirations and achievement of African American adolescents to the tension created by conflicting abstract and concrete goals. For example, the Black students Mickelson surveyed expressed an abstract desire to attend college and obtain professional careers, but further probing revealed that they actually believed their futures would be less promising. Mickelson's (1990) research also suggested that the achievement of Black students is far more likely to be influenced by their concrete perceptions of opportunity than by the abstract aspirations they articulate to adults.

As the chapter's opening two quotes illustrate—Black youth express the positive impact of having a Black President, yet many of these same youth view entertainment and/or sports as the primary vehicles of social mobility. We critically examine the perspectives of these high school students and question the notion that career opportunities are perceived to be equally accessible to all students. In fact, as we suggest throughout the book, poverty and racism prevail in and out of schools. These factors generally have consequences for the educational plight of students of color, even those who are believed to be doing well.

THE ACADEMY FOR BOYS IN AN URBAN HIGH SCHOOL

According to its 2009 mission statement, Smith Male Academy is an initiative designed to increase high school graduation rates for "underrepresented promising male students." Different high schools in the Sandy Unified School District (SUSD) have instituted various types of academies for boys. For example, at another high school in the district, the Male Academy is an elective course that students attend daily, while the Smith High School Academy is an after-school club with several meetings per month. The implementation format (as a club or elective course) has important consequences for how members and other stakeholders understand their involvement and for how well the initiative will succeed. However, in this chapter, the focus is not on the implementation format, but on how participation in this group facilitates school engagement and buffers the negative labels assigned to males of color within and outside of schools.

SMA, like the larger high school where it was situated, emphasized college readiness and college success. The aim was to bolster male students' interests in pursing distinct professional career options. In fact, both the school and the academy did not emphasize an athletic culture, and teachers and adults in the community worked together to expose Academy students, and in particular student-athletes, to careers outside of sports. The emphasis on non-athletic and non-entertainment careers has implications for the findings of this chapter.

While the program was developed to address the low high school graduation rates of Black and Latino students in the SUSD, it is not reserved only for students who are struggling academically. SMA members included the high school senior class president and vice president, star athletes, college-bound students, students who are making up credits, C-average students, and students returning from continuation school for a second chance at graduating from their home school. This heterogeneity is an important feature. By including students of different achievement levels, the school encourages relationships among students who are members of very different social and academic circles. The tacit goal is that the high-achieving students, with pro-academic social networks, will have a positive influence on those who are struggling.

For descriptive purposes, Smith High School (SHS) is located in a largely urban city in Southern California. During the 2007–2008 academic year, 4,364 students were enrolled and the average class size ranged from 27 to 30 students. Together, Latino and White students constituted 71.8% of the school population, 33 and 38.8% respectively. African Americans represented 13.7% of the student population, Asians are 10.6%, and the remaining 3.9% were classified as "others." The number of SHS students who qualify for free or reduced lunch is lower than the district average—48.4 and 67% for SHS and the district, respectively. Only 9.8% of SHS students are English Language Learners, compared with a 24.7% average at the district level.

The district comparison data illustrate two notable features of SHS. First, SHS, although located in a middle-class community, also draws from affluent and working-class neighborhoods. This results in a student body that is highly diverse economically, ethnically, and in terms of academic preparation. Overall, the school serves a less vulnerable student body than the district as a whole. Second, SHS is one of four high schools in the district chosen as a Top U.S. High School by *Newsweek*, based, along with other markers, on the number of students who are enrolled in Advanced Placement courses. These features are important to consider before and during the study because they influence the culture of the school, students' experiences in the community, and their interactions with peers from different socioeconomic and racial backgrounds.

SMA STUDENTS' PERSPECTIVES ON THE OBAMA PRESIDENCY

In assessing the potential impact of Obama's presidency, students shared feelings of positive transformation in society's expectations of African Americans. They also communicated a sense that the doors of opportunity would dramatically open for Blacks. Jonathan offered a vivid and thorough explanation:

> Most African Americans expect us to not even make it out of high school. When an African American gets a doctorate or master's, you know it's a very rare thing and most African Americans celebrate that— when something like that does happen—because they say, "Dang, you know he made it" or, "It's like when Obama became president." You know, a lot of African Americans were like "You know we finally have one of our people in there" . . . we can actually do something where it's no more of that excuse of "Oh, I'm African American."

Here, Jonathan prefaced his explanation with the observation that, historically, society has placed low expectations on the academic achievement of African Americans. However, in assessing the meaning of Obama's presidency, he described how a Black man reaching the highest office in the land dramatically changed the mind-set of African Americans. He observed how, in light of Obama's election, current and future generations of African Americans should not use the long history of racial oppression as an excuse to underachieve.

Thus, Obama's presidency may influence some in the African American community to take more responsibility for their actions. This harmonizes with Obama's stance regarding the African American community, as he has often articulated that individuals should embrace the past but avoid using it to make themselves victims. Jonathan equated the achievement of a person earning a doctorate or master's degree with someone clinching the presidency. These are the achievements of people who have "made it." The students' assessments suggest that Obama's presidency extends beyond a purely political influence. It is applicable to a student thriving in any academic setting. Students were able to locate Obama's historical stature among the procession of notable figures crucial to the Civil Rights Movement. This was evidenced by Kiel's ability to understand how Obama's success fits within a long line of American achievements—from Harriet Tubman's courageous efforts in the Underground Railroad all the way to Martin Luther King Jr.'s triumph in giving "us our rights, so that [Obama] could get in the White House."

The students' comments indicated that Obama's presidency was more than an individual achievement—it was about honoring the triumphs of all the important figures in African American history. Students viewed Obama not only as a role model, but also as the culminating embodiment of the tireless civic and judicial efforts exerted by Black leaders and common citizens throughout the past. It is apparent that these students perceive Obama's presidency as a victory in the long struggle for civil rights in the African American community. The election impacted all African Americans and served as a bright ray of hope for future generations. Obama's presidency paved the way for African Americans to realize their dreams, despite the nation's long history of racial inequity.

The symbolic power of Obama's presidency powerfully impacted African American students. Kevin elaborated on the significance of electing a Black President:

> People were really proud of that. They say the Black face in the White House . . . that should motivate you to do better. So maybe . . . you can do whatever you wanna do. Him [Obama] becomin' president kinda raised the bar on what you're doing . . . he motivated us.

The students at SHS were not old enough to participate in the 2008 elections, yet the influence of Obama's victory resonated powerfully with them. Kevin's feelings exemplify the symbolic image of a Black person in office and how the election served as a motivating force to help African Americans broaden their career interests and to persevere in a world of limited opportunities. Indeed, this student captured the spirit of many African Americans and others around the world—people for whom Barack Obama stands as an iconic symbol of hope and freedom.

Finally, students keenly predicted that Obama's presidency would change the way that society looks at Black males. Todd exclaimed, "[Obama] has opened the door for every race and has proven that you can actually do something with yourself. You don't have to have that person looking down on you saying that you're not going to make it." Thus, from the students' observations, the opportunity structure has opened for members of the African American community. Students alluded to the fact that society now has a higher expectation for African Americans, suggesting that race may become less of a mediating factor in determining their career aspirations. Therefore, it will be interesting to examine how students in a school environment geared toward developing academic scholars reflect on their career aspirations and expectations in this time of change.

CONFLICTING PERSPECTIVES ON ASPIRATIONS AND EXPECTATIONS

In a school and in an academy that emphasized academics and career pathways, a large number of Black males wanted to become entertainers or athletes. We found that, in terms of socioeconomic status, academically oriented students came from similar backgrounds as students interested in careers in entertainment and professional sports. Socioeconomic status did not have a discernible impact on students' career aspirations and expectations. In addition to the fact that 12 of the students were student-athletes, it is important to note that 8 of these student-athletes would continue to aspire to careers in entertainment and athletic arena.

It was surprising to hear that many Black youth, even after their involvement in an after-school program that promoted college and professional careers, still preferred to pursue a career in the non-academic field. Confirming what Conchas (2006) demonstrated years ago, African American males placed a high value on athletic fame and perceived college as the pathway to achieving it. While students in the Conchas study and those in the present study acknowledged the importance of college, they made certain compromises on their academic aspirations so they could still pursue football or basketball. Instead of dropping education altogether, they used it as a way to get into college to improve and show off their athletic talents. This is no fault of their own, but of their perceptions of the limited opportunity structure.

Students functioned under the plan that if their sports endeavor failed, they would use the skills acquired in their classes to pursue traditional careers. Drake, for instance, a student on the football team, who often boasted about the academy's rigorous academic culture, elevated sports as his career choice. When asked about his career aspirations, Drake responded that he had a plan A, B, and C, "so A is the NFL [National Football League], B is some form of engineering or real estate, but if that doesn't work I was looking into law enforcement." Like many of his African American peers, expectations in the athletic and entertainment industry still held precedence for Drake, while a career in an academic field remained as a backup plan. Certainly, Drake's football dreams seemed contradictory to his earlier admission that "fitting the stereotype" bothered him, observing that people can fall into the stereotype like "dominoes."

But perhaps most important in these findings is Drake's assessment of the odds of one person becoming a professional football player.

Interviewer: So you have ten athletes and out of those ten, how many do you think will become a superstar?
Drake: Two.
Interviewer: So you have ten smart kids and they stay in school, how many of those kids will become doctors or lawyers?
Drake: Probably eight or nine of them.

Interestingly, Drake believed that the chance for an individual to become an athletic superstar is small in comparison to that of an individual who pursues academic stardom. Yet even Drake's seemingly gloomy prediction was off by quite a bit. Research shows that only 0.08% of high school seniors playing football will ever be drafted by an NFL team (Newlin, 2010). Furthermore, only a fraction of those drafted become NFL regulars.

Moreover, findings indicate that even some of the students' aspirations to go to college were guided by their inclination toward sports. Drew, for instance, had strong aspirations to pursue higher education, ranked his college prospects starting with the "University of Texas . . . then UCLA probably number two, and USC number three, but [he] think[s] Georgetown or Georgia Teach was number three or four." He admitted that his list was determined by "playing college basketball video games and watching college basketball." In a separate and more extreme example, a student justified his desire to enroll in a Minnesota college because the school colors were purple and yellow—the same color as his favorite professional teams, the Los Angeles Lakers and the Minnesota Vikings. Despite the fact that students have exhibited a more optimistic view regarding education and the opportunities therein for social mobility, some college aspirations continue to be determined exclusively by a preference toward athletics.

The following sections attempt to shed light on this perplexing phenomenon, as expressed through student perspectives on being Black males, on racism and school, and on the impact of poverty. Although the students were part of a thriving social and academic environment, outside forces greatly mediated their conflicting aspirations and expectations.

PERCEPTIONS OF BEING BLACK IN THE UNITED STATES

Students were assessed about their perceptions of being Black to illustrate the effect of racial stereotypes on their career aspirations and expectations. Ben, a hard-working 17-year old student aspiring to become an architect, was asked about the portrayal of African Americans. He candidly replied that, "so many things for the negative side, like we're seen as loud, violent . . . talking super loud in theaters, we ruin it for everybody. We're the ones gang-banging, shooting people, going to jail." Like Ben, many students described media portrayals of African Americans as negative, showing them as volatile, with a tendency to clash with social norms. Students articulated that these negative media attributes would transfer to real-life perspectives, leading to frequent encounters with the law.

In addition, students agreed almost unanimously that society portrayed Black males as completely indifferent toward education. Howard's (2008) "assassination of the Black male image" largely captures the perceptions of these students. In Howard's piece, the Black male is often portrayed on a spectrum from the "docile or the bewildered slave, to the hyper-sexed brute, to the gregarious Sambo, the exploitative pimp or slickster to the super athlete and entertainer" (p. 966). Society's projection of such harmful stereotypes of African American males could have a detrimental effect on how these students perceive themselves. Jonathan, motivated to become a sociologist, shared his thoughts about his inability to resist the onset of negative stereotypes. He admitted that "when so many people telling you that 85 or whatever percent . . . of African Americans fail . . . you start to believe it, you know, so it gets harder and you're . . . just going to wind up like everybody else so why even try." Here, we can see how facts and statistics, which appear to be couched within a scientific or empirical context, can be misleading for these youth, whether they are true or not.

In fact, a majority of the students acquired their negative conceptions of African Americans in large part through the media, which affected the way the students were treated in their schools. Ken, a student, described the reality constructed by the media—one that reinforces a social ordering. This order relegates minorities, particularly African Americans, to lower-class status.

> You rarely see a Black or Latino boss, you always see the Caucasian man and it's in everywhere. It's in TV, it's in movies, magazines, wherever you look, and you always see either the Black or Latino . . . they're at a little desk working and the boss is always coming in to check on them.

Thus, the media's expansive influence on movies, TV shows, and magazines occupied a significant portion of the students' lives, making it difficult for them to escape the proliferation of these negative stereotypes.

Moreover, the socio-historical nature of these stereotypes retained such a strong effect on the students' self-esteem that some students admitted that they needed to academically outperform their historical predecessors. Frustrated by societies' unfavorable projection of African Americans males, Bill argued that "you hear this all the time . . . and you're going to keep on hearing it, just show everybody that you can do better than what they say that you're doing." Not content with fitting the mold shaped by numerous negative stereotypes, it is clear that students aspired to create a more positive conception of African American males—by working to change societal perceptions.

Jonathan proclaimed that his parents continually reminded him about his disadvantage in life by asserting that, "You're always going to have a strike against you because of the color of your skin . . . it's been engraved into my skull that you know I have to try harder than everybody else just because of the color of my skin and in some cases that is true because you still have racist people." On an individual level, these students could be viewed with the hardship of having a chip on their shoulders, but ultimately they had the shared experience of trying to break various stereotypes that had a noticeable constraint on their career aspirations and expectations.

PERSPECTIVES ON RACISM AND SCHOOL

The racial discrimination felt by the African American males was evident in their experiences at school. Students agreed that a racial and ethnic-based social ordering was influential in defining the school culture. A thoughtful Black and Filipino student, Cliff, openly asserted that "African Americans would be on the bottom . . . then Latinos, then Asians, then Caucasians [ordering them from lowest to highest]." In the students' eyes, the school had a preconceived notion of which racial groups would succeed or end up at the bottom. A majority of the students did not delineate how the social ordering system could vary, depending on certain group attributes. Instead, they presumed that the hierarchy would uniformly apply to all aspects of their schooling life, including academics, extracurricular activities, social status, and discipline. A student named Drew supposed that this ranking was determined by the "order of the highest test scores." This was indicative of his experience in an AP English class, since "it was only me and another Black student . . . but the majority . . . is Caucasian students." It is apparent that students' appraisal of the social ordering system is not coincidental to the presence of tracking in the school system. This racial ordering mirrors how we perceive success on a larger societal scale.

Many students shared their discomfort in acknowledging the presence of racial discrimination in the classroom. Jeffrey made this assessment regarding how teachers held particularly low expectations toward African Americans: "They're not going to teach as good . . . they're not gonna give them as much information . . . 'Why give it to them, they don't know.' It's probably what their mind is saying." This observation suggests that teachers' academic expectations of their students may vary depending on students' race. As a result, the teachers' prejudices may influence youths to temper their career aspirations and hopes of achievement. Drew also supported the notion that teachers' expectations might be based on racism. He said, "some of my teachers didn't expect me to do good. They didn't verbally say it but I could see how their actions were. They didn't expect me to be the one answering the questions in class and actually doing my homework and trying to go to tutoring and get a better grade." While enrolled in his AP English class, in an attempt to disrupt the low academic expectations held by teachers, Drew sought to distance himself from unfavorable African American stereotypes.

Students spoke candidly of their perceived notions of success. These perceptions proved crucial in understanding whether or not their aspirations and expectations were aligned closely with academically oriented goals. Interestingly enough, the students' goals were closely aligned with Mickelson's (1990) delineation of abstract and concrete goals. Many of the students' responses showed that they held a vague conception of reaching success, thus exhibiting an abstract goal orientation. "I think that a high school student is successful," one student stated, "if they work hard in the classroom but they still remain close to their friends and they have goals, which are the main thing for me, and I think you're successful." When students plan their goals abstractly, they may lack tangible markers that determine school success, for example, reaching a certain GPA or enrolling in more advanced courses.

An abstract concept like effort may contribute to students' success, but such concepts are not necessarily indicative of a student striving for success in school. Another student further elaborated about his perception of academic success:

> Success in school. Doing all you can and putting your best foot
> forward no matter what. Getting the best grades you can—no matter
> what, that is. You can be successful and have a D or you can be
> successful and have an F. As long as you're putting all your work, and
> all of your heart.

Here, we can imagine the risk of a student conceptualizing success in terms of doing the "best work" possible, even if those efforts result in low grades. It may be difficult for students to set a high bar of expectation when many around them expect very little of them.

However, in contrast to these abstract goal orientations, some students framed their goals more concretely. Kiel, an aspiring architect, outlined his plan in specific details. He asserted that he wanted to maintain at least a 3.0 GPA at the academy and then attend 2 years at a city college before transferring to either a local state university or a local research university so that he could obtain a degree in architecture. It is evident that students who frame their goals concretely value the importance of setting tangible markers as indicators of success. The success of Kevin's concrete plan is consistent with the reality of his academic situation, since he is ranked as one of the highest-achieving students in the academy.

PERCEPTIONS OF POVERTY AND OUT-OF-SCHOOL ISSUES

Throughout our discourse with students about their career aspirations and expectations, there was a general consensus that the students could not quite escape various problems stemming from poverty and other social-related issues in their communities. In our interview with Todd, he provided an explanation of why Blacks and Hispanics possessed the lowest prospects in terms of graduating and becoming successful. He pointed to "gang problems, family problems [and] you have peer pressure." In reference to the topic of gangs, Todd commented that students are often tempted to" let that [gang membership] take over their lives and then they start saying 'oh this is not for me' and start putting themselves down and saying that they can't do it even though they are smart enough inside." From the students' perspectives, it is apparent that the pressure of joining gangs can have a destructive impact on their self-awareness and career aspirations. Indeed, the gang culture can seep into every aspect of students' lives, generating damaging consequences, even if they have no desire to become a gang member.

Furthermore, some students who were knowledgeable about the gang situations existing on and off school grounds explained that tensions between Blacks and Hispanics were often high. Jay elaborated that "the tension between Hispanics and Blacks is like, maybe I guess it's over territory . . . some Black people felt, you know Hispanics kinda came . . . into Southern California and they started livin' in their neighborhoods and stuff." The explanation sheds light on how some of the animosity and gang violence between Blacks and Hispanics may have developed. From a historical perspective, the students were mindful about poverty, and economic deprivation led to gang tensions in their neighborhoods. This provides a more critical understanding about the importance of poverty in gang formation and how marginalization continues to be a significant element in their home lives.

In fact, the students advocated for their school to encourage an open and continuous dialogue on the impact of poverty and the consequences of racism in their lives. Kiel commented on the topic of racism and whether he adopted the belief that schools should strive to adopt a post-racial perspective:

Interviewer: Some people don't talk about race a lot, you know. So if
    you feel uncomfortable with any of these questions . . .
Kiel: Like . . . I feel like it's something that should be talked about . . .
    people try to deny like…there's like racial barriers and stuff.

As Kiel's comments show, schools should not presume a post-racial
society since racial barriers, at many levels, are still intact. Kiel seems troubled by the notion that people want schools to declare colorblindness when,
in fact, racism exists. Students valued the significance of bringing racism
to the forefront in dealing with various issues stemming from poverty and
gang-related activities. They desired to explore how these issues impact their
aspirations and expectations.

COMPLICATING STUDENT PERSPECTIVES
IN A TIME OF CHANGE

The strength of this case study lies in the advantage of collecting the responses
from academically engaged African American males who were able to speak
openly about their racial experiences in school and in their communities.
The method of counter-storytelling (Solórzano & Yasso, 2002) was particularly effective, not only in providing the details needed for a rich and vivid
account, but also in delivering an honest description of the realities present
in school. Narratives projected in the mainstream media often overshadow
these realities. Through in-depth interviews and key insights from the students' diverse backgrounds, the students were able to provide perspectives
on the impact of Obama's election in the context of African American history and the long, ongoing struggle for civil rights and social equity.
    Many students articulated that Obama's election represented the break-
ing of a racial glass ceiling and that the students could now aspire toward any
career occupation. However, speaking to our discourse concerning how African Americans are stereotyped in the media and society, students reflected
a heightened stress and discomfort as they dealt with these distorted depic-
tions. In regard to the impact of racism in school, students provided schemas
on how racial identities were socially ranked and how these categories were
institutionalized by the school's tracking system. Students observed that these
past racial projects coalesced in their schooling experience, which refined
and tempered their optimism regarding a post-Obama effect on schooling.
In addition to the existence of racism in the students' schooling life, students
underscored the importance of poverty and racism in their home and neighborhood life as manifested through gang and peer-related pressure.
    Most interestingly, we found that the influence of Obama's election did
not cause a discernable effect on the students' career expectations. Students
still communicated a desire to enter the entertainment and professional

sports domains, career paths not indicative of an academic culture. In light of these findings, it is clear that future research should address racism and poverty as crucial elements that may serve to impede students' academic performance and, ultimately, their career interests.

Although our predictions indicated optimism in African American students as they acknowledged significant gains in their community, our findings support the notion that students still harbor a distrust and skepticism toward the fairness of a schooling system that has yet to adopt a colorblind approach to opportunities. Although the students were exuberant about the effect and potential of Obama's election, the impact of racism and negative stereotypes may have had an overbearing effect in diminishing their optimism. Therefore, it was crucial to examine the attitude-achievement paradox as a partial explanation for why students did not quite fully embrace an upward transformation in their career expectations. Employing a framework that delineates between students' abstract and concrete attitudes toward education helped reconcile the paradox of optimism in the post-Obama era with unwavering hoop dreams and Hollywood.

It is imperative to use these students' opinions and experiences to shed light on important policy implications that ought to be considered in school practices. In *Equity and Empathy: Toward Racial and Educational Achievement in the Obama Era*, Carter (2009) provided a strong caution to schools that "dismiss the relevance of race too quickly" in a climate where students are still hesitant to interact with each other across racial lines (p. 293). The author asserted the need for initiatives to amplify racial awareness in school, which is the "ideal site for social change" (p. 295). Thus, even, perhaps especially, in the midst of the Obama's presidency, a proactive discourse on racism needs to be sustained. Similarly, Pollock (2004) highlighted the relevancy of racism in schools through a study concerning conversations about the process of racial categorization among students, teachers, and administrators. The collective perspective of the students' racial experiences was vital to informing school administrators about redrawing race boundaries used to "identify and monitor the students," thus serving as an impetus for enacting positive change in the school culture (Pollock, 2004; Warmington, 2009, p. 293). Therefore, it is important for schools to sustain discourse on racism as a means to create a more equitable environment for students.

CONCLUSION

For the country, the election of Obama ushered in a moment of renewed hope and optimism. This chapter, however, suggests that it may be premature to expect that Obama's election has halted the long historical oppression of African Americans. Our case study presenting student perspectives presents evidence that poverty and racism are prominent factors in Black male students' career aspirations and expectations. Although we advocate for strong supportive networks in school that create for optimism and success, it is not enough to dismantle the opportunity gap. We must remain critical of larger historical and structural forces that impact African American youths' perceptions of the opportunity structure. However, it remains crucial that conversations regarding poverty, marginalization, and racism should be sustained in fostering a healthy and racially tolerant school environment. We suggest that it will take more than one individual to break the insidious class and racial glass ceilings, even if that individual happens to be the President of the United States of America.

Chapter 9

Conclusion

The Possibilities of
Comprehensive School Reform

*What's most overwhelming about urban poverty is that it's so difficult
to escape—it's so isolating and it's everywhere. . . . Your school isn't
likely to have the right books or best teachers. You're more likely
to encounter gang activities than after-school activities. And if you
can't find a job because the most successful businessman in your
neighborhood is a drug dealer, you're most likely to join that gang
yourself. Opportunity is scarce, role models are few, and there is little
contact with the normalcy of life outside those streets.*
—Barack H. Obama, *Announces Presidency*

In this book, we concur that poverty, racism, and social marginalization among
boys of color often lead to street socialization. Instead of receiving social support from families and schools, street youth receive it from peers or strangers.
In doing so, street boys develop mind-sets shaped by street realities and choose
their outlets accordingly. Street socialization undermines and transforms the
otherwise normal course of human development for marginalized youth in
ways that institutionalize a street subculture. This is not simply a personal
choice, but the consequences of poverty and marginalization, something that
is mostly outside of the hands of youth coming of age in "overwhelming" circumstances of "urban poverty." This unfortunate scenario creates clear paths
to prison, and constricted opportunities for social mobility. In this book, we
have shown that for a fortunate few, *streetsmart* paths have been redirected in
time to follow trails toward *schoolsmart* ways.

In our analysis, multiple marginality details the academic and social
disengagement of street youth. The framework describes the relegation of
various groups or individuals to the margins of society, where social and
economic conditions result in powerlessness. The process of neglect and
suppression occurs on multiple levels as a product of forces in play over a

long period of time of economic deprivation. Although most youth in these communities are exposed to a street subculture of marginalization, not all boys become disengaged and join gangs. In Chapter 8, for example, we present how academically engaged African American boys in an all-male academy still cope with the harsh pressures of their urban Southern California environment. Poverty, outside-of-school influences, peer pressure, stereotypes of African American men, and racial inequalities within their high schools shape and undermine these boys' college and career aspirations and expectations. In an effort to challenge inequalities directly, street-socialized boys need to be equipped with the necessary resources. They need access to avenues that lead to productive adult lives.

Educational strategies for youth ought to be informed by the roots of highly concentrated poverty: dangerous places, stressed families, homelessness, overworked schools, reliance on street role models that have been hypersocialized inside the criminal justice system, poor health, and no jobs. There is still hope for youth who grow up street-socialized in such economically deprived circumstances. Gang and non-gang youth who grow up in hypersegregated neighborhoods need the opportunity to become productive 21st-century citizens and to fully compete in a global labor force.

Previous chapters covered a great deal of terrain about out-of-school and in-school programs that structure success. These programs establish the foundation for networks and resources that have the potential to generate social and academic success in poor neighborhoods. To conclude this book, we elaborate on the notion of social capital and suggest an optimistic—yet difficult—agenda for educational policy and practice. It will be impossible to improve the condition of boys of color until the social and political will surfaces to build ecologies of social and economic opportunity.

POOR PEOPLE'S SOCIAL CAPITAL AS MARGINALIZED SOCIAL CAPITAL

Community-based organizations and schools are two institutions that show significant promise in collaboratively addressing the needs of marginalized youth. Such programs have the potential to reengage street kids while keeping those who are doing well off the streets. The portraits of Jared (Chapter 2), Samuel (Chapter 3), and Pedro (Chapter 4), along with the other case studies presented in this book, shed light on the factors necessary to reengage boys into promising paths. Research on career academies found in Chapter 7, for instance, demonstrates the long-term positive impact on the engagement and wages of boys of color. As we have shown, understanding the synthesis of time, people, and place is necessary in formulating balanced strategies around social capital. People are the key to the equation—what Stanton-Salazar (2010) coins as "institutional agents." *But let us now ask, is acquiring social capital enough?*

Although the negative relationship among racism, class, and academic achievement is fairly consistent, there is evidence that a small number of schools and students in low-income communities are performing at high levels. Though confronted with numerous obstacles, certain students and schools are able to overcome these challenges to achieve high levels of academic performance. In particular, there is evidence that some recent immigrant students demonstrate exceptional resilience and manage to excel academically despite numerous hardships (Conchas, 2001). Furthermore, a sizeable body of literature examines the social capital that enables *some* low-income students and *some* schools to perform well in school (Oseguera et al., 2010). However, we must critically examine the value of the types of social capital available to the poor.

Most poor people, especially poor ethnic minorities, do not have the social capital recognized by the "mainstream" as the capital necessary for social and academic success. Poor people's social capital differs greatly from that of the middle-class or that of the elites. The poor are not connected to institutions or individuals in power positions—positions that can facilitate advocacy (Lareau & Weininger, 2003; Ream & Palardy, 2008). Street-socialized youth in marginalized communities often seek other street-socialized youth for information, status-seeking, identity formation, and, perhaps, protection from violence in the streets. Some youth join gangs in the absence of programs and adults who might otherwise mentor them and demonstrate that there is a better life off the streets. Simply put, not all forms of social capital lead to productive resources and may result in negative consequences; in fact, even with the best of purposes, not all forms of capital are valued in society.

Social capital in poor and neglected communities—even with the best intentions—can at best be described as "marginalized" social capital. In effect, marginalized social capital allows poor people to simply "get by" or "cope" in dealing with their circumstances. Although marginalized social capital has the potential to keep some youth off the streets, resources gained through these networks might be insufficient to mainstream all young men into society. There are programs that do an exceptional job of building relationships among schools, families, and communities. These programs help ameliorate the rampant despair in hypermarginalized poor neighborhoods, but, sadly, they remain exceptions to the norm.

This book highlights processes that attempt to structure success in order to figure out what works. As researchers who are embedded within the community, we are concerned with the life prospects of inner-city youth and seek solutions to the damaging consequences of institutionalized cycles of poverty and neglect. Unfortunately, the programs in schools and in communities that seem to work well currently only help a few. These small projects do not change the social structure of poverty that produces and reproduces marginalization in schools and in society. A few boys of color do beat the odds, but the majority do not. This is not to say that helping a few to reach their potential is not important, because saving youth from the grasps of prison demands our attention. But more needs to be done.

THE IMPORTANCE AND LIMITATIONS
OF PROMISING PRACTICES

The case studies in this book demonstrate the importance of social capital in youths' ability to break out of poverty. We show how the success of community-based organizations and innovative school programs provide intangible resources. These resources, which often lead to social engagement and mobility, are gained through networks and relationships. Our personal histories underscore the strengthening power of these connections. The two of us could have not have attained the educational and economic mobility we currently experience without the adults and peer mentors throughout our lives. To this day, we remember elementary school teachers who took us under their wing and community centers that took us off the streets, providing tutors, mentors, sports, meals, field trips to colleges, and a variety of out-of-school activities—rich, nourishing experiences that the sons and daughters of those born with resources take for granted. Social networks and relationships embedded before school, during school, and after school are essential to the social mobility of all youth and, in particular, those growing up poor. It is these relationships, namely with key adults, which impart the important information youth need to move forward in their lives.

We strongly recommend that policy and practitioner leaders work to implement programs that promote the kind of social capital that matters. While such programs will not eradicate poverty, they are the best hope for a breakthrough to the mainstream. What are the alternatives— joblessness and/or prison? Those who practice and make policy must begin to brainstorm innovative ways to address street socialization and school failure in poor communities, especially in a demographically changing country in which the children of immigrants make up a substantial population in public schools.

Current educational reform initiatives do not tackle inequality at its roots; if they did, they would generate policies aimed at eradicating poverty. Those that shape legislation and policy need to stop putting the onus on schools, school leaders, and teachers for the disturbing educational trends that show declines in achievement over time. Because of systemic inequalities, they need help from the social, the political, and the economic domains. We are in a crisis, and a crisis demands immediate attention, sacrifice, and political will.

EQUIPPING YOUTH FOR ADULTHOOD

The effect of poverty on youths' physical and mental health begins early and often continues to leave its mark well into the adolescent years. There exists a strong connection between growing up poor, childhood health, and academic performance. Children are negatively affected by poverty throughout their lives in many domains, especially when poverty persists throughout their lives. Policy efforts to assist poor families, in order to strengthen children's chances of succeeding in school, need to start early; such approaches would link educational issues to environmental issues.

We offer a few strategies and action areas that, taken together, will bring us closer to improving the life chances of boys of color who are growing up poor:

School improvement efforts: Prisons and the military are doing a better job at seducing our young men than our schools. We need quality preschools and K–12 schools to have curricula that explores career themes. We need opportunities for higher education that are available to all youth. In order to make a difference, we need school improvement efforts that work through the Pre-K-to-college pipeline. Due to their proximity to poor communities, community colleges are an important component of the success of the educational endeavor. Often, they provide a second chance to many young people.

Enhanced programs for out-of-school hours: Youth spend large parts of their time outside of schools. Therefore, as a means to narrow the income gap, we need an education strategy that includes the crucial out-of-school hours—before school, after school, and summer school. We need to supply poor youth with the out-of-school programming that the middle class or the elite take for granted. Often, community-based organizations do an excellent job of working with schools to achieve these goals.

Promotion of healthy lifestyles: It is well documented that youth who are born and grow up in poverty are more likely to suffer from a host of mental and physical health issues that can greatly impact their ability to learn. School improvement efforts should augment health services for children and include families. Of course poor youth can learn, but we can't expect kids to learn if they are not eating well, have behavioral issues, and are being raised in stressful environments.

Enhancement of the built environment: Distressed inner-city neighborhoods are far from pleasing. Sadly, most are concrete jungles with very little green spaces for children. Schools and community centers are run-down and crowded. Instead of playing in lush verdant parks, which are often available in most middle- to high-wealth areas, kids find refuge in the streets. Places like Detroit, downtown Los Angeles, and Oakland, for instance, suffer from low levels of investment. We must invest in these neighborhoods and promote spatial justice.

Provision of stable housing: How can children learn if they are constantly on the go, without a place to call home? Although parents may be working a 9-to-5 job (or two), most don't make enough to rent a suitable home. Often, families with little mobility occupy motel rooms near their places of employment. These are often cheaper than permanent housing, but kids end up being heavily exposed to street life. School reform efforts ought to augment housing needs and provide education for poor working families.

Enhancement of youth employment opportunities: Youth need high aspirations and expectations to attain high-quality jobs and therefore need to stay in school to achieve them. However, many youth in poor communities and schools have a hard time envisioning the link between schooling and careers. Often, their role models are entertainers or athletes who wear expensive clothes and jewelry and drive fancy cars. In reality, very few can live up to these unrealistic expectations. Therefore, school improvement efforts need to include alternatives for social mobility through college and career opportunities.

We recommend that reform efforts need to align themselves with labor to prepare youth for a contemporary global economy. Career Academies, for instance, offer youth small learning environments that focus on career themes and have partnerships with employers and higher education. These academies have the potential to foster school success (including the attainment of a post-secondary degree) and create high career optimism. The aim is not to continue to track boys of color into vocational tracks, but to increase expectations that they will pursue high-paid careers in a knowledge-based economy.

Juvenile and criminal justice system reforms: Attention should be given to the draconian policies that keep boys and men of color within prison walls instead of outside them. Our current system creates a revolving prison pipeline that places a higher priority on hiring prison guards than on producing caring and effective schoolteachers. Incarceration breaks up families, further perpetuates inequality, and prevents marginalized populations from entering the social and economic mainstream. Often there remains a disconnect between school programs and correctional facilities. Persistent marginalized communities instill anomie, apathy, and the loss of hope. School reform efforts should not be limited to suppression strategies such as campus police, zero tolerance, metal detectors, and traditional pushout/ kickout policies. School reform efforts need to augment the transitional and academic needs of neglected youth, delinquent youth, and youth returning from correctional facilities.

Elevation of the importance of boys: Boys of color are often character-ized in society as deficient. That is, they are stereotyped in ways that are det-rimental to youths' self-esteem. Often, Black and Latino men are viewed as a menace to society—drug dealers, gang-bangers, lazy, loud, and dangerous. These images are embraced by the status quo, reinforced through the media, and have an unquestionable impact on public policy. School reform efforts and policy should work hard to characterize boys of color as untapped assets—vital to their communities and society.

These issues are not mutually exclusive and, as such, should be tar-geted holistically. In so doing, society must be proactive and not reactive in addressing the negative circumstances affecting youth who grow up poor.

CONCLUSION

Schools are not immune from the social ecology of poverty and therefore new social and economic policies are simultaneously required to promote college and career readiness for all. While good teachers are instrumental in school success, they are not able to eliminate inequality outside of the schoolyard. Therefore, it is the combination of good teachers in addition to good social and economic policies that is better able to affect systemic change. Educational reform that embraces a comprehensive agenda is an imperative to the economy. Understanding of this phenomenon will ensure the wherewithal to build communities of opportunity that improve the life chances of boys of color.

Appendix A

A Portrait of a Chicano Sociologist from the City of Good Fortune

On a balmy summer day in 1981, two young brothers climbed alone into the hills. To the boys—black-haired, dark-skinned Gil, 12 years old, and brown-haired, light-skinned Jessie, 7, the hills by their Ventura, California, neighborhood were "mountains" and they were headed for a grand adventure. These mustard-colored slopes, once described by Spanish settlers as part of "the land of everlasting summers," were originally named San Buenaventura—"good fortune." That's what Gil and Jessie wanted—good fortune and, maybe, some adventure, too. As they hiked, their neighborhood, The Avenue, fell behind and below them and, along with it, all thoughts of schoolwork and trouble and fighting. No father working 13 hours a day. No mother fighting and working to feed her family on 50 dollars a week. No bus rides every day to a distant school. No money up here, either, but maybe they could find some kind of . . . treasure.

When they reached the top of a ridge, Gil turned and looked back. From here, The Avenue looked tidy, all squares and straight lines. In the distance, the Pacific Ocean yawned, sucking in the horizon. Gil looked down at Jessie. "Let's go," Gil told him. Jessie obeyed and they trudged on. Their feet crunched in the crispy, summer-dried grass.

Gil didn't know which one of them saw the shrubs first. But there they were—clusters of ripe, wild raspberries. The boys scrambled to the bushes, sat down, and gorged on the dusky fruit, warm and sweet. With their ashy overlay, the odd-shaped clusters looked dirty, but inside, the raspberries were juicy and clean. The boys stuffed themselves until Gil noticed the dropping sun. He told Jessie it was time.

With red fingers and chins, they headed home, leaving the world of wild fruit, hawks, and birds with colored breasts. They were halfway down the hill when it started. Jessie began to act funny—complaining that he was itchy. He scratched his chest and stomach incessantly. Gil pulled up Jessie's shirt and saw red welts. *What happened?* They hadn't seen any snakes or bugs or anything like that. Gil yanked his brother's hand, rushing him home. Entering the house, Gil told his mother something was wrong with Jessie's skin and that they didn't do nothing wrong. Only ate raspberries.

Gil's mother, Evelia, took charge and when Gil went to bed, she continued, as she had been doing for hours, fanning and lightly scratching Jessie's welts. As Gil drifted off to sleep, he wondered, *How come we could both eat the same thing but I didn't get sick? Only Jessie, not me.*

It is spring 2010, and Gil, now forty-one, hasn't been back to The Avenue for quite some time. He hasn't seen Jessie for a long while, either. In his car, he speeds north from Orange County, where he is a professor of education at the University of California, Irvine. He leaves in the middle of the night—2:30 a.m. It's time.

He leaves the landscaped, manufactured greenery of Irvine, a planned city of carefully modulated colors and weight limits for dogs. However, no weight limits for humans. Accelerating onto the 405 freeway, Gil passes South Coast Plaza, the largest, most upscale mall in California. He's heading back to his childhood home, where his mother still lives. As he drives, Gil's stomach churns—maybe it's guilt, maybe it's regret, because he hasn't made this trip for some time. Success as an academic has moved him away from the neighborhood—to Berkeley, to the University of Michigan, to Harvard, and now to UC Irvine. *But isn't this what I wanted—to get away?* His mother often tells him that he should work at a university close to the neighborhood. She promises to fix up her garage and make it a room for him. His mother's home, purchased for $49,000 in 1979, is the crowning glory of years of her hard work and sacrifice. Gil hasn't reconciled the feelings he has for the place. It is his hearth. It is his forge. It will always be there for him and, as a Chicano success story, it will always be what he left behind. Out of the corner of his eye, Gil sees the lights from the refineries of Wilmington. He turns the radio up.

THE CONCHAS FAMILY

Gilberto Conchas was born in 1969 to José and Evelia Conchas, Mexican immigrants from San Jerónimo, a small farming town in the state of Jalisco. Their third son, Gil, has two older brothers, Celso and José Luis (called "Joe"); one younger brother, Jessie; and a sister, the youngest — Jenny. Married in México, the couple already had two sons when the elder José applied in 1966 to be a guest worker for the United States Bracero program, which legally allowed for temporary importation of Mexican contract laborers. He was accepted. Leaving his wife and children behind, he traveled alone for 3 or 4 years throughout the Southwest, picking strawberries, tomatoes, and grapes. Later, José avoided discussing these years, but when he did, he spoke of clashes with Teamsters over competition for jobs and getting sprayed by his employers with lice-killing chemicals. When the guest worker program ended, Gil's father stayed in the United States and, no longer considered a legal worker, began to experience police raids on top of his other ongoing challenges.

Back in México, Evelia went months without receiving money from her husband. She soon began taking in sewing and making cheese and yogurt to earn income. When she had saved enough, she headed for California to find her husband. Because Evelia's parents were landowners, a privileged group when it came to getting visas to visit the United States from México, she was able to fly legally to California with her two little boys.

She located the address of her husband's dwelling in San Diego and, with their two boys standing behind her, Evelia knocked on the door. José, not knowing of his family's arrival, stood frozen in shock. Evelia nudged their two sons forward—past responsibilities come to life, a resurrection of the family. Taking back its space in José's life, the family moved forward. During this period, Gil was conceived and he was born in 1969. In 1973, Jessie, was born.

The family moved to southeast San Diego, to a predominatly African American neighborhood near Logan Heights, where they lived through Gil's kindergarten year. Gil's father obtained a job as a welder. His parents rented a cockroach-ridden, dirty duplex, which Evelia feverishly sanitized.

In 1972, when Gil was 3, a woman knocked on doors throughout the neighborhood, telling parents about a new program, Head Start, which would prepare preschoolers for kindergarten. José and Evelia had third- and fourth-grade educations, respectively. They decided to enroll Gil.

Head Start, launched in 1965, was a comprehensive program offered to families at the dawn of Lyndon B. Johnson's Great Society. The components of the program included social services, health, nutrition, education, and parent involvement. But Gil, an unwilling preschooler recruit, didn't want to go and his dad carried him, kicking and screaming, to the first day of the program. After being forced to attend, Gil loved Head Start. The only part of school that he didn't like was the stolen jackets.

FROM THE CITY OF STOLEN JACKETS
TO THE CITY OF GOOD ADVENTURE

Gil remembers San Diego as the city of stolen jackets. Almost all the Conchas boys had at least one jacket stolen while living there. In desperation, Gil and his older brother went out one time hunting for one of his stolen jackets, but they never found it. All the stolen jackets just disappeared.

Once, noticing that Gil didn't have a winter jacket, a teacher gave him an old one, which had been sitting unclaimed in the lost-and-found bin. Gil watched as his mother scrubbed the garment clean, scrubbing until her knuckles were raw.

When Gil finished kindergarten in 1975, the family had to move. José had lost his welding job. An acquaintance of José's told him that there were good-paying jobs available at a mushroom plant in Ventura. Evelia and José loaded up the pickup truck, which had no camper shell—parents in the front and furniture, bags, mattresses, and children in the back. Heading north on Interstate 5 to Ventura, six-year-old Gil and his brothers huddled in the truck bed, holding a blanket tightly as the wind fought to rip it out of their hands.

The family settled in the west Ventura neighborhood known as The Avenue. In the 1920s, the area had been home to roughnecks drilling for oil. Now, in the mid-1970s, the 18-block-long, four-block-wide strip was just a poor neighborhood. The Conchas family, all six, moved into a two-bedroom, one-bath home. José got two jobs—cleaning a country-western bar and picking crops. He had to leave the house at 4:30 a.m. each day. For years, Evelia, who hadn't yet worked outside the home, had often declared that the family needed to purchase a house, a place that would give them lasting value. José, tiring of Evelia's constant push to buy a house, told her that if she wanted a home, she would have to go to work. So she did. Over the next 5 years, Evelia worked 6 days a week, 10 hours a day. She cooked all the family's meals, cleaned the house, and did laundry on her one day off.

About this time, in 1976, the school district began busing Gil to 1st grade at an elementary school located about 30 minutes away from his neighborhood. During the 1970s and 1980s, many school districts required mandatory busing, aiming at desegregation, under the supervision of federal courts. Gil's neighborhood was predominately Latino. His new school was in a wealthier, white neighborhood.

Because his surname was Conchas, the school's administration, without any language testing, placed Gil in a class labeled English as Second Language (ESL), even though he was already bilingual; of course, he was not proficient in either "academic" Spanish or English. Soon, Gil, a budding extrovert, became chief tutor and advocate for his classmates, who were mostly recent Mexican immigrants. He helped them with their work and made them laugh. His classmates faced bullying, not just from white kids, but from *cholos*—third- and fourth-generation Mexican Americans. Early on, Gil became their defender. An insult against his Mexican classmates was the same as an insult against his mother and father. Gil straddled both worlds.

BUILDING SUPPORTIVE ADULT RELATIONSHIPS

The chirpy, gregarious boy soon caught the eye of his teacher, who quickly sized up his love of life and interest in the world around him. Mrs. Campbell, short and stocky with frizzy salt-and-pepper hair, wore Mr. Magoo glasses, spoke terrible Spanish, and laughed all the time. Gil's parents liked her and started bringing large bags of mushrooms to meetings. They began to trust her to take Gil on various adventures. When Gil made his First Communion, Mrs. Campbell and her husband became his godparents. They brought Gil along on many family adventures. One of the Campbells's two children, Little John, was the drum major for the University of Southern California band, a hallowed position.

He remembers going with the Campbells three times to Pasadena for the Rose Bowl Parade and Game. On the Saturday afternoon before the game, the Campbells' large new motor home would rumble up to the Conchas home in The Avenue. Picking him up, they'd lurch down the freeways to Pasadena. Gil remembers the enormous, vivid floats—moving giraffes and spaceships, towering buildings, singers, dancers—and the drums, beating so loud that you could feel them in your chest. And the smell of roses.

For 3 years, until he moved away, the Campbells included Gil in their family activities. Gil flourished with the extra attention. He tried to get good grades and succeeded, almost always earning straight As. He liked success and enjoyed his school friendships.

ARTS AND CRAFTS AND DIRTY DIAPERS

Very early in childhood, Gil decided that he didn't want his parents' lives. He was just too lazy, he concluded. He saw their weathered hands and he witnessed the exhaustion of his mother as she worked, on her only day off, to lug dirty clothes to the nearest Laundromat. One time, Gil helped her wash and fold 26 loads of laundry. He remembers carrying plastic bags of dirty diapers on his handlebars, embarrassed by the smell that erupted as he emptied them at the Laundromat. He would take them anyway. But he didn't want to do it forever. He could maybe do better. Maybe go somewhere like USC—somewhere beautiful and far away.

When Gil entered 4th grade, the school district stopped busing him and assigned him to his neighborhood school. Now the white kids would be bused to The Avenue. Gil began to grow closer to friends from his neighborhood—a whole group of them. One of them, William, had a lot of nice material items—things that Gil didn't have. He had an Atari system and all the kids played Pac-Man at his house.

When the group of friends got bored, all of them would head over to the local community center, a 5-minute walk from Gil's house. When Gil started going to the center, Jimmy Carter was President and funds for after-school programs were plentiful. In the summer, Gil spent up to 8 hours a day there. During the school year, he was often there for 3 or more hours. There was tutoring. Some days, the recreation leaders organized sports teams and the boys played softball and basketball or pool. Gil did so well at pool that eventually his older brother Joe took him to pool halls and, paired up with Gil, raked in some money—no one suspected that the little boy and his brother were hustlers.

When he wasn't playing sports, Gil worked on arts and crafts at the center, with art teachers available to provide materials and encouragement. Gil went on field trips—to the circus, to the zoo, and to the theme park Magic Mountain. In the fall, all the kids worked together to make a haunted house for Halloween. Eventually, as the boys grew older, the center took them to visit colleges. When they visited the colleges, Gil remembered visiting USC with the Campbells. USC was majestic. Gil had seen it himself. School was a good thing.

THE FIRST CONCHAS-STYLE THANKSGIVING

One Thanksgiving Day, during his elementary school years, Gil announced to his mother that the Conchas family should have a Thanksgiving like all the other families at his school. All week his classmates had chattered about the holiday, about the turkey and the stuffing, the pies and the football games. His teacher had decorated the classroom with Pilgrims and Indians. Gil was hooked—he wanted a Thanksgiving, too.

Mama, we have to have a bird!
But why, *mi hijo*?
Because all the other families have one and because we are thankful.
Thankful for what, *mi hijo*?
When the Pilgrims came here, they had dinner with the Indians that
    were here.
So are we thankful for killing the Indians after that dinner?
Mama—no! I want a bird, Mama, for us.

Evelia went into her room and emerged with a 5-dollar bill. "Okay," she said, "go and buy us a chicken and I will cook it."

Sticking the bill deep inside his pocket, Gil set out. He headed to the neighborhood store. Closed for the holiday. There was another store nearby. He trudged by empty lots, small homes with cars on their front lawns, and various auto repair and pawnshops until he found another small market. It was closed as well. Rain started falling, making Gil blink as his eyelashes filled with droplets. Gil made up his mind. This day wasn't going to be another day that the Conchas family didn't belong. Their family was going to be the same as everyone else's today. He kept walking, a small figure on almost empty streets. An occasional car passed and threw up a rooster tail of water. Gil just ducked. He walked for 2 hours and finally found a store open, bought his chicken, and walked another 2 hours home. His mother kept her promise and it was the first Conchas family Thanksgiving. Evelia did it for Gil, but as far as she was concerned, she had a different American dream in mind.

A MEXICANA DEEP IN THE HEART OF CALIFORNIA

By 1979, Evelia had finally saved enough money to purchase a home. José found them a property just down the street. It was a two-bedroom, one-bath house in the front and a two-bedroom, one-bath house in the back. The entire property cost $49,000. When moving day came and she and the children moved all their belongings down the street, using a child's wooden red wagon, Evelia was thrilled to see her dream come true. She made dozens of trips, back and forth, while Gil's dad rested on his day off.

One morning in 1980, Evelia, as she did every day, got up early do her chores. She had more plans. They had the house, but the needs of the children kept increasing and she thought that they might even be able to get another house one day. So she didn't mind getting up early, packing lunches, and working until her hands cramped up on her. She finished her chores, leaving the house tidy, and headed to the bus stop.

She arrived at her destination, where her equipment was stored. Putting on her hat and headlamp, she stepped into the building, leaving the cool morning air for the steamy darkness inside. Almost immediately, the smell of ammonia hit her, burning her eyes. She reached into her pocket with scarred hands, remembering to put on her gloves. She couldn't risk doing what she had to do without them. It was hard to see and she carefully stepped on the slick surface, looking for a path to the bed.

That day, the bed was on the third floor. The slim, curly-haired, hazel-eyed woman climbed slowly and deliberately to her destination. She patted her hip to make sure her knife was there. It was. It was important, every time she did this, to be careful of each step, careful not to make a mistake. Now on the third floor, she located her targets, thousands of them—*Agaricus bisporus*—common white button mushrooms. Here they lay waiting for her to twist off their little heads, to cut off their stems, to sort and place them in bins. She was the fastest picker in the building, faster than her husband. Evelia bent over the little white domes, stark and clean against the mix of manure and horse urine-soaked straw, and that's when it happened. Her foot slipped on the wet, wooden slats and, grasping at air, she fell three stories. Landing on the first floor in a sitting position, other workers rushed to her side, but 40-year-old Evelia, in the midst of the pain from the disc that had just ruptured in her back, could only think of the baby, her fifth, tucked inside her womb.

FOURTH-GRADE INTERPRETER

Two weeks later, Evelia yelled from the back of the house in Spanish, "*Mi hijo . . .* Gilberto, get ready to come with me to the doctors." Ten-year-old Gil, bent over his homework at the kitchen table, immediately closed his book and jumped up. Arm in arm, they stepped out, his mom walking slowly due to her back injury and due to the fact that she had, miraculously, remained pregnant after the accident.

The two moved slowly down the street toward the bus stop—the small, sturdy, black-haired son carefully adjusting his speed to match the pained stride of his mother. His eyes watched her, alert for signs that she was in pain, but his mother was, as always, stoic. You could only see something was wrong from the way she was walking and the way she grasped the rail, holding her breath as she climbed onto the bus. Her lips were pressed together—resolute—but she needed Gil today to help her get what she needed from the doctor.

For 5 years, since kindergarten, Gil had served as interpreter for his mother, so today was nothing new. He had, for years, been writing the checks used to pay the family's bills. He attended his own parent-teacher conferences, learning quickly that he could filter comments to benefit himself. Any glowing comments about his performance made it through, but if a teacher said he talked too much, well, Gil would omit that information—"She says I'm doing great, Mama." But today, at the doctor's, he couldn't fool around like that. He knew that his mom could never work again at the mushroom plant and that there were some other people who were helping his mother to get money because she got hurt at work. He had to do things right.

When they arrived at the medical office, after seating his mother, Gil strode to the counter. His head barely rising above the Formica lip, he greeted the receptionist and signed his mother in—"Evelia Conchas." Sitting down, he waited until the receptionist, waving a clipboard, called out to his mother. Gil sprang to his feet and grabbed the clipboard. "I'll do it. I know how." The receptionist didn't look too sure.

Gil looked at the papers. The first page he could fill out by himself. His mom's name, address, date of birth, stuff like that. He had done this stuff before. But the second page was different. There were two outlines of a person, one from the front (it had a face on it) and one from the back. Gil was puzzled but he read the directions and figured things out.

"Mama, you have to tell me where it hurts and I have to mark it here on the pictures with a cross."

This was pretty easy, because even though his mom didn't speak English, she could just point and there really wasn't much translating. They finished the papers quickly, Gil returned the clipboard, and soon the nurse opened a door and called for Evelia. Gil walked into the hallway with her. "I'm the interpreter," he told the lady and kept walking.

VISITING *EL CARNALITO—*
MY LITTLE BROTHER

Gil shuts down the engine of the car. He is finally here—back home. He sees the silhouette of his mother in the window, waving at him. She is so much slimmer now than she was only a few years ago. She used to weigh about 185 pounds. But a few years back, she visited a doctor and he told her that her cholesterol and blood pressure were too high. Since then, Evelia has adopted a vigorous program of diet and exercise. She never eats red meat, rarely eats chicken, only eats brown rice, and chooses to buy as many food items as possible from her store of choice, Trader Joe's—"La Tienda de José." Without fail, she religiously walks 2 hours a day. She wants to live a long life. She has a special reason.

Gil sees that she has recently had her curly hair colored and her nails done. He is happy to see that because he likes to see her have nice things. Sometimes he gives her extravagant gifts—a $700 dinner for Evelia and her sisters, when he knows she is happy just to spend time with him eating a 5-dollar foot-long turkey Subway. Gil remembers that long ago, when Evelia couldn't work anymore, she often wore bathrobes all day as she scrubbed, folded, and cooked. He remembers, as a child, going into a store with her. He was embarrassed when some White friends saw them there—together. He had to introduce his friends to his mother, who was in her robe, with her hair nappy. Gil cannot tolerate that he ever felt that way about his mother and his shame is such that he cannot make it up to her. So he buys her Ferragamo shoes.

His mother engulfs him in a hug when he enters. She has a little bag ready to go, because there's no time to waste. Gil's taking her to visit Jessie, because Evelia, after all these years, still doesn't drive. Along with Gil, Jessie's left The Avenue behind. Two of Gil's nieces are going with them. Gil tells his mother that he didn't forget the quarters. They'll need a lot of quarters today. They pile into Gil's car and head, once again, north. They have a 3- to 4-hour drive ahead of them. They speak quietly in Spanish as the car speeds through the dark. It's 4:00 a.m.

THE STREET-SOCIALIZED AVENUE YOUTH

When Gil reached junior-high-school age, he and his friends grew more aware of the neighborhood gang. Gil had heard that the local gang and their affiliates had been around since the late 1960s to early 1970s, but when Gil came of age, in the early 1980s, most of the founding generation of gang members was no longer active in the neighborhood. Gil never felt pressure to join, never had any gang members try to jump him in, and didn't count one gang member among his many friends. Gil witnessed a few smoking pot in the park, sniffing silver paint from white tube socks, keeping an eye on their territory, but their ranks were diminished compared to a few years earlier.

As powerful and deadly and as organized as gangs have become, they have an inherent weakness. Unlike sports teams or city councils or boards of directors, organizations that maintain a set number of members, gangs cannot ensure stability in their "roster." It is impossible to predict, with any accuracy, how many members of a gang will be active in any given year. How many will die in an anonymous hail of bullets? How many will overdose? How many will go to prison? Additionally, there are, each year, gang members who, perhaps because they father children or perhaps, because they've seen enough to know that things aren't going to end well for them, decide to mature out of the gang. Because of these sources of attrition, there are years where the pull of the gang is weaker than normal in a neighborhood—like a trough between punishing ocean waves. Gil and his cohort, because of the timing of their adolescence, landed in such a trough. But behind them, another wave was coming. It hit right about the time that Gil's younger brother, Jessie, reached his 12th birthday. Jessie didn't have to do anything to make it happen. The wave came to him. He could wheel his arms, kick and try to break free of the current, but it was a big wave.

THE CHICANO SCHOOLBOY

Gil maintained his straight-A average throughout middle school and entered high school in 1983. He could compete toe-to-toe academically with any student. But he didn't try to become close friends with "those kids"— upper-middle-class White and Asian kids. He knew he didn't belong in their groups. He knew his place. He kept close to his friends from the neighborhood, almost all C students, and they kept him close as well. Gil started to notice how they subtly began to protect him, to maneuver him out of harm's way, to close ranks when a threat appeared. Once, when a schoolmate came to the track field to beat Gil up—to "crush" him—a group of his friends surrounded him and prevented the assault.

Saved from the thrashing, Gil sensed, more and more, that his friends wanted him to be different—that they were proud of him. He remembered Mrs. Campbell and help from other teachers along the way. And whenever he considered his future, he saw, in his mind's eye, his parents' hands— what they looked like after they came home, before they could wash and clean their nails. A strange combination of confidence and fear began to move in him. He was proud of his parents' work and sacrifice, but he was averse to picking mushrooms in the dark. It would be different for Gil. He was going to go to college.

In addition to school, Gil worked whenever he could. First, he worked with a man, Juan, who sold leather goods at the local swap meet. On weekends, Gil would rise early and join Juan, setting up their wares in the dark. Juan paid Gil 20 bucks a day—to work from 5:00 a.m. until 8:00 p.m. at night. He bought himself Levi's and Izod polo shirts. When he got his work permit, he worked at a fast food place, taking orders from the drive-up customers. He soon figured that he could yell out the real orders to the Mexican immigrants cooking the food and then he could ring up false, smaller orders on the cash register, allowing him to pocket the difference. For some reason, even though math was his worst subject, his calculations were excellent in the fast food environment. He was just being "streetsmart" and he always wanted more. *Be smart or let someone else outsmart you.*

But Gil never cut corners in school, because there were no shortcuts to obtaining a scholarship to a top university. So he studied and continued working part-time and running track and field and cross-country. Gil became the president of MECHA, an acronym for the Movimiento Estudiantil Chicana/o de Aztlán (Chicano Student Movement of Aztlán). The group's advisor at the high school, Mr. Carillo, encouraged them to form a peer group in order to prepare college applications and write admissions essays.

MECHA, founded in the 1960s, is a student-led organization that stands for different things depending on who you ask. To some, MECHA is a nationalist, separatist organization that seeks a reconquest of the American Southwest by descendants of the supreme Aztecs. But to many Chicanos, that conclusion is mistaken and is based on comments of individuals taken out of context, not on the mission statement of the organization. Instead, to many Chicanos, the mission of MECHA is to increase support for higher education of Latinos. Gustavo Arellano, a journalist from the OC *Weekly*, which is published in Orange County, California, notes that all of the MECHA members from his college graduated (Arellano, 2006). Other MECHA groups have seen similar successes.

Gil applied to several University of California campuses—San Diego, Santa Barbara, UCLA, and Berkeley. One day, in the middle of this process, Gil's father came home and declared, "Gilberto, you are going to Berkeley."

Gil asked his dad what he knew about Berkeley. José said that he didn't know anything except that his boss said that Berkeley was the best and that was the school that Gil was going to go to. Gil was accepted to all the UC campuses he applied to, but in the end . . . he chose Berkeley. He received a full scholarship. And going with him to Berkeley were three friends—all fellow MECHA members.

LEARNING
STREETSMART WAYS

As Gil prepared to leave home, Jessie wasn't doing well. Gang membership in The Avenue had surged over the last 4 years, partially because some gang members were released from prison and partly because many of the children of the older "*veteranos*" were coming of age. Things were different at the community center, too. President Ronald Reagan, elected in 1980, had cut funding for Volunteers in Service to America (VISTA) and for the Community Development Block Grant program (CDBG), which funded community development activities, including maintenance of community centers, anti-poverty programs, and community-building activities. The community center was still open, but now it was lightly staffed and its programs drastically cut. The days of field trips and cultural activities were over. Just like Gil, Jessie was out of the house most of the day, but instead of visiting colleges and making collages, he and his group of friends, about 15 of them, were out on the streets. Each of the 15, except for Jessie, had familial connections to the local Avenue gang. He managed to stay clear from gang membership, but many of his barrio peers were deeply involved.

Jessie shrugged school off as being for sissies. Although extremely academically gifted, he started to get into trouble—fistfights and talking back to teachers. Jessie seemed conflicted since has failed him and many others like him in the community. For instance, when Jessie was still in middle school, a teacher blamed him for something that he swore he didn't do. In the principal's office with his accuser, Jessie turned on the teacher and called him a liar. The principal thought something was off. She knew Jessie. Usually, when he was caught doing something wrong, Jessie would smirk or laugh. This magnitude of a response was out of character. She made a decision. She told Jessie that she believed him and he calmed down. The principal smoothed things over between the teacher and Jessie, and no charges were filed over the incident. Often, it only takes one individual who cares, but in Jessie's case, and others like him, he needed the entire "village."

CALIFORNIA GOLDEN BEARS
OR BUST

As Jessie prepared to enter high school, Gil, 350 miles north, settled into dorm life. Dropped off at an ugly dorm, after crying on the drive north, Gil took a deep breath and started enjoying himself. He made friends quickly and, just as quickly, blew through two roommates. The first, Vietnamese and Catholic, didn't approve of Gil's penchant for having a few friends over at night to socialize. The second, a baseball player from Orange County, argued with Gil heatedly over the issue of affirmative action. Fed up, Gil thought, *F— it, I'm going to the Chicano Theme House.* Casa Joaquin Murrieta is, as described in its latest application, "a co-ed residence located blocks from the UC Berkeley campus . . . Casa has evolved into a multi-ethnic, academic-residential, collaborative center that promotes social justice, leadership development in a very respectful, hands-on and engaging environment." Plus, Gil today laughingly admits, "There, everyone thought the same."

The leaders at Casa pushed Gil out of his comfort zone. They expected academic effort and results. On entering the university, Gil had failed the English essay exam, so he spent hours in the computer lab and with tutors, working on his English writing skills. It was the first time in his life that Gil had free access to computers. He learned how to deviate from the rigid five-paragraph writing model that had worked for him throughout high school. His peers in the dorm pushed him as well. *Gil, don't be lazy. Go back down to the lab and rewrite this piece.* He listened and went back downstairs to the lab again and again. Some of his peers were good writers and they gave their time to help Gil. Gil passed the English exam and flourished in the high-achieving, supportive climate. His efforts paid off.

Gil impressed the director of Casa and she introduced him to sociologist Denise Segura at the University of California, Santa Barbara. Professor Segura helped him to secure two summer internships, both pivotal in his future success. The first, with the Summer Academic Research Institute, allowed Gil to carve out and present his own research project comparing job satisfaction between Mexican immigrant and Mexican-American women. He found a passion and interest in research related to social equity. He learned to use the computer to crunch numbers. His second internship was with the American Sociological Association's Minority Opportunity Summer Training—MOST. This internship, designed to recruit and prepare graduate students of color for top doctoral programs, had its effect on Gil. As a result of his involvement with MOST, no longer satisfied with a bachelor's degree, Gil aimed his sights higher—at a Ph.D.

EVELIA ATE TOO MUCH CHILE

With all that he was doing, Gil didn't get back to Ventura very often. But he called whenever he could. From a distance, he heard that Jessie was still getting into trouble, but managing to do well in school. Unbeknownst to the family, Jessie was getting more entrenched in street life, even though he wasn't an official gang member. Evelia still thought that the only problem with Jessie was that he was a little hot-tempered. At this point, she even joked that maybe it was because of how she ate too much chile during her pregnancy—"Es que comí mucho chile."

One day, calling from school, Gil, as he had done for several years, tried to talk Jessie into going out for the track and cross-country teams. But Jessie didn't want to be around White people. Gil told him to make a stand.

"You go and make the team. You compete and you prove you can beat them. That's the point!"

Jessie listened. He tried out for the teams, making them. He became a track star. He started tending to his studies, and his grades rose and he started getting As and Bs. The family started to make plans for Jessie to spend some time with Gil during the summer up at Berkeley. But Jessie still spent time with his homies.

"They are my friends. This is where I live. This is what we do."

Up in Northern California, Gil tried, whenever he could, to work and make extra money. He ran a tutorial program at a high school in Oakland. He secured a job as director of youth Activities, on an educational cruise line sailing through the glaciers of Alaska. He was on the ship when, on May 3, 1992, he received another phone call from home. After listening to the caller, he wanted to fly home immediately. But he couldn't leave his employer hanging. So he gave notice and made plans to leave in one month and head home to Ventura. His family needed him. To interpret, as he had so many years ago. To support, Jessie, 16, had been arrested for second-degree murder.

SENTENCED 16 YEARS TO LIFE

Jessie was 17 when he was ordered to stand trial as an adult. Gil, along with his parents, was in the courtroom for every hearing. Gil occasionally saw a single tear slide down his mother's face as she looked at the back of her youngest son, who wore an orange sweat outfit with the words "Juvenile Hall" on the back. Gil looked across the courtroom at the parents of the boy who had died. They were the same kind of folks as Gil's—poor, working Mexican immigrants. Over the course of the trial, Gil could tell that each set of parents felt pain for the other. He saw it in small courtesies—glances and gestures. Somehow, both sets of parents, less than one full generation into their foray into the United States, with so much in common, had been pitted against one another. *Why?*

On May 17, 1993, the judge sentenced the now 18-year-old Jessie to the harsher of the two possible sentences—16 years to life. The trial was over. The authorities took Jessie away.

FROM GOLDEN BEARS TO MICHIGAN WOLVERINES

After the trial, Gil returned to his studies. Now, on top of his natural ambition, he wanted to work so that he could somehow help Jessie and others like him. He and Jessie talked and Jessie held on to the hope that he would do well enough to get paroled. Then he planned to live with Gil and go back to school. Gil loved the idea of having his little brother with him on campus. He applied to eight graduate programs and was accepted at all of them. He chose the Ph.D. program in sociology at University of Michigan. It was a 5-year program, during which he would achieve a master's and a doctoral degree. After he got used to the weather, which wasn't easy for a brown boy from California, Michigan opened up his world to all the varieties of Latinos in the world—Puerto Ricans, Cubans, South Americans.

While at Michigan, Gil was awarded the Rackham Doctoral Fellowship, in support of outstanding doctoral candidates. Gil wanted his scholarship to lead to action, because he knew that Terri Campbell, West Park Community Center, MECHA, Casa Joaquin Murrieta, his internships, and all of his mentors had provided a scaffolding for him to work toward success. Jessie didn't have much of a scaffolding—only the web of failure offered by the street. With renewed vigor, Gil completed his coursework and exams and returned to Oakland to research and write his dissertation. Gil earned his Ph.D. in sociology in 1999.

INSIDE PRISON WALLS

The car pulls into the parking lot of the state prison. It's 7:30 a.m., and when he exits the weather-controlled car, Gil feels the promise of scorching sun. He sees it all around him in the cracked, parched earth. The prison's 129 acres are surrounded by concertina wire and an electric fence. Nothing gets in or out without notice. Every time a bird flies onto the fence and dies, it must be reported to the Department of Corrections.

The prison is the most overcrowded in California's system, sometimes housing prisoners at over 250% of its capacity. The male-only population sleeps in dorms of up to 200 prisoners. The chorus of 200 snorers is the least of a prisoner's worries. For someone who lives looking over his shoulder, it's not an easy night's rest. Jessie couldn't sleep for weeks after he was moved here from another prison.

The four of them prepare to wait in line. They've followed all the rules. None of them wear denim clothing, so as not to be confused with inmates in the event of an emergency. No hats, tobacco, chewing gum, purses, or cameras. Evelia and her granddaughters cannot wear underwire bras. No spaghetti-strap tops or skirts that reach higher than 2 inches above the knees. No writing materials or books. They are each allowed to bring one pack of tissue, unopened. They can bring 10 photographs. Each person is allowed to carry up to $50 in change, which is why Gil and his mother have so many quarters. They need over $100 today, to pay for their food from the prison vending machines. They're ready to be searched for contraband. After 2 hours in line, they make it in.

When they enter the visitation room, the guards bring in Jessie. His expression is kind, but he looks beat down and stressed. Gil knows that Jessie will have a different face when the family leaves. He must, if he is to survive. His skin is burned from time spent in the prison yard. Jessie's mom busies herself with making sure that everyone has enough food, leaving Gil to do most of the talking with Jessie. She basks in the enjoyment of watching her sons together. She hopes and prays, due to her diet and exercise regimen, to be alive when Jessie gets out. It is her greatest dream.

The brothers talk about what's going on back home with all the nieces and nephews. One of Jessie's fellow inmates is in the visiting room and Jessie calls him over and introduces him to Gil: "This is my brother. He's a professor and he writes books. He was a professor at Harvard and now he is at the University of California, Irvine." The inmate shakes Gil's hand, his head angled down slightly, his eyes looking up with respect.

Gil continues talking to Jessie. As they talk, Gil looks into Jessie's eyes. They connect. The feelings that are too tender to speak, for fear of disturbing the lightness and warmth of the visit, come out in their eyes. When Gil looks into Jessie's eyes, he sees the same 16-year-old from before—it's the same green eyes. But there's been years since Jessie was that boy, almost 20 years and two unsuccessful parole hearings. There is strong and penetrating spark in Jessie's eyes and Gil feels a chill, a foreshadowing. Gil knows that he is witnessing something he doesn't want to voice. His little brother is now a man, he has matured, and he is ready for life. He is an untapped intellectual and personal resource that society can benefit from. The family stuffs themselves with food from the prison's vending machines, and the visit ends with tight hugs and promises of visits soon to come.

LIKE A BIG *CHINGÓN*—A REAL BAD-ASS

Months later, Gil is in his home office. He receives a collect call from Jessie. Whenever he calls, Jessie likes Gil to verbally paint pictures for him, pictures of the outside world, of things he wants to see. Usually Gil talks about the weather or trips he has taken or news from home. Today, Jessie has a certain picture already in mind.

Jessie: Just do what I say.
Gil: Okay, okay.
Jessie: This is what I want you to do. I want you to put your feet up on your desk, with your computer right there, acting like a big *chingón*—like a real bad-ass.
Gil: I'm doing it, Jessie.
Jessie: That's right. A big chingón. Talking to me.

And from far away, over the phone line, Gil hears his little brother laugh. And, for just a second, a flash of time, they are children once more, standing on the ridge again, high above The Avenue—above it all.

A Portrait of a Chicano Anthropologist from the City of Angels

LOS ANGELES, CALIFORNIA, 1954

His face a few inches from the ground, 16-year-old Jimmy lay still under the pallet stacked with lumber, his face submerged in fumes of concentrated port wine, moldy earth, and grass. The downtown Los Angeles lumberyard was dark, pressed under an indigo summer night, except for the swinging arcs of flashlights. It would have been silent, except for the sound of the police breaking bottles. The flashlights searched for Jimmy and his cohorts from the 32nd Street gang, trying to root them out. Jimmy was still angry that he hadn't run away in time. His stomach contracted and he vomited, but he held his position, fearing any movement that would hasten discovery. There were 3 inches of space between his mouth and the spattered ground. The police could find him at any moment.

This had been his first time consorting with the gang, although he had walked among them since early childhood. Some gang members had called out to Jimmy and his friend Jaime earlier in the evening—"Jimmy, Jaime! Come here!" Jimmy couldn't say no. Actually, he felt proud that he had been singled out for attention. Since early childhood, Jimmy had watched the young men who ruled the neighborhood—they had the "juice," they had the clothes, they had the respect.

Even if Jimmy had wanted to resist the call that night, he would have been a fool to reject the invitation. Getting on the wrong side of the 32nd Street gang would have left him a vulnerable target as he walked to school, rode his bike to work, or showed his face outside his Maple Avenue house.

During Jimmy's childhood in the 1940s, gangs had little to no money, as gang involvement with drug sales hadn't yet exploded. There was no financial gain to seduce Jimmy, yet Jimmy still felt a visceral pull—a thrill at being recognized. And as for what was going on inside Jimmy's brain, he had to consider a disincentive known to all young boys from his neighborhood—a simple truth: Don't dismiss the gang. Or else.

Stretched out under the pallet, Jimmy pondered his fate. Almost all of Jimmy's sponsors for the evening, all 32nd Street members, had long disappeared, hopping the fence when the police arrived and dispersing into the warren of streets and alleyways. But Jimmy hadn't run away. He had suffered the dueling reactions of an amateur, which resulted in paralysis. When Jimmy saw the lights of the police cars approaching and heard his friends yell out warnings, half of his brain told him to run from that which can trap you and the other half told him to listen to he who is in charge. So, tangled up with excitement and terror, when the patrol car rounded the corner and approached the lot, it was too late for escape, and Jimmy, rousing from his terror at last, squeezed under the nearest pile of wood. He waited. And listened. He wondered what he would look like with handcuffs . . . standing on his front porch in front of Mama. The space of time between the sounds of bottles shattering lengthened and then . . . stopped. Silence.

He wondered, was this how it was going to be from now on? For a long time, Jimmy had been dressing like a gang member—Dickies pants, thick-soled Price shoes, which were even cheaper copies of the cheap Stacey Adams shoes worn by the gang. Tonight, Jimmy had felt like part of 32nd Street. Sitting around with them, drinking a mixture of wine and lemonade, adding in a few beers, feeling the satisfying buzz—all of this followed by the rush of breaking bottles on the ground. A loud sound, festive and violent. It was an evening of revelry unmatched in Jimmy's experience, which ended abruptly when someone in the neighborhood called the cops.

Bolitas de Chile

Jimmy thought of his friend Jaime, who had started the evening with him and skipped out before all the trouble. That was just like Jaime. Jimmy had known Jaime, the son of a single mother, since they were 4 years old. Smaller than Jimmy, Jaime had a wiry frame, wavy hair, and heavy, Boris Karloff eyebrows. Jaime's even features—firm jaw line, full lips, straight nose—balanced out the eyebrows, and the combination made him look a little intense. This wasn't a bad effect for a teenager hanging out in the streets of downtown Los Angeles. Jimmy, due to the length of their friendship, was unimpressed by Jaime's intense expressions and spent almost every day with him—on the streetcars, in the streets, inside the Santo Niño Community Center. They were *"bolitas de chile,"* little balls of chile rolling around in the elements, blowing whichever way the wind took them. All the fun was outside, going to the Pike in Venice on the streetcar or playing street games—marbles; mumbly-peg, which was a rather dangerous game played with pen knives; tag; and cops and robbers.

Despite Jimmy having two parents at home, Jaime's mother had the tighter rein on her son, and that's what had made the difference this night. That was why Jimmy was face down in a lumberyard and Jaime was safely ensconced in his house. Jaime and Jimmy knew some of the gang members—Teddy, Foxy, and Burt—guys who were respected for their power and influence on the street. But there had been dozens of guys headed to the lumberyard tonight and Jaime and Jimmy didn't know most of them. Before they even made it to the lumberyard, though, Jaime was snatched away. A high-pitched voice, made ghostly by the wind, grasped at them: "¡Jaiiiiiime! Jaiiiiiiiiiiiiime!" They turned and there was Jaime's mother, just a small point in the distance, standing in the street, waiting. The dutiful Jaime fell back, turned around, and went home. Now, stuck in the darkness, Jimmy had time to reflect.

Friends and Competitors

Jaime and Jimmy had been, for years, both friends and competitors. One day, when they were children, some friends had cajoled Jaime into fighting Jimmy. They circled Jaime: "Come on, Jaime, beat him up, beat Jimmy up, you can take him!" So Jaime walked over and shoved Jimmy. Forced to action in front of all their friends, Jimmy gave Jaime a nice sock in the smackeroo and Jaime started crying, but he was strong enough to make one final move—Jaime grabbed Jimmy's sweater at the collar and hung from it, sobbing as his body slowly sagged to the ground, the garment ripping in half. Then, with the knowledge of how much sweaters cost, Jimmy felt tears come to his eyes. By the end of the fight, both boys were crying.

Jaime sold newspapers, just like Jimmy, and from time to time the two argued over the right to prime selling spots. Jimmy had discovered a "rich people" spot at the Los Angeles Coliseum—a mother lode for a small newspaper boy on game day. Jimmy would stand there and mine the bigwigs who passed by, week after week. Jimmy bragged to Jaime about his special selling spot, where he had received a one-dollar tip from the Oscar-nominated actor Lewis Calhern. Jaime, being a smart little fellow, figured that if planted himself 5 feet in front of Jimmy on game day, he could do pretty well. Jimmy didn't agree with Jaime's thinking and this led to yet another argument between the two. They would go a couple of weeks without speaking, but eventually their friendship and long history would win out.

Both boys had to work. Jimmy had been earning his own money since he was 10, and from that age, he bought all his own clothes, paid his own fare on the streetcar, and covered the costs of any entertainment. He did a lot of things without adult supervision—like traveling long distances by streetcar.

Bee Rock

One day, 8-year-old Jimmy and 6-year-old Dicky, Jimmy's younger brother, took off on the streetcar with a group of 12-year-old boys from the neighborhood. It was early afternoon when they left. Neither Jimmy nor Dicky told their mother that they were leaving. They paid the 10 cents to the conductor and jumped on the H streetcar, taking it down to Sixth Street and Vermont, where they transferred to the V car, which took them all the way to their destination—Griffith Park. One of the largest urban parks in the nation at 4,310 acres, it was waiting to be explored.

The big boys led the way to the trail to Bee Rock, a sandstone formation that resembles a bee hive and sits high above Los Angeles. After climbing over a mile to the summit, the boys could see the distant San Gabriel Mountains and, in the foreground, the sprawling high rises of downtown. Jimmy thought that there was a giant bee hive in Bee Rock—that's what the big boys told him—so he felt brave to be so close to the thousands of bees that he thought were buzzing nearby. After wrestling around at the summit and throwing a few rocks, it was time to start home. They retraced their steps down the trail, but at the bottom, one of the older boys told Jimmy and Dicky that there wasn't enough money for them to take the streetcar home. They were going to walk back. It was about a 10-mile walk, most of it along the Los Angeles River. Taking off their shoes, they waded for a time in the water, trying to catch crawdads and splashing each other. Several of the older boys, who had tied their shoelaces together, draped them over little Dicky's neck, making him carry them. They all started getting tired as the sun started to descend. It was almost 10:00 at night before Jimmy and Dicky finally made it back to Maple Avenue. Their mother was furious. She looked at them, both dusty and dirty, and threw them into the bath tub. As she scrubbed them, she berated them. Every now and then, as words failed her, she slapped one of them on the back. Jimmy still thought the adventure was worth it, especially since Dicky seemed to get most of the slaps.

LOS ANGELES, CALIFORNIA, 1954

That love of adventure was how Jimmy came to be alone now . . . in the dark lumberyard. But at least the cops were gone. Like a smelly prairie dog, Jimmy emerged from his hole headfirst. At 120 pounds and 5'7" tall, with a short torso, Jimmy was a "long-legged sardine." His flat fish-like body had served him well tonight, enabling him to scurry into a tight spot. Jimmy looked around. Two other youth emerged. Out of the 25 or 30 that had been in their original group, only three remained. There was Jimmy. Then there was Burt, a youth friendly to Jimmy. Unfortunately, the third straggler was, of all people, Beto.

Crazy Beto

Beto had a face like the Sub-Mariner, the Marvel comic book superhero/antihero. Beto's black eyebrows were straight lines arching outward and upward. His triangular head, face, and widow's peak matched the lines of his eyebrows, making his entire face appear to be slanted upward—other-worldly and, in the right light, demonic. Beto also had some of the Sub-Mariner's personality—the hot-tempered, vengeful side. Beto was crazy. Real crazy—a legitimate *vato loco*. None of the three remaining boys knew it that night, but in the not-too-distant future, Beto would take up residence at a state mental hospital. But that was far off and, tonight, Beto was free.

Despite sharing seeing Jimmy almost daily, each time Beto's eyes lit on Jimmy, it was as if he were seeing him for the first time. Beto would have no flash of recognition in his eyes—just a blank expression, followed shortly after by an expressed desire to kick Jimmy's ass. Tonight was no exception.

As the three youths walked away from the lumberyard Beto asked Burt who the hell this "Jimmy" was and if he was part of the neighborhood. Burt, trying to protect Jimmy, reassured Beto, "Yeah, yeah, we know him." A lonely synapse must have fired in Beto's brain, igniting a fragment of a memory associated with pleasure, because Beto's face lit up—"Heyyyy, we never jumped him in, then." The vestiges of port wine in Jimmy's system bolstered his spine and Jimmy *knew*—he just *knew*—that he could take Beto. It was Beto's time. Sure, it would change Jimmy's life forever, because Beto, after getting his ass kicked memorably, would finally remember Jimmy. But Jimmy could live with that. As Jimmy waited, fists clenched, Burt intervened: "Hey, Beto, no . . . no, this is Jimmy." And then . . . Beto backed off.

"I Thought You Wanted to Be an Athlete"

The tension over, the three walked down 23rd Street toward Santo Niño Community Center, the focal point of their neighborhood—the place that provided arts, crafts, and guidance for the children and the place that served as the main landmark for the gang. It was here, safe back in their own territory, that they parted and Jimmy continued alone. Shambling along, he considered his options: go home now or go home later. Deciding that in his mother's eyes being late was better than being drunk, Jimmy turned and headed in a new direction. He stumbled past the aged houses and headed toward Bobby Lopez's place. Jimmy knew that Bobby, his older sister's boyfriend, had a broken-down car that had been sitting on a side street for months—a 1948 12-cylinder Lincoln Continental Coupe. Horsepower didn't matter at the moment—just that the car was unlocked and that it had a big back seat, perfect for the situation at hand. Jumping into that seat, Jimmy slept for what seemed like a couple of hours and awoke feeling a little more in control of his faculties. Good enough to go home, he figured. He headed off to Maple Avenue.

The hinges on the front door of Jimmy's 1870s-built house hadn't been connected for months, so he had to enter with care. He used both hands to pull the front door out of its frame like a puzzle piece. After stepping inside, he carefully plugged the door back into the rectangular hole. There—nice and secure. He turned around.

He came face to face with his mother, her eyebrows knitted in worry, her mouth pursed in anger—"Cheemi, where were you?" Jimmy started to walk through the living room, figuring the less time his mother could observe his face, the better. Maybe she wouldn't notice. She was easy to fool. She was always working, either in the house cleaning and cooking or helping at the restaurant or working at menial jobs. She was an inside person, following the inside rules. She couldn't speak English. Jimmy's world was much bigger and he knew she couldn't figure out a lot of things. She was tall, with brown, wavy hair, which was always pulled back into a bun. Despite penetrating green eyes, all her children knew her for the innocent she was—a woman who had kissed a man for the first time on her wedding day. A woman who received an envelope of cash each week from her husband to pay for groceries. She could wield a wooden hanger from time to time, but Jimmy knew that he could handle Mama. But he was glad Daddy wasn't home yet from his job at Union Station. Jimmy had to get to bed quickly.

"I'm okay, Mama. I'm all right." Jimmy's head was pounding in rhythm with his footsteps as he grabbed a glass of water and went to bed. By now, enough of his older siblings had moved out that Jimmy and his younger brother, Dicky, shared a bedroom. Within 30 seconds of his head hitting the pillow, all went black.

Waking up, Jimmy summoned Dicky, 14 years old, gave him some coins, and asked him to go to the store and buy a soda for his big brother. Maybe a cold drink would quench Jimmy's thirst and take away the fog that had settled in his brain. So far, everything was going well. The previous night was starting to look good in Jimmy's memory and he was starting to feature as the hero of the story—surviving the police, surviving Beto, gaining the respect of the gang, and now avoiding any repercussions at home. His soda was coming, but Jimmy had to use the bathroom. So he walked out of the bedroom and there was his father, sitting and reading the newspaper. A tall, thin, dark-skinned man, with a large nose and glasses, his father didn't look up. Jimmy glided by, trying to be invisible.

"Hey, Jimmy," a quiet voice from the living room rang out.

Jimmy froze.

"I thought you wanted to be an athlete."

"Yeah, Daddy. . . . I did."

"Oh . . . okay," his father replied, a wave of shock briefly moving across and off his face. He turned back to the *Herald Examiner,* shaking it straight with both hands. Jimmy, head down, returned to his bed. It could have been worse, he thought. Way worse.

It was the first time Jimmy had been staggering drunk. It was the first time he had hung out with the 32nd Street gang. It was the first time he had faced possible arrest. It was the first time he had heard that kind of disappointment in his father's voice. It was the morning of his first hangover. It was the summer of 1954.

LOS ANGELES, CALIFORNIA, 1938

When Patricio and Magdalena Vigil brought their newborn son, Jimmy ("James" on his birth certificate), home from the hospital in 1938, their Maple Avenue home was situated in a predominatly White, middle-class neighborhood. The house they rented, built in the 1870s, had been built somewhere else, no one knew where, and transported, no one knew by whom, to Maple Avenue. But the structure was planted solidly on Maple Avenue and the Vigils raised seven children within its white wooden walls.

Jimmy was the sixth of seven children. He was born when his parents were in their 40s. Both parents were Mexican American transplants from Texas and neither had made it beyond grade school. Magdalena, Jimmy's mother, left school at the end of 3rd grade. Patricio made it all the way to 6th grade, which was pretty far for a Mexican American in Texas at the time. But Patricio could read and write in Spanish and English and, because of his abilities, worked his way up to the position of assistant manager in the shipping department of a railroad. When the company promoted his manager, Patricio felt certain that he would move into the vacant position. Instead, the company hired a White man and had Patricio train him. Patricio, humiliated, shortly thereafter moved his family to California. He never spoke to his children about what happened in El Paso. After a brief time in San Diego, the family settled in downtown Los Angeles, where Patricio took a job at Union Station.

Jimmy was a Depression baby, born at the tail end of the worldwide economic collapse. Like most working-class families of this era, the Vigils survived through shared sacrifice, effort, and some small provisions—courtesy of Franklin Delano Roosevelt's New Deal. In one respect, the timing of the Depression could have been worse for the family. Most of the children entered their teenage years during this period and were old enough to quit school and go to work. Consequently, none of Jimmy's five older siblings, who included one brother and four sisters, completed high school. They all went to work.

The Siblings

Jimmy's older brother, Pat, 16 years old when Jimmy was born, left home when Jimmy was a toddler. He, along with hundreds of thousands of unemployed American young men, joined FDR's Civilian Conservation Corps (CCC) and headed off to perform manual labor on government lands. These young men built many of the bridges and roads in our national parks. Only poor youth qualified to work with the CCC—66.75% of the workers came from families on relief, 29% were from families living below the average standard, and 3% had no families at all. When Pat left, the family didn't have to feed and house him, plus the CCC sent some money home to help out the family. After his stint with the Corps ended, Pat enlisted in the Army. It was the day after the bombing of Pearl Harbor.

Jimmy never forgot the day his brother returned from World War II. Jimmy and his mother used to enjoy going to movie theaters and watching double features. Jimmy would cuddle next to his mother for hours on end. It was one of the few times he wasn't running around and one of the few times he had his mother to himself. One day they were sitting in a theater when Pat walked in, wearing his dress uniform. First Magdalena gasped and then she jumped to her feet. Tears of joy ran down her face as she hugged her son tightly to her chest, leaned back to look at his face, and then hugged him again. Jimmy barely knew Pat, but the memory of his brother the hero returning from war stayed with him forever.

Jimmy's eldest sister, Viola, a quick-witted extrovert, had a knack for finding relatively easy jobs. She made sandwiches for little vending machines at the Automat and worked doing clerical work at Top Records, a budget label that specialized in what Jimmy calls "half-ass dirty records." A little of Tops Records must have rubbed off on Viola, because she had an appetite for the same type of bawdy humor, which proved a delight to all her family, including her children, nieces, and nephews. Later, she worked at See's Candies and fulfilled the entire family's appetite for chocolate by bringing home the conveyer belt rejects. Every child in her extended family knew where to find the big bag of misshapen chocolate clods—sitting ugly and delicious in her refrigerator.

Jimmy's three other sisters, Nany (short for Magdalena), Bea (Beatrice), and Loy (Eloisa) as teenagers worked in factories wiring generators. Nany and Loy doted on their much younger brothers—Jimmy and the 2 years younger Dicky, who was the final child born to the family. Every Friday afternoon, Jimmy and Dicky waited, squirming in anticipation, on the front steps of the Maple Avenue house. Their faces scrubbed and their shirts clean, they peered down the street, waiting for Nany and Loy. They watched for the familiar two figures approaching, their hair tied up in scarves, their sweaters buttoned over greasy overalls. *There they were!* All patience gone, the boys would jump and run. Nany and Loy would grab their little brothers by the hand and they would all march over to the five-and-ten store, where Jimmy and Dicky each got to spend 25 cents on anything they wanted. Every Friday.

One Friday, Nany and Loy were late. Dicky and Jimmy were waiting in their usual spot. *What happened? Aren't we going to go to the store?* But the boys didn't move—they didn't want to give up hope. Finally, in the distance, Jimmy spotted his sisters, but they were walking funny, each of them with one arm trailing over their heads, behind their bodies. Then Jimmy saw them, he saw THEM—they were pulling kites—one for Jimmy and one for Dicky! The sense of gloom and lost hope transformed into joy, and the boys laughed and embraced their sisters, all locked together, as the kites swayed and trembled above them.

Home Alone

Compared with their older siblings, Dicky and Jimmy had it easy, because the worst effects of the Depression were over by the time of their births. Still, money was in short supply and the two boys were often unsupervised, both inside and outside. They had few toys and no books. No one taught them their ABCs or read them stories. Jimmy was 10 years old before he learned the difference between odd and even numbers. The only reading material in the house was *Motion Picture* magazine. Outside the house, some older neighbor boys provided access to "Tijuana Bibles," eight-page pornographic comic books. The family ate simply—*guisos* (stews) and fish balls (made from whole fishes, heads and filets included). They often ran out of all but the basics by each week's end. By midweek, Jimmy often couldn't even find a piece of fruit for a snack. He blamed Dicky for eating all of the food. Dicky blamed Jimmy for being picky.

One Taste Lasts a Lifetime

One day, when he was still small, Jimmy was walking along the street with his sister Viola, and they came up on Gus's hamburger truck. Gus, a White, wrinkled World War I veteran who often picked his nose as he stacked the lettuce and pickles, worked in the neighborhood selling grilled burgers and Jimmy always noticed when Gus was working. The delicious smell of the burgers wafted through the air. Jimmy never ate out, unless you count the once or twice a year that the family went to Clifton's Cafeteria, which sometimes fed poor people for free. So, Jimmy, on this day, prepared, as usual, to walk by Old Gus when Viola suddenly stopped and dug into her purse. She bought one hamburger. She gave Jimmy one bite. It was his first bite of a grilled burger. The taste of that bite is still in Jimmy's mouth 62 years later.

Newspaper Boy

As much as Jimmy's sisters adored him, he couldn't escape the economic realities of the times. At 10 years of age, Jimmy was sitting on a porch with five or six other kids when a white man approached—"Hey, you guys want to work? Make some money? Sell newspapers?" The boys looked at one another and decided well, heck, yeah, they wanted money. So the man, Mike Johnson, loaded the boys up with copies of the *Los Angeles Mirror*, an afternoon tabloid that the *Los Angeles Times* had launched that day. Dumped on a corner, Jimmy sold two newspapers in three hours and he made a nickel. The papers cost a nickel apiece, but Jimmy had to pay Mike two-and-a-half cents to cover the cost of each paper. After that day, all of the other boys quit except Jimmy. He stuck with the job for the best part of the next 6 years. Despite his dismal start, Jimmy eventually sold a lot of papers and figured out how to make and save money.

Each day, when the school bell rang, he jumped on his bike and careened home to change his clothes, putting on a denim jacket and pants so that the newsprint wouldn't ruin his regular clothing. Back on his bike, he rushed to buy his papers and get to his corner. If he was late, his regular customers would buy their papers from someone else. If he didn't sell all his papers, he would be out the money he had paid for them. Sometimes, on days when sales were poor, his bosses would take pity on him and buy back the papers, but there were no guarantees.

At 3:00 p.m. on weekdays, he'd be on the corner of 16th and Main yelling, "Read all about it! Get your newspapers here free! Five cents tax!" It was a great spot—about a mile from downtown—and Jimmy eventually averaged 50 or 60 papers a day. Each day, after Jimmy took care of his regular customers, who came by on foot and by car, he grabbed a copy of every L.A. paper—the *Examiner*, the *Times*, the *Mirror*, the *Daily News*, and the *Herald Express*—and rushed off to make his daily run to the offices of *La Opinión*, the Spanish-language newspaper for Los Angeles.

La Opinión bought the papers from Jimmy so that they could get a jump on the news. Technically, they didn't have permission to start writing from Jimmy's papers—they were supposed to depend on their own news feed, but their news feed was always a day late and the reporters didn't want to wait to start writing their pieces. The sportswriter, Rudy Garcia, liked Jimmy, but made fun of him for not speaking Spanish. Jimmy showed up at *La Opinión* with the papers like clockwork and, on top of paying him for the papers each day, the writers gave Jimmy a big bag of groceries to take home to his family each Christmas.

But one day Jimmy decided to quit. He had grown tired of hearing how his friends were just chilling out and playing after school every day. Others were joining sports' teams. Jimmy didn't want to be so damn dutiful anymore and he tired of the grueling routine—5 days a week plus many weekends, when he worked at Los Angeles Coliseum selling special football editions. In the summer, he sometimes delivered papers from 5:00 to 7:00 a.m., followed by working a corner from 10:00 a.m. to 6:00 p.m. He decided that he was done for with the newspaper business. He would break the news first to his big sister Loy. She was the softest, sweetest of his older sisters and he knew she would understand. With an appropriately worried, serious look on his face, he approached her one evening—"Loy, you know what?"

"What, Jimmy?" She looked at him kindly.

"I'm getting . . . [Jimmy paused at the sight of her face, his throat constricting and his voice quavering in her indulgent presence] . . . I'm getting . . . I don't get to play sports after school. I'm getting tired of working . . . I want to quit."

Loy's face changed—she looked at Jimmy real cold—looked through him, really, without looking him in the eyes. She said, in a low, flat voice, "You're not going to quit. You keep working." And she turned and walked away. This was a new Loy—not the one who had given Jimmy a kite only a few years before. Jimmy didn't quit. Even a few years later, when he was a 16-year-old newspaper boy, still standing on the corner, embarrassed for his 18-year-old girlfriend to see him as she passed by on the streetcar, he kept working.

Jimmy headed home about 6:30 p.m. each night. Over time, he learned to save money. His brother-in-law told him, "Make a dime, save a nickel." So that's what Jimmy did. It took him some time, making 2.5 cents profit per paper, but he averaged about $15.00 per week and eventually saved $225, enough to buy his first car, a 1941 Ford, which he purchased for $150. He and his little brother, Dicky, who also began selling newspapers, bought the family their first television, a Zenith. The two brothers had nagged their parents for years to get a TV.

LOS ANGELES, BEFORE AND AFTER THE DEPRESSION

Poverty slammed the entire country during the Depression, but Los Angeles took the punch in its own way. Founded in 1781 by the Spanish, the small pueblo of Los Angeles had grown into a dream by the time the Depression hit—site of the 1932 Olympics and thousands of acres of orange groves, home to movie stars and Hollywood film studios, a Mediterranean climate and a history steeped in the legends of the Californios. Marketed for White tourists, with the carefully constructed image of Olvera Street portraying the peaceful, sleeping, subservient Mexican past, the city held many attractions. Streetcars traversed the city, delivering tourists and residents alike to Macy's Department Store; theatergoers to the Mayan, the Roxie, and the Million Dollar; and club hoppers to the Coconut Grove in the Ambassador Hotel, where they could listen to the sweet baritone of Bing Crosby. One could spend the morning at the beach and then take a train up a steep incline to the top of Mount Lowe, "Earth's Grandest Mountain Ride." From its peak, one could see Long Beach and Catalina Island. Cawston's Ostrich Farm, located in nearby Pasadena, exhibited transplanted ostriches from Africa. The Depression had caused many of these businesses to wither and die as tourists, almost all of them White, stayed away.

World War II transformed Los Angeles into an industrial center for manufacturing related to war production. Poor whites, "Okies," flocked to Los Angeles and, as part of the Great Migration from the South, so did large numbers of African Americans. Despite the fact that 12,000 Mexicans were deported in the early 1930s, Mexicans continued to immigrate to the city, joining Mexican Americans who had already been there for several generations. Many new immigrants sought work in the booming factories. Racial and ethnic tensions increased as the demographics of the city shifted and a sense of competition for space and jobs arose.

The Rise of Charitable Organizations

Charitable organizations arose to meet the needs of the new minority populations. The Catholic Youth Authority offered classes, sports, and field trips. In Jimmy's neighborhood, El Santo Niño Community Center was a refuge for the neighborhood children.

Jimmy also became involved in the Woodcraft Rangers, founded in 1922 by naturalist-author Ernest Thompson Seton. Before founding the Rangers, Seton's home in Connecticut had been vandalized by a group of local boys. Seton decided not to prosecute, and instead he invited the boys to his home for a visit, which included telling stories and learning how to identify birds, swim, and canoe. This event led to the founding of the Woodcraft Indians in 1902. The name of the organization changed to the Woodcraft Rangers, but the principles Seton took from his respect for Native American cultures endure in the current organization—a quest to seek knowledge, pursue truth and beauty, increase tolerance and understanding, and improve social and environmental conditions through "personal and collective action." Jimmy and his neighborhood friends took part in many Woodcraft Ranger activities, but still spent the majority of their time out in the neighborhood, on the street. And sometimes, Jimmy already knew, the street was not very tolerant. He saw it himself. And he knew the stories.

Sleepy Lagoon and the "Bad Mexican"

On August 1, 1942, as a result of a fight between rival groups of Mexican American youth, 22-year-old José Díaz died, due to blunt force trauma. The fight took place at Sleepy Lagoon, a reservoir in southeast Los Angeles. Both groups in the fight were part of the *"pachuco"* subculture, made up of youth who adopted their own style of speech and, most famously, their own style of dress—the zoot suit. The zoot suit style, expressed with a long jacket, loose pants, swinging chains, and a porkpie hat, was a marker for delinquency and negative perceptions of Mexicans, despite the fact that many non-delinquent youth and even some Whites wore zoot suits. Some *pachucos* were gang members, but many were not. However, the *Los Angeles Times,* in the wake of the Sleepy Lagoon trial, fueled negative perceptions by, for example, referring to *pachucos* as organized bands of marauders (Sherman, 1943).

In a city already churning from the rapidly growing convergence of so many diverse immigrants, the trial of the defendants in the Sleepy Lagoon case became a focal point as ethnic tensions exploded in bigotry and a hungry, feverish desire for retribution. As a result, the trial of the case resulted in 12 murder and 5 assault convictions. Throughout the trial, the court deprived the defendants of basic civil rights. They were forced to wear zoot suits throughout the trial and prevented from sitting near or communicating with their attorneys. The judge allowed an expert witness to testify that Mexicans were hard-wired for criminal violence, due to their Aztec ancestors' bloodlust. Eventually, in 1944, the U.S. Court of Appeals overturned the convictions, but the tide of violence had already risen and washed across Los Angeles.

After the Sleepy Lagoon trial, violence began to erupt between White servicemen and Mexican Americans. Two fights between zoot-suiters and military personnel led, within a few days, to thousands of servicemen marching through the streets in order to find and assault Latino youths, not just zoot-suiters. In one incident, about 200 sailors took taxis to an East Los Angeles neighborhood, where they found Mexican American youth, many of them 12- and 13-year-olds. The sailors took clubs to the boys, stripped them of their zoot suits, and burned the clothing in a street bonfire. On another evening, servicemen invaded a movie theater and pulled Latinos, African Americans, and Filipinos out of their seats, throwing them into the street and beating them. Finally, national attention and condemnation of the actions, including a rebuke from Eleanor Roosevelt, halted the attacks. The Marine and Navy commands declared Los Angeles off-limits to all members of the military. The violence ended, but the image of the "bad Mexican" endured.

Beans, Spooks, Buddhaheads, and Fades

For most of his childhood, Jimmy had felt comfortable in the mix of working-class residents in his neighborhood. Post-Depression, different races and ethnicities abounded, but they shared the common denominator of being working-class. So racial and ethnic differences were noted matter-of-factly. Jimmy was a "bean" and he knew he was a bean. Wasn't nothing wrong with it. Nothing personal. Sometimes a person needed a little more identifying information.

For example, Jimmy recalled, one might say, "You know Jimmy?"

"I'm not sure. Jimmy who?"

"You know, Jimmy, the Bean—Jimmy."

"Oh, okay, yeah, yeah."

No hard feelings.

So, African Americans were "spooks." Japanese were "Buddhaheads" and Whites were "fades." Jimmy believed that the "fades" probably used to have more color, lots of generations ago and, well, time and the sun had taken their toll.

Bimini Baths, Facing De Facto Racial Covenants

Despite the egalitarian nature of the multicultural working-class neighborhood Jimmy experienced in his earliest years, there had always been parts of Los Angeles that weren't welcoming to the dark-skinned, especially African Americans and Mexicans. Bimini Baths, located below Griffith Observatory, was a place that Jimmy only got to go to a few times, but what fun it was! West of downtown, built in 1900 over natural hot springs, the baths provided hot and cold pools, deep and shallow pools, splashing pools and soaking pools. For 25 cents, a kid gained all-day admission and could paddle about, jump off the high dive, and play himself into exhaustion. There was even a small beach, but Jimmy and his friends didn't spend their time sitting around on the sand.

One day, Jimmy and his friends took the H line to Vermont Avenue, where the baths were located. Joining the group that day was Kiki Macias, a boy with much darker skin than Jimmy. When Jimmy paid his admission and entered, he turned and saw that Kiki had been stopped at the door and forbidden entrance, a victim of one of the de facto racial covenants that, along with the legal racial covenants that existed to prevent certain races and ethnicities home ownership in certain areas of the city, prevailed to ensure the privilege of white Angelenos.

After Kiki was held back, the rest of the boys, showing the characteristic generosity of prepubescent males, shrugged off the insult to their friend and frolicked all day in the baths. They came out to find Kiki in an adjacent lot, kicking rocks. He had waited all day for their return.

Violent Teachers, Violent Students

As Jimmy approached his teen years, even his neighborhood began to show tension. It showed up first at school—in the teachers' behavior. With rare exception, the teachers seemed enraged by the cruel hoax society had played on them. When, only a few years earlier, they had been able to teach only White, well-prepared middle-class children, they now had to deal with African Americans, Okies, and Mexicans, students from working-class families who chattered in class and came from homes with no reading materials. Corporal punishment was legal and seemed like a good solution to the new challenges. One teacher at Jimmy's school, who only had one arm, swung it like a log against the heads of many of her dull, misbehaving charges.

The atmosphere around Jimmy, at school and on the street, was one of latent aggression, and Jimmy figured out different ways to meet the challenge of violence that he faced. He had at least six fights in elementary school, almost all of them forced on him. Because he had some boxing training, courtesy of the Catholic Youth Authority, he held his own or dominated in most cases. Usually, he would use his quickness to hit his opponent with a few good jabs and punches and that would do the trick. The fight would be over.

But one night, when he was walking with his sister's boyfriend, Pete, an ex-con later sent to San Quentin prison for murder, Jimmy crossed paths with an older group of boys from a different neighborhood. One of the boys challenged him and Jimmy responded with some of his patented punches, right in the face—executed perfectly. Pete stood back, letting Jimmy take care of the situation. Breathing heavily and confidently expecting his victim to stagger backward, Jimmy was surprised to see that the boy barely moved. Instead, his body visibly coiled in readiness, his eyes narrowed in resolve, and his lips curled, exposing his teeth. Quickly Jimmy cried out, "I don't want to fight. I'm a good boy. I want God to like me." The other boys started laughing at this outburst and Jimmy never suffered a retaliating blow. As he and Pete walked home, he felt the older man's disgust fall upon him—thick and silent. But he was glad to have an intact face. Nobody had ever been so unaffected by Jimmy's best jabs. In this case, retreat was Jimmy's choice, but he couldn't retreat every time. If you did that, you were screwed.

One day at school, Emilio, a chunky boy, saw Jimmy's face pressed up against a screen door and, standing on the other side of the door, he slapped Jimmy—hard—in the nose. Jimmy, enraged, sprinted out of the classroom, caught up with the lumbering Emilio, grabbed him by both lapels of his jacket, and, nose to nose, hissed into his face, "If you do that again, I'll kick the shit out of you." He never saw Emilio again.

Advancing, retreating, posturing, enduring—it was all part of surviving and forging a street identity, which garnered some degree of respect and immunity from bullies.

As an ill-prepared Mexican American in the era of corporal punishment, Jimmy didn't have immunity from his teachers. One of them, exasperated by his dullness and constant chattering, stretched out her arm to its fullest length, cupped her palm, and swung with all her power, hitting Jimmy's ear with a resounding clap. Something inside his ear popped and a great pain emanated from his ear. The pain lasted for weeks. Yet Jimmy said nothing at home. If he told his parents, he risked yet another clobbering. For the rest of his life, his ear bothered him. Eventually, he suffered hearing loss and every now and then, the ear would bleed.

Jimmy Strikes an Effective Pose

After several years on the receiving end of rubber hoses, paddles, kicks, and slaps, Jimmy developed an effective coping strategy. He began to execute it in 5th grade, when he had Mr. Berry, who Jimmy knew could hit with a powerful, gut-clenching force. Jimmy learned to strike a pose during class—he would turn his elfin face upward, raise his eyebrows, and assume what he figured was an attentive expression. It worked—he stopped getting hit. But also, to his great surprise, he began learning. He began to read for pleasure, an activity previously untapped. For the next 2 years, he got As and Bs, and as he prepared to enter junior high, the administration targeted him as potentially gifted. His future appeared bright. Unfortunately, he met Ronnie Daniels on the first day he attended John Adams Middle School. Together, they would compete in a race to the bottom of all things academic.

Fun with Ronnie

Jimmy was still friends with Jaime, who was a good student, but the alchemy between Ronnie and Jimmy produced glorious adventures and bad grades. Between trips to the Pike, where the boys tried to lure girls into the Tunnel of Love, the boys found success where they valued it most—on the street.

Jimmy continued selling newspapers, but developed a new interest and a new nickname—"Killer"—referring to his popularity with the female population. Ronnie occasionally stole Jimmy's girls, one of these thefts occurring in the Tunnel of Love, but Ronnie graciously refused to brag or acknowledge this thievery, out of respect for the friendship.

To the Suburbs: Life in Norwalk

In 1954, shortly after Jimmy's lumberyard experience, Jimmy's parents told him that the family would be moving. Jimmy's sister Nany had already purchased a home in the city of Norwalk, California, 17 miles southeast of downtown Los Angeles. His parents didn't like how much time Jimmy and Dicky spent hanging out in the streets. Using the G.I. benefit of Jimmy's eldest brother, Patrick, they purchased a small home adjacent to their daughters' in suburban Norwalk. Jimmy hoped that there would be some "fine chicks" there.

At this time, Norwalk was one of the fastest-growing cities in America. Its name dates back to 1874, when the Anaheim Pacific railroad crossed the "North-Walk," the stagecoach stop between Los Angeles and Anaheim. Its name shortened to Norwalk Station, it became a destination during the 1880s land boom, when people from across the country rushed to buy land in Southern California's sunny clime, which had only recently been connected to the rest of the nation. Soon, the city even boasted the state's largest ostrich farm. Located only a few miles from Hollywood, the city was the location for the filming of the 1946 film noir *The Postman Always Rings Twice*, starring John Garfield and Lana Turner.

But by the early 1900s, Norwalk main business was dairy-related—the city was known as "Heart of the Valleys." When Jimmy arrived in 1954, it remained a dairy town. The smell of manure and methane dominated. When Jimmy arrived with his family, he smelled opportunity. He looked forward to the change, to the new girls, to the new friends. There were no newspaper boys in Norwalk, so it was a fresh start for Jimmy. On the first day of school, he put on his Price shoes, combed his hair, carefully dressed, and walked out the door as the All-American boy. Like Archie from the comics, he envisioned himself getting dates with a "Veronica" or a "Betty." It took a few days for him to realize that he wasn't who he thought he was in this new place. Here, with the Dutch American children of the dairymen, he discovered that he was really just a "chili choke." That was what he heard, anyway.

To make things worse, he enrolled in Excelsior High School as a sophomore, meaning that almost all the other students had already had 1 year to form cliques. He made few friends, but he did get himself a girlfriend, a year younger, a good student, and a Mexican American like Jimmy. Soon he was spending most of his time with her. But it wasn't enough. He missed Los Angeles and all its smells, parties, and the sense that, when you went out for the evening, anything could happen. He started driving his father to work at Union Station, then heading over to the old neighborhood. The first time he made the return trip, he hadn't seen Jaime in a month. Jaime, his off-and-on nemesis for so many years, ran over and embraced Jimmy. So did the rest of the neighborhood. They hit parties, proms, events at hotels. During this time, they started smoking pot, alongside the alcohol they had already been drinking for a couple of years.

Jimmy's dual existence worked well throughout high school. Eventually, because he no longer worked daily selling newspapers, he was able to join the football team and, by his senior year, became the starting quarterback. His grades remained less than mediocre—Cs and Ds, except for his consistent As in Physical Education. No one at home asked about his grades. No one suggested he shape up and consider college. Only one man, a long time earlier, had given Jimmy any input on a potential career. He was a customer of Jimmy's when he was a newspaper boy. The man told Jimmy that he looked like he could make a good police officer. So while at Excelsior, Jimmy remembered the man's advice and joined the Future Law Enforcement Officers club.

He worked summers at a car wash, the high school years went by, and before he knew it, it was senior year. He maintained his steady below-average performance for the first semester. Then, at the beginning of second semester, his final few months at the school, Jimmy had an epiphany. *I figure that I'm smarter than most of these other students. I'm going to try.* At the end of the semester, Jimmy received straight Bs. He was smart. And he knew he could have done even better.

Marriage, Fatherhood, College

Jimmy still had his '41 Ford and he still had a couple of hundred dollars saved, so he decided to embark on adulthood. He married his high school girlfriend when he was19, in August 1958, and they had their first child, a daughter, the following June. Life suddenly accelerated.

So he enrolled at Cerritos College, a junior college that had free tuition. Jimmy's parents, after years of not mentioning education, offered to pay for his books. Jimmy studied harder. His wife worked full-time and Jimmy worked as well, for a time as a janitor. By this time, his dream of being a police officer had faded and now he wanted to be a physical education teacher, so he took courses toward that major. For the first time in his life, he read entire books. He found himself fascinated by history. He stayed up late, underlining his books, saving them all. He would look at his bookshelf and think, *I read that one . . . and that one . . . I read a chapter in that one.* He read anthropology, sociology, early childhood development, and psychology. He applied to transfer into California State University, Long Beach. He was accepted.

Cal State Long Beach didn't have free tuition. It was 50 dollars per semester. Jimmy's parents continued to pay his books, and now they offered to pay his tuition. By now, Jimmy and his wife were expecting their second child—a son. During the first semester, Jimmy ended up on academic probation. He wasn't ready for the caliber of the students and for the more advanced writing skills that were required at the university level. So he had to take remedial English.

Jimmy made it through remedial English, changed his major to history, and graduated. Shortly thereafter, he obtained a job teaching elementary school. In the summer, he worked as a recreation leader. He had his third and fourth children—both sons. Four years passed.

Pursuing a Master's Degree

Jimmy began to consider going to graduate school. No one gave him the idea. There were no mentors at that time for minority students at Cal State Long Beach. Getting his bachelor's degree could have been enough for someone in his shoes—he was the first in his family to graduate from high school. But dreams of obtaining a master's degree began to tickle his brain. He decided to apply to the school of his dreams—UCLA. He carefully filled out the application and, after weeks of waiting, was rejected.

Disconsolate, he walked to the academic counseling office at Cal State Long Beach, where he saw a brochure advertising a fellowship available for minority students to attend graduate school. He applied, under the program's rules, to Sacramento State as well as the University of Denver. Weeks later, he received a thick envelope in the mail. Sacramento had accepted him! Then, a short time later, he received another envelope—Denver had offered him a position as well. He chose Sacramento and headed north with his family—four children under the age of 10. He was 29 and his wife was 28. His library grew larger and so did his dreams. He started to think that some day he might be able to write books.

El Movimiento

This was 1968 and El Movimiento, the Chicano Movement, was in full stride. Jimmy found a personal renaissance during this time. No longer just an overachieving "chili choke," Jimmy embraced a new, proud identity as a Chicano. Until this time, Jimmy worked for personal satisfaction and achievement. Now, a dawning sense of community with others embraced him and he began to envision a life's work, a passion, a political philosophy—a way to help fellow Chicanos. And the way was not one of weakness; it was a way of power and assertion. This was all new. He met the academic Octavio Romano, from Berkeley, who inspired him. Jimmy joined the Brown Berets and also joined a group of Chicano educators from throughout the southland.

Shortly after the family's arrival in Sacramento, Jimmy's marriage fell apart and, with a divorce soon to follow, his wife moved and took the children back to Norwalk. Jimmy stayed and completed his master's degree in social science. The divorce destabilized Jimmy—his children and wife were gone—but he forged forward, even though it was difficult to concentrate on his reading and writing. Nevertheless, during this time, he was published for the first time, in the *Sacramento Hornet*, which was the university's newspaper. The name of his article: "Pachuco Yesterday. Vato Loco today." For the first time, someone wanted Jimmy's academic input. He began to dream bigger dreams—dreams of obtaining a doctorate.

Doctoral Studies

In 1969, after obtaining his master's degree, Jimmy had about 10 different job options. But his dream of attending a certain Los Angeles university surfaced from the depths of his memory, and he joined, as Academic Staff, the High-Potential Program at UCLA. Here, for 2 years, he taught minority students who had been underserved in their earlier academic careers in order to prepare them for the opportunity to attend the university. During the same time period, he obtained a second master's degree, this time in Anthropology.

1971 turned out to be a momentous year for Jimmy. He met his future second wife in a graduate student seminar, began a UCLA fellowship to obtain a Ph.D., and obtained a job teaching at Chaffey College, a community college located in Rancho Cucamonga, California. The fellowship came about in an interesting manner. Jimmy had already begun to pursue, with the help of limited financial aid, a Ph.D. in History when he heard about an offer available for graduate students pursuing Ph.D.s in Anthropology. The new fellowship offered a monthly stipend, full tuition, and funds available for research. It was too good to pass up, and Jimmy obtained the fellowship and decided to pursue his Ph.D. in Cultural Anthropology. But he still had financial hurdles to overcome.

He married for the second time in 1972 and his wife gave birth to a daughter in 1973. As a father of five, Jimmy couldn't pay child support and take care of his family on the monthly stipend offered via his fellowship. But the terms of the fellowship required that he only could teach classes at UCLA. No outside, additional work was allowed. Jimmy made the tough decision to secretly continue working at Chaffey. As he puts it, "I had all these kids—these 'mudsuckers'—and I needed to take care of them." He kept his mouth shut and juggled multiple roles.

He moved his new bride and infant daughter to Rosemead, briefly, and then to Ontario, California, so that their main abode would be near Chaffey. Three days a week he drove to UCLA to fulfill the requirements of his fellowship—attending seminars and teaching. At the end of each day at UCLA, he would drive home to Ontario, so that he could prepare for his teaching duties at Chaffey. Every other weekend, on a Friday night, he drove for 1 hour and 15 minutes to pick up his first four children in Huntington Beach. They would climb into his 1968 Volkswagen camper van and he would drive them to visit for the weekend. On Sunday night, he would deliver them back home. In between, late at night, he read, studied, and began work on his dissertation. His young wife took care of all the household responsibilities and cared for all their children so that Jimmy could concentrate on his studies. As time went on, she also became his research assistant.

While at UCLA, Jimmy did a favor for a well-established professor. He needed access to high school students for some research, and Jimmy provided the professor with the contacts. The professor wanted to show thanks to Jimmy, so he invited him to his office for a meeting. There, he offered to chair Jimmy's Ph.D. committee, with the only condition being that Jimmy would take the professor's seminar the following semester. Jimmy knew how important the professor could be to Jimmy's career. But he had to say no.

His job at Chaffey, the job he needed to support his family, conflicted with the schedule for the seminar. But Jimmy couldn't tell the professor that he had a second job—it would jeopardize everything. All he could say was, "No, I can't take your class." The professor then rescinded his offer, which ended up impacting Jimmy heavily.

Finally—a Professor

If Jimmy had been able to attend the seminar, he likely would have been championed by the professor, who would have helped Jimmy to secure a position as a professor at a university—most likely within a year of receiving his Ph.D. Instead, after Jimmy received his Ph.D. in 1975, he waited 7 years for a university position. During this time, he and his wife had another daughter. It was only after the publication of his first book, *From Indians to Chicanos*, that Jimmy was able to move on from Chaffey College. His accepted his first professorship—at the University of Southern California—in 1981. In 1982, he and his wife added a seventh child to their family, another daughter.

Two passions marked this period of Jimmy's life—both personal and academic. Having a lot of children fueled the passion to "keep my head above water." His academic passions evolved over time—beginning with the desire to study racial relations between peasant populations and Mestizos in Central America—a topic he researched in Guatemala— and continuing into research on culture change and urban anthropology.

As a busy academic, Jimmy doesn't look back very often. But when asked to do so, he admits that,

> I'm surprised that I did what I did. I reached a level that never in my wildest dreams would I think I was capable of [reaching.] I credit most of it to what happened in the sixties—the striving for civil rights for minorities and for affirmative action. But I also have to say that I pushed. I pushed myself. I finally began to see that I had the ability to be a writer, to be a researcher, to be a professor. All that I wished for and worked for came to pass. The best is that I didn't sell out . . . The most beautiful feeling was that I didn't make any compromises.

Due to their father's example and some of his "push," all seven of Jimmy's children have obtained college degrees. Of the seven, four have obtained advanced degrees—one has a law degree, one has an MBA, and two have master's degrees. A fifth is currently working on a master's degree.

UCLA, 1988

"Come on, Jaime, let's get the hell out of here," Jimmy nagged. His childhood friend Jaime gathered up his notes and answered, with just a bit of irritation in his voice, "All right, all right, we're going. If you're going to come, don't complain so much! Besides, you're the one that's making us stop at your office." Their dress shoes clicked on the polished floors as they walked down the halls of UCLA's Haines Hall toward the elevator. Jaime, a Presiding Judge of the Los Angeles County Juvenile Court, had just given a lecture on Psychology and the Law. He had lured Jimmy to the lecture with the promise of martinis and dinner afterward. Jimmy, as always, didn't want to waste time getting to their destination.

The two stepped into the elevator and Jimmy pushed the button for the third floor. The doors shut. The elevator couldn't move fast enough for Jimmy—the martini, extra-dry with extra olives, was waiting. Jimmy glanced at Jaime and something caught his eye. Jaime was wearing a suit and tie, but that wasn't it. It was Jaime! What the hell was Jaime doing standing here? What was he doing here? They used to sell papers at the Coliseum before Bruins games. Jaime was looking at Jimmy, too, and in that instant, they each knew what the other was feeling. Wordlessly, they reached for each other. Each of them wrapped his arms tightly around the other with a big hug, *un gran abrazo*.

Notes

Introduction

1. Even though individuals or families are able to climb out of economic poverty, Lewis argues that a culture of poverty would be reproduced by generations of the poor and would last for some time. In our work, we locate institutions that promote the social mobility of the poor; however, much more structural reform is needed to combat the economic marginalization that people face.

2. By not blaming the individual, our work contributes to debunking deficit models in education, such as Ruby Payne's (2005) recent arguments about poverty (e.g., *A Framework for Understanding Poverty*). See the article by Gorski (2006) and the article by Bomer, Dworin, May, & Semingson, P. (2008) for thoughtful critiques of Payne's work.

Chapter 5

1. See Vigil (2002, second edition). *Personas Mexicanas: Chicano high schoolers in a changing Los Angeles*. Belmont, CA: Thomson Custom Publishing for a full discussion of the study.

Chapter 7

1. Although this book concentrates on boys, we include the voices of both boys and girls to show the general impact of these small learning communities. As with the other research-based studies, the names and characteristics of students and the school have been changed to ensure confidentiality.

2. In the portraits of Samuel and Pedro, we observe how work-related internships assisted these young men later in life. Samuel's experience in pouring concrete enabled him to open his own business, and Pedro's internship while in community college mediated his higher sense of optimism for himself and later for his son.

3. In California, there exists a high school reform initiative coined "linked learning." Linked learning "connects strong academics with real–world experience in a wide range of fields, such as engineering, arts and media, and biomedical and health sciences—helping students gain an advantage in high school, col-

lege, and career" (ConnectED website). The Irvine Foundation has embraced this high school reform strategy, and linked learning pathways have been implemented throughout California high schools. See, for example, the work of the Career Academy Support Network (CASN), ConnectEd, Education Trust West, National Academy Foundation, and UCLA's IDEA, to name a few organizations that promote college and career success.

4. It is important to note that while significant to the success of many youth, Career Academies are not without limitations. Namely, these high school reform efforts have the potential to reproduce the status quo in terms of tracking via career theme (for instance, Engineering versus Hospitality and Transportation), equity issues around who enrolls in in certain Academies, uneven recruitment processes, Academies serving too few students, and many excluding English language learners. Future research should uncover best practices in Career Academies that demonstrate success around equity issues.

References

Advancement Project. (2006, Spring). Arresting development: Addressing the school discipline crisis in Florida. A report prepared by Florida State Conference NAACP, Advancement Project, NAACP Legal Defense and Educational Fun, Inc.

Alonso, A. A. (2004). Racialized identities and the formation of black gangs in Los Angeles. *Urban Geography, 25*(7), 658–674. doi:10.2747/0272-3638.25.7.658

Anderson, E. (1990). *Streetwise: Race, class and change in an urban community.* Chicago: University of Chicago Press.

Arellano, G. (2006, June 15). Raza isn't racist. *Los Angeles Times.* Retrieved from http://www.latimes.com/news/opinion/commentary/la-oe-arellano-15jun15,0,3083983.story

Banks, J. A. (2001). Citizenship education and diversity: Implications for teacher education. *Journal of Teacher Education, 52*(1), 5–16. doi:10.1177/0022487101052001002

Banks, J. A. (2008). *An introduction to multicultural education.* Boston: Pearson, Allyn & Bacon.

Bauman, R. (2008). *Race and the war on poverty: From Watts to East L.A.* Norman, OK: University of Oklahoma Press.

Blackwell, A. G., & Pastor, M. (2010). Let's hear it for the boys: Building a stronger America by investing in young men and boys of color. In C. Edley & J. Ruiz de Velasco (Eds.), *Changing places: How communities will improve the health of boys of color* (pp. 3–35). Berkeley: University of California Press.

Bolivar, J. M., & Chrispeels, J. H. (2011). Enhancing parent leadership through building social and intellectual capital. *American Educational Research Journal, 48*(1), 4–38. doi:10.3102/000281210366466

Bomer, R., Dworin, J. E., May, L., & Semingson, P. (2008). Miseducating teachers about the poor: A critical analysis of Ruby Payne's claims about poverty. *Teachers College Record, 110*(12), 2497–2531.

Bourdieu, P. (1986). The forms of capital. In J. G. Richardson (Ed.), *Handbook of theory and resistance for the sociology of education* (pp. 241–258). New York:Greenwood Press.

Branch, T. (1989). *Parting the waters: America in the King years, 1954–63.* New York: Simon & Schuster.

Burstall, S. A. (1894). *The education of girls in the United States.* New York: Macmillan. Cammarota, J. (2004). The gendered and racialized pathways of Latina and Latino youth: Different struggles, different resistance in the urban context. *Anthropology & Education Quarterly, 35*(1), 53–74. doi:10.1525/aeq.2004.35.1.53

Carter, P. L. (2005). *Keepin' it real: School success beyond Black and White.* New York: Oxford University Press.

Carter, P. L. (2009). Equity and empathy: Toward racial and educational achievement in the Obama era. *Harvard Educational Review, 79*(2), 287–297.

Chávez, L. (1992). *Shadowed lives.* New York: Harcourt Brace Jovanovich.

Chávez, L. (2008). *The Latino threat: Constructing immigrants, citizens, and the nation.* Palo Alto, CA: Stanford University Press.

Coleman, J. S. (1988). Social capital in the creation of human capital: The ambiguous position of private schools. *American Journal of Sociology, 94,* 95–120.

Colvin, R. E. (1995). Bilingual education rift divides state teachers union. *Los Angeles Times.* Retrieved from http://articles.latimes.com/1995-06-05/news/mn-9792_1_bilingual-education

Conchas, G. Q. (2001). Structuring failure and success: Understanding the variability in Latino school engagement. *Harvard Educational Review, 70,* 475–504.

Conchas, G. Q. (2006). *The color of success: Race and high-achieving urban youth.* New York: Teachers College Press. Conchas, G. Q., & Clark, P. A. (2002). Career academies and urban minority schooling: Forging optimism despite limited opportunity. *Journal of Education for Students Placed at Risk, 7*(3), 287–311. doi:10.1207/S15327671ESPR0703_1

Conchas, G. Q., & Noguera, P. A. (2004). Understanding the exceptions: How small schools support the achievement of academically successful Black boys. In N. Way & J. Chu (Eds.), *Adolescent Boys in Context* (pp. 317–337). New York, NY: New York University Press.

Conchas, G. Q., & Pérez, C. C. (2003). Surfing the "model. minority" wave of success: How the school context shapes distinct experiences among Vietnamese youth. In C. Suárez-Orozco & I. Todorova (Eds.), *New directions for youth development: Understanding the social worlds of immigrant youth* (pp. 41–56). San Francisco: Jossey-Bass.

Conchas, G. Q., & Rodríguez, L. F. (2008). *Small schools and urban youth: Using the power of school culture to engage students.* Thousand Oaks, CA: Corwin Press.

Conchas, G. Q., & Vigil, J. D. (2010). Multiple marginality and urban education: Community and school socialization among low-income Mexican-descent youth. *Journal of Education for Students Placed at Risk, 15*(1–2), 51–65. doi 10.1080/10824661003634963

Cureton, S. R. (2000). Justifiable arrests or discretionary justice: Predictors of racial arrest differentials. *Journal of Black Studies, 30*(5), 703–719.

Cureton, S. R. (2002). Introducing Hoover: I'll ride for you, gangsta. In C. Ronald Huff (Ed.)., *Gangs in America III* (pp. 83–100). Thousand Oaks: Sage.

Daly, A. J. (Ed.). (2010). *Social network theory and educational change.* Cambridge, MA: Harvard Education Press.

Darder, A., & Torres, R. D. (2004). *After race: Racism after multiculturalism.* New York: New York University Press.

Datnow, A., Hubbard, L., & Mehan, H. (2002). *Extending educational reform: From one school to many.* New York: Routledge Falmer.

Delgado-Gaitan, C. (1991). Involving parents in the schools: A process of empowerment. *American Journal of Education, 100*(1), 20–46. doi:0195-6744/1001-0002$01.00

Díaz, D. R. (1993). La vida libra: Cultura de la calle en Los Angeles este. *Places, 8*(3), 30–37.

Dillon, S. (2009, January 23). Study sees an Obama effect as lifting Black test-takers. *The New York Times.* Retrieved from http://www.nytimes.com/2009/01/23/education/23gap.html.

Donato, R., Menchaca, M., & Valencia, R. R. (1991). Segregation, desegregation, and integration of Chicano students: Problems and prospects. In R. R. Valencia (Ed.), *Chicano School Failure and Success.* London: Falmer, 27–63.

Edley, C., & Ruiz de Velasco, J. (Eds.). (2010). *Changing places: How communities will improve the health of boys of color.* Berkeley: University of California Press

Fashola, O. S., & Slavin, R. E. (1997). *Show me the evidence!: Proven and promising programs for America's schools.* Thousand Oaks, CA: Corwin Press.

Feliciano, C. (2006a). Beyond the family: The influence of pre-migration group status on the educational expectations of immigrants' children. *Sociology of Education, 76,* 281–303.

Feliciano, C. (2006b). *Unequal origins: Immigrant selection and the education of the second generation.* New York: LFB Scholarly Publishers.

Gándara, P. (1995). *Over the ivy walls: The educational mobility of low-income Chicanos.* Albany, NY: State University of New York Press.

Gándara, P., & Contreras, F. (2009). *The Latino education crisis: The consequences of failed social policies.* Cambridge, MA: Harvard University Press.

Gibson, M. A. (1988). *Accommodation without assimilation: Sikh immigrants in an American high school.* Ithaca, NY: Cornell University Press.

Gibson, M. A., & Ogbu, J. (1991). *Minority status and schooling: A comparative study of immigrant and involuntary minorities.* New York: Garland.

Gonzales, G. (1990). *Chicano education in the era of segregation.* Philadelphia: Balch Institute Press.

Gordon, M. (1964). *Assimilation in American life: The role of race, religion, and national origins.* New York: Oxford University Press.

Gorski, P. (2006, February 9). The classist underpinnings of Ruby Payne's framework. *Teachers College Record,* www.tcrecord.org.

Goyette, K. A., & Conchas, G. Q. (2002). Family and non-family roots of social capital among Vietnamese and ethnic American children. *Review of the Sociology of Education: Schooling and Social Capital in Diverse Cultures, 13,* 41–72.

Gullatt, D. E., & Lemoine, D. A. (1997). Truancy: What's a principal to do? *American Secondary Education, 1,* 7–12.

Gutiérrez, K. (2008). Developing a sociocritical literacy in the third space. *Reading Research Quarterly. 43*(2), 148–164.

Harry, B., Kingner J., & Moore, R. (2000, November 17). *Of rocks and soft places: Using qualitative methods to investigate the processes that result in disproportionately.* Paper presented at the Minority Issues in Special Education conference, Harvard University, Cambridge, MA.

Hegewisch, A., Williams, C., & Henderson. A. (2011). *The gender wage gap.* Washington, DC: Institute for Women's Policy Research.

Hehir, T. (2005). *New directions in special education: Eliminating ableism in policy and practice.* Cambridge, MA: Harvard Education Press.

Howard, T. C. (2008). Who really cares? The disenfranchisement of African American males in pre K-12 schools: A critical race theory perspective. *Teachers College Record, 110*(5), 954–985.

Huff, C. R. (Ed.). (2002). *Gangs in America.* Thousand Oaks, CA: Sage Publications.

Hurtado, A., & Gurin., P. (1995). Ethnic identity and bilingualism. In A. Padilla (Ed.), *Hispanic psychology* (pp. 89–103). Thousand Oaks, CA: Sage Publishing.Katz, J. (1988). *Seductions of crime: Moral and sensual attractions in doing evil.* New York: Basic Books.

Katz, M. (1986). *In the shadow of the poorhouse: A social history of welfare in America.* New York: Basic Books

Kemple, J., & Snipes, J. (2000). *Career academies: Impacts on students' engagement and performance in high school.* New York: Manpower Demonstration Research Corporation.

Kemple, J., & Willner, C. (2008). *Career academies: Long-term impacts on labor market outcomes, educational attainment, and transitions to adulthood.* New York: Manpower Demonstration Research Corporation.

Kozol, J. (2005). *The shame of the nation: The restoration of apartheid schooling in America.* New York: Crown. Lareau, A., & Weininger, E. B. (2003). Cultural capital in education research: A critical assessment. *Theory and Society, 32*(5–6), 567–606. doi:10.1023/B:RYSO.0000004951.04408.b0

Lauria, M., & Miron, L. F. (2005). *Urban schools: The new social space of resistance.* New York: Peter Lang Publishing.

Lee, S. J. (1996). *Unraveling the model minority stereotype: Listening to Asian American youth.* New York: Teachers College Press.

Lewis, O. (1959). *Five families: Mexican case studies in the culture of poverty.* New York: Basic Books.

Lewis, O. (1965). *La vida: A Puerto Rican family in the culture of poverty—San Juan and New York.* New York: Random House.

López, N. (2003). *Hopeful girls, troubled boys: Race and gender disparity in urban education.* New York: Routledge.

López, N. (2011). Racially stigmatized masculinities: Conceptualizing Latino male schooling in the United States. In P. Noguera, E. Fergus, & A. Hertado (Eds.), *Disenfranchisement of Latino males: Contemporary perspectives on cultural and structural factors* (p. 35). New York: Routledge.

López, M., & López, G. (2010). *Persistent inequality: Contemporary realities in the education of undocumented Latina/o students.* New York: Routledge.

Maxwell, J. (1996). *Qualitative research design: An interactive approach.* Thousand Oaks, CA: Sage Publishing.

Maxwell, N. L., & Rubin, V. (1997). *The relative impact of a career academy on postsecondary work and education skills in urban, public high schools.* Hayward, CA: The Human Investment Research and Education Center.

Mehan, H., Villanueva, I., Hubbard, L., & Lintz, A. (1996). *Constructing school success: The consequences of untracking low-achieving students.* New York: Cambridge University Press.

Mickelson, R. A. (1990). The attitude-achievement paradox among Black adolescents. *Sociology of Education, 63*(1), 44–61.

Moll, L., Amanti, C., Neff, D., & Gonzalez, N. (1992). Funds of knowledge for teaching: Using a qualitative approach to connect homes and classrooms. *Theory into Practice, 31,* 132–141.

Moore, J. W. (1991). *Going down to the barrio.* Philadelphia: Temple University Press.

Moore, J. W., & Pinderhughes-Rivera, R. (Eds.). (1993). *In the barrios: Latinos and the underclass debate.* New York: Russell Sage Foundation.

Moran, R. (1987). Bilingual education as a status conflict. *Critical Law Review, 75*(1), 321–362.

Moran, R., & Carbado, D. W. (2010). *Moran and Carbado's race law stories.* New York: Thomson Reuters/Foundation Press.

Murnane, R. J., & Levy, F. (1996). *Teaching the new basic skills: Principles for educating children to thrive in a changing economy.* New York: Free Press.

Nagourney, A. (2008). Obama elected president as racial barrier falls. *New York Times.* Retrieved from *http://www.nytimes.com/2008/11/05/us/politics/05elect.html?pagewanted=all*

Newlin, C. (2010). *Estimated probability of competing in athletics beyond high school.* Retrieved November 5, 2010, from http://www.ncaa.org/wps/wcm/connect/ncaa/NCAA/Academics+and+Athletes/Education+and+Research/Probability+of+Competing/Methodology+-+Prob+of+Competing?pageDesign=Printer+Friendly+General+Content+Layout

Noguera, P. A. (2001). The trouble with black boys: The role and influence of environmental and cultural factors on the academic performance of African American males. *Urban Education, 38,* 431–459. doi:10.1177/0042085903038004005

Noguera, P. A. (2003). *City schools and the American dream: Reclaiming the promise of public education.* New York: Teachers College Press.

Noguera, P. A. (2008). *The trouble with Black boys and other reflections on race, ethnicity, and the future of public education.* San Francisco: Jossey-Bass.

Noguera, P. A., Hurtado, A., & Fergus, E. (2011). *Understanding the disenfranchisement of Latino men and boys: Invisible no more.* New York: Routledge.

Oakes, J. (2005.) *Keeping track: How schools structure inequality* (2nd ed.). New Haven: Yale University Press.

Obama, B. (2007). *Announces presidency.* Retrieved from http://chicago.about.com/od/chicagopeople/a/ObamaRunSpeech.htm

Obama, B. (2008). *A more perfect union.* Retrieved from http://www.journalism.org/node/11860

Ogbu, J. (1987). Variability in minority student performance: A problem in search of an explanation. *Anthropology and Education Quarterly, 18*(4), 312–334. doi:10.1525/aeq.1987.18.4.04x0022v

Ono, K., & Stoop, J. (2002). *Shifting borders: Rhetoric, immigration, and California's Proposition 187.* Philadelphia: Temple University Press.

Orfield, G. (2004). *Dropouts in America: Confronting the graduation rate crisis.* Cambridge, MA: Harvard Education Press.

Oseguera, L., Conchas, G. Q., & Mosqueda, E. (2010). Beyond family and ethnic culture: Understanding the preconditions for the potential realization of social capital. *Youth & Society.* doi: 10.1177/0044118X10382030.

Payne, R. K. (2005). *A Framework for understanding poverty.* Highlands, TX: Aha! Process.

Plant, A. E., Devine, P.G., Cox, W. T., Columb, C., Miller, S. L., Goplen, J., & Peruche, M. B (2009). The Obama effect: Decreasing implicit prejudice and stereotyping. *Journal of Experimental Social Psychology, 45,* 961–964.

Pollock, M. (2004). *Colormute: Race talk dilemmas in an American school.* Princeton, NJ: Princeton University Press.

Portes, A., & Bach, R. L. (1985). *Latin journey: Cuban and Mexican immigrants in the United States.* Berkeley, CA: University of California Press.

Portes, A., & Hao, L. (1998). E *pluribus unum*: Bilingualism and loss of language in the second generation. *Sociology of Education, 71*(4), 269–294.

Putnam, R. D. (2000). *Bowling along: The collapse and revival of American community.* New York: Simon & Schuster.

Quadagno, J. (1994). *The color of welfare: How racism undermined the war on poverty.* New York: Oxford University Press.

Rafael, T. (2007). *The Mexican mafia.* New York: Encounter Books.

Ream, R., & Palardy, G. (2008, June). Re-examining social class differences in the availability and the educational utility of parental social capital. *American Educational Research Journal, 45*(2), 238–273.

Rios, V. (2011). *Punished: Policing the lives of Black and Latino boys.* New York: New York University Press.

Rodríguez, L. F., & Conchas, G. Q. (2009). Preventing truancy and dropout among urban middle school youth: Understanding community-based action from the student's perspective. *Education and Urban Society, 41*(2), 216–247. doi:10.1177/0013124508325681

Rong, X. L. (1996). Effects of race and gender on teachers; perceptions of the social behaviors of elementary students. *Urban Education, 31*(3), 261–290. doi:10.1177/0042085996031003003

Roth, J., & Hendrickson, J. M. (1991). Schools and youth organizations: Empowering adolescents to confront high-risk behavior. *Phi Delta Kappan, 72*, 619–622.

Rothstein, R. (2004). *Class and schools: Using social, economic and educational reform to close the Black-White achievement gap.* Washington, D.C.: Economic Policy Institute.

Saenz, V. B., & Ponjuan, L. (2009). The vanishing Latino male in higher education. *Journal of Hispanic Higher Education, 8*(1), 54–89.

Sánchez-Jankowski, M. (1992). *Islands in the street: Gangs and American urban society.* Berkeley and Los Angeles: University of California Press.

Sánchez-Jankowski, M. (2008). *Cracks in the pavement: Social change and resilience in poor neighborhoods.* Berkeley: University of California Press.

Simpson, C., & Pearlman, A. (2005). *Inside the Crips: Life inside L.A.'s most notorious gang.* New York: St. Martin's Press.

Solórzano, D., & Yosso, T. (2002). Critical race methodology: Counter-storytelling as an analytical framework. *Qualitative Inquiry, 8*(1), 23–44.

Spindler, G., & Spindler, L. (1990). *The American cultural dialogue and its transmission.* Bristol, PA: The Falmer Press.

Stanton-Salazar, R. D. (2001). *Manufacturing hope and despair: The school and kin support networks of U.S. Mexican youth.* New York: Teachers College Press.

Stanton-Salazar, R. D. (2010, October 11). A social capital framework for the study of institutional agents and their role in empowerment of low-status students and youth. *Youth & Society.* doi:10.1177/0044118X10382877

Stanton-Salazar, R. D., & Dornbusch, S. M. (1995). Social capital and the social reproduction of inequality: The formation of informational networks among Mexican-origin high school students. *Sociology of Education, 68*, 116–135.

Stern, D., Dayton, C., & Raby, M. (2010). *Career academics: A proven strategy to prepare high school students for college and careers.* University of California, Berkeley, Career Academy Support Network.

Stern, D., Raby, M., & Dayton, C. (1992). *Career academics: Partnerships for reconstructing American high schools.* San Francisco: Jossey-Bass.

Suárez-Orozco, C., Pimentel, A., & Martin, M. (2009). The significance of relationships: Academic engagement and achievement among newcomer immigrant youth. *Teachers College Record, 111*(3), 712–749.

Suárez-Orozco, C. E., & Suárez-Orozco, M. (1995). *Transformations: Migration, family life, and achievement motivation among Latino adolescents.* Stanford, CA: Stanford University Press.

Suárez-Orozco, C. E., & Suárez-Orozco, M. (2001). *Children of immigration.* Cambridge, MA: Harvard University Press.

Tapia, M. (2011). Gang membership and race as risk factors for juvenile arrest. *Journal of Research in Crime and Delinquency, 48*(3), 364–395.

Taylor, P. S. (1934). *An American Latino frontier.* Chapel Hill: University of North Carolina Press.

Telles, E. E., & Ortiz, V. (2009). *Generations of exclusion: Mexican Americans, assimilation, and race.* New York: Russell Sage.

Tita, G., & Abrahamse, A. (2004). *Gang homicide in LA, 1981–2001.* California Attorney General's Office.

U.S. Census Bureau. (2010). *Educational attainment in the United States 2010.* Retrieved from http://www.census.gov/compendia/statab/

Uslaner, E. M. (2001). Volunteering and social capital: How trust and religion shape civic participation in the United States. In E. M. Uslaner (Ed.), *Social capital and participation in everyday life* (pp. 104–117). London: Routledge.

Valdez, A. (2007). *Gangs across America: History and sociology.* San Clememte, CA: Law Tech Custom PublishingValencia, R. R. (Ed.). (1991). *Chicano school failure and success: Research and policy agendas for the 1990s.* London: The Falmer Press.

Valencia, R. R. (2010). *Dismantling contemporary deficit thinking: Educational thought and practice.* New York: Routledge.

Valencia, R. R., & Alburto, S. (1991). The uses and abuses of educational testing: Chicanos as a case in point. In R. R. Valencia (Ed.), *Chicano school failure and success: Research and policy agendas for the 1990s* (pp, 203–251). London: Falmer Press.

Valenzuela, A. (1999). *Subtractive schooling: U.S. Mexican youth and the politics of caring.* Albany: State University of New York Press.

Vigil, J. D. (1988a). *Barrio gangs.* Austin University of Texas Press.

Vigil, J. D. (1988b). Group processes and street identity: Adolescent Chicago gang members. *Ethos, 16,* 421–445. doi 10.1525/eth.1988.16.4.02a00040

Vigil, J. D. (1997). *Personas Mexicanas: Chicano highschoolers in a changing Los Angeles.* Dallas, TX: Harcourt Brace.

Vigil, J. D. (2002a). Community dynamics and the rise of street gangs. In M. M. Suárez-Orozco & M. M. Paez (Eds.), *Latinos! Remaking America* (pp. 97–109). Berkeley: University of California Press.

Vigil, J. D. (2002b). *A rainbow of gangs: Street cultures in the mega-city.* Austin: University of Texas Press.

Vigil, J. D. (2003). Urban violence and street gangs. *Annual Review of Anthropology, 32,* 225–242. doi:10.1146/annurev.anthro.32.061002.093426

Vigil, J. D. (2007). *The projects: Gang and non-gang families in East Los Angeles.* Austin: University of Texas Press.

Vigil, J. D. (2010). *Gang redux: A balanced anti-gang strategy.* Long Grove, IL: Waveland Press.

Vigil, J. D., & Yun, S.C. (1990). Vietnamese youth gangs in California. In C. R. Huff (Ed.), *Gangs in America* (pp. 146–162). Newbury Park, CA: Sage Publications.

Warakoo, N. (2011). *Balacing acts: Youth culture in the global city.* Berkeley: University of California Press.

Warmington, P. (2009). Taking race out of scare quotes: Race-conscious social analysis in an ostensibly post-racial world. *Race, Ethnicity and Education, 12*(3), 281–296.

Wehlage, G. G., & Rutter, R. A. (1986). Dropping out: How much do schools contribute to the problem? *Teachers College Record, 87*(3), 374–392.

Wheeler, B. G. (1993). *Black California: The history of African-Americans in the Golden State.* New York: Hippocrene Books.

Willis, P. E. (1977). *Learning to labour: How working class kids get working class jobs.* Farmborough, England: Saxon

Wilson, W. J. (1996). *When work disappears: The world of the new urban poor.* New York: Knopf.

Yosso, T. J. (2005). Whose culture has capital? A critical race theory discussion of community cultural wealth. *Race Ethnicity and Education, 8*(1), 69–91. doi:10.1080/1361332052000341006

Zhou, M., & Bankston, C. L. (1998). *Growing up American: How Vietnamese children adapt to life in the United States.* New York: Russell Sage Foundation.

About the Authors

Gilberto Q. Conchas is executive director of the Career Academy Support Network (CASN) at the University of California, Berkeley, and associate professor of education and Chancellor's Fellow with joint appointments in Chicano/Latino studies and sociology at the University of California, Irvine. He received his Ph.D. in sociology form the University of Michigan, Ann Arbor. Previously, he was assistant professor at the Harvard Graduate School of Education and senior program officer with the Bill & Melinda Gates Foundation. His work focuses on inequality, with an emphasis on urban school systems. He is the author of *The Color of Success: Race and High-Achieving Urban Youth* (2006) and co-author of *Small Schools and Urban Youth: Using the Power of School Culture to Engage Students* (2008). He has been a visiting professor at the University of California, Berkeley; University of Southern California; San Francisco State University; University of Washington; and the University of Barcelona.

James Diego Vigil is professor of social ecology at the University of California, Irvine. He received his Ph.D. in anthropology from University of California, Los Angeles, and has held various teaching and administrative positions. As an urban anthropologist focusing on Mexican Americans, he has conducted research on ethnohistory, education, culture change and acculturation, and adolescent and youth issues, especially street gangs. This work has resulted in publications such as *From Indians to Chicanos: The Dynamics of Mexican American Culture* (third edition, 2012), *Personas Mexicanas: Chicano Highschoolers in a Changing Los Angeles* (1997), and *Barrio Gangs* (1988). His recent books include *A Rainbow of Gangs: Street Cultures in the Mega-City* (2002) and *The Projects: Gang and Non-Gang Families in East Los Angeles* (2007), which examine family life in a housing project. *Gang Redux: A Balanced Anti-Gang Strategy* (2010) has most recently been published.